Young Medieval Women

To Our Parents

Young Medieval Women

Edited by
Katherine J. Lewis,
Noël James Menuge &
Kim M. Phillips

St. Martin's Press
New York

YOUNG MEDIEVAL WOMEN

St. Martin's Press, Scholarly and Reference Division,
175 Fifth Avenue, New York, N.Y. 10010

First published in the United States of America in 1999

Printed in Great Britain

ISBN 0-312-22130-4

Library of Congress Cataloging-in-Publication Data

Young medieval women/edited by Katherine J. Lewis, Noël James Menuge & Kim M. Phillips.
p. cm.
Includes bibliographical references and index.
ISBN 0-312-22130-4 (cloth)
1. Women--History--Middle Ages, 500–1500. 2. Young women--Europe--History. 3. Civilization, Medieval. I. Lewis, Katherine J., 1969–
II. James, Noël M. III. Phillips, Kim M.
HQ1143.Y68 1999
305.4'09'02--dc21 98-48753
CIP

CONTENTS

List of Figures

List of Contributors

Joanna L. Chamberlayne is a doctoral candidate at the Centre for Medieval Studies, University of York where her DPhil on English Queenship 1445–1503 is in its final stages of completion. She has an article forthcoming on the coronation rites of queens in fifteenth-century England.

Lilas G. Edwards holds a BA from the University of Texas and an MA in Medieval Studies from the University of York. She has published an article on androgyny and Joan of Arc in *Medieval Life* and is currently pursuing an acting career in Austin, Texas.

P.J.P. Goldberg is lecturer in history at the University of York. He is the author of *Women, Work and Lifecycle in a Medieval Economy: Women in York and Yorkshire* c. *1300–1520*, *Women in England* c. *1275–1525*, and the editor of *Women in Medieval English Society*. He has also published numerous articles on medieval women.

Kristina E. Gourlay is a doctoral candidate at the Centre for Medieval Studies, University of Toronto, where she is working on a study of western medieval textual representations of Muslim women. She is the author of 'La Dame à la Licorne: A Reinterpretation' (Gazette des Beaux-Arts, September 1997).

Noël James Menuge is currently working as a landscape historian in Cambridge. She is a doctoral candidate at the Centre for Medieval Studies, University of York, where her DPhil on wardship is in its final stages of completion. She has published on wardship in romance and law and on landscape history.

Katherine J. Lewis is a research associate at the Centre for Medieval Studies, University of York, from where she holds a DPhil in Medieval Studies. Her study of the cult of St Katherine of Alexandria in late medieval England is forthcoming from Boydell and Brewer. She also has articles forthcoming on aspects of the cults of St Katherine and St Margaret.

Isabelle Mast holds an MA in Medieval Studies from the University of York. Her DPhil, written at the University of Oxford, is a study of the representation of women in Gower's *Confessio Amantis*. She is currently working in the City of London.

Kim M. Phillips is lecturer in history at the University of Auckland and holds a DPhil in Medieval Studies from the University of York on the topic of young womanhood in late medieval England. She has published an article on medieval ideas of feminine beauty and has forthcoming articles on women and youth in the Middle Ages, gesture in romance and conduct literature and rape in late-medieval England.

INTRODUCTION

Where once feminist historians bemoaned the absence of works on medieval women, they are now able to revel in the riches produced within this field each year. Given such abundance, one might ask what virtue lies in producing a volume specifically concerned with *young* medieval women? Our view is that its value lies in its contribution to two fields of history, as two historiographies converge in this collection. These are the historiographies of women, and of youth.

The value of focusing on a particular phase in the life cycles of medieval women becomes apparent when we consider the shifts in emphasis which have marked the theory of women's history since the 1980s. One of the major shifts has been towards emphasizing the particularity of certain groups of women, and recognition of the differences in identity between one group and another. Where, in the early days of women's history, 'women' of the past were viewed and studied as a category unto themselves, revelations from Black history and Marxist history in particular had, by the early 1980s, cast serious doubt on the validity of viewing 'woman' as a stable category in history.[1] As Joan Scott writes in her introduction to a recent collection of important essays on the theory and method of women's history, women's history in the later 1990s has come to be characterized by a difficult tension between the political importance of maintaining 'woman' as a valid category of historical analysis, and the equally politically useful recognition of the historically-constructed nature of the identity 'woman'. This latter recognition has produced the understanding that 'women', being produced historically rather than naturally, are also constructed according to a range of other historically-produced identities, including class, race, ethnicity, occupation, and life-cycle stage. The danger of the latter view is that it has the potential to erase the category 'woman' both from history and contemporary political thought, thus rendering the project of feminism obsolete.[2]

Here we wish neither to lose sight of gender as a fundamental category of historical analysis, nor to imply that it is somehow of superior significance to other categories. Rather, it is recognized that gender identities are intermingled with and modified by other aspects of identity. One key aspect of identity which is being paid increasing attention as a modifier of medieval women's gendered identity is the life-cycle stage occupied at a given time. The importance of life-cycle identities should be immediately apparent on looking at medieval women. For such women, social circumstances, legal rights, access to economic resources, and representation in textual and visual forms all varied according to their life-cycle phase, as well as according to other aspects of identity including social status and regional identity.

The recent spate of studies on widowhood have paid witness to the often marked difference in circumstances experienced by married women and widows.[3] Given the common Middle English references to women as 'maids, wives and widows', we can see that as wives and widows are receiving separate attention, it is time now to pay more notice to maidens.[4] Young medieval women have already received scattered attention within medieval social history. P.J.P. Goldberg's extensive studies of female service and marriage strategies in late-medieval England are particularly important here.[5] Valuable contributions are also available in Caroline Barron's study of education for London girls, and Judith Bennett's and Barbara Hanawalt's interest in the differing experiences of young English males and females within the peasantry (and, for the latter, in late-medieval London).[6] Richard Smith has provided extremely useful comparative studies of service, marriage and family forms in late-medieval England and Tuscany, while Christiane Klapisch-Zuber's demographic studies of fifteenth-century Tuscany have produced studies of female service in that region.[7] Interdisciplinary contributions have also begun to be made to the topic of young medieval womanhood, notably Felicity Riddy's reading of a fourteenth-century Middle English conduct text within both the context of its production, and of its reception over the next century-and-a-half, pointing to the meanings of this particular work concerning young women and its changing relevance to them during a period of intense social change.[8]

Despite this increasing interest, until now no single monograph or essay collection has appeared on the subject of young womanhood. This collection aims to go some way toward filling that gap. But while making a particular contribution to medieval women's history, it is hoped that it will make an equivalent contribution to the field of studies of medieval youth. This field, growing out of Philippe Ariès study of childhood and the debate which ensued, focuses on the more cultural than social 'notion' of youth or adolescence, and has a fairly extensive historiography.[9] Yet, to date, the notion of youth for girls or young women, rather than boys or young men, has almost always taken a secondary position. Barbara Hanawalt, after attempting to incorporate the experiences of girls into her account of London childhood and youth as much as of boys, acknowledges that she has not granted the former as much space as the latter and that female youth may have been defined so 'differently from boys' as to warrant separate study.[10] Although several studies of medieval youth have included female experience or representations in their analysis, the issue of the influence of gender identity upon youthful identity tends not to be made a focus.[11] Even the most recent substantial contribution to the field, despite the sophistication of its editors' approach, pays far less attention to young girls than boys in its essays on medieval young people.[12] Honourable exceptions to this tendency towards gender-blindness include James A. Schultz's updated and more extensive work on youth in Middle High German literature, and Stanley Chojnacki's very insightful study of adolescence and gender in Renaissance Venice.[13]

Through a process of academic 'affirmative action', we hope that this collection's focus on young women will help to redress the gender imbalance in approaches to medieval youth. It seeks to illuminate our understanding of the lives and experiences of young medieval women located within specifically defined settings and represented in particular sources. The individual studies which it contains focus on the later medieval period, roughly defined as the fourteenth and fifteenth centuries; geographically, there is an emphasis on England with the inclusion of comparative material from a wider north-western European context.

This collection is an interdisciplinary one, where interdisciplinarity is taken to mean an approach which crosses the traditional disciplinary boundaries, both in terms of the kinds of sources which are usually seen as the preserve of a particular discipline, and in terms of the kinds of methodologies and theoretical frameworks within which such source materials are analysed. This is true for the collection as a whole, as well as for the individual studies which it contains. The contributors are specialists within the broad academic disciplines of history, literature and art-history, but all of their work is informed by an interdisciplinary methodology of some kind. This is true even where the focus of an individual study rests largely on sources drawn from a single discipline. This is due in no small part to the fact that all of the contributors, at some point in their academic career, have studied or worked at the Centre for Medieval Studies within the University of York. The Centre has long been committed to an interdisciplinary approach to the study and understanding of the medieval world, and the lives of the men and women who lived within it.

Interdisciplinarity provides a solid context within which to investigate young medieval women, as it allows us to uncover the relationship between representation and reality. Do the depictions of young women to be found in a variety of literary and visual sources reflect or distort the actual experiences of young women as revealed in documentary sources?[14] Within this book this issue is explored with reference to a variety of sources and discourses; romances, saints' lives, legal records, manuscript illuminations, collections of *exempla*, theological and liturgical material, various forms of didactic literature and embroidery. Within individual articles answers to this question are proposed in relation to young women drawn from particular socio-economic, geographic or cultural contexts. These are often supported or illuminated by the findings of other contributors. Thus some general conclusions both about conceptions of young womanhood and the key themes which characterize it as a stage in the female life cycle do emerge.

Kim M. Phillips' article serves as a conceptual introduction to the concerns of the collection as a whole. In it she utilizes an interdisciplinary methodology to demonstrate that the stage in women's life cycle which she terms 'maidenhood', is the perfect age of woman's life as conceived within late-medieval English culture. This age spans the period between puberty, which occurs between twelve and fourteen, and adult womanhood, defined as the time at which women are perceived to be ready for marriage and motherhood and occurring from the late teens to early twenties. An explanation of the historical and other evidence which defines young womanhood in women's life cycle forms one part of the discussion here. However, most of the article examines the evidence which suggests maidenhood, the period when a woman is sexually mature yet chaste, as the perfect age of woman. The Middle English poem *Pearl*, the lives of the virgin-martyrs, and visual representations of the Virgin Mary during her assumption and coronation all substantiate the argument. In each case the female figures represent a pinnacle of femininity and in each case they are represented as young unmarried women. This article thus provides an account of perceptions of youth as a stage in women's life cycle and contributes to an understanding of ideals of femininity within late-medieval English culture. It also proposes a model of women's life cycle based on radically different principles from the model of the ages of man.

In this way Phillips explores maidenhood as a paradigm, or a set of signifiers. These were by no means of relevance only to women who were actually at that stage in their life cycle. The next two articles illustrate this point by demonstrating the ways in which the vocabulary of maidenhood was actually appropriated by and for certain medieval women some of whom were neither young, nor maidens. Leading on from Phillips' discussion of virgin-martyrs as pinnacles of femininity Katherine J. Lewis considers the dissemination of the hagiographic narratives of their lives within certain social and cultural settings, as a means of determining the influence they had in the education of young women in medieval England. She moves away from past readings of these texts as displaced rape narratives, or as of relevance only to consecrated virgins and argues for a more sophisticated and positive understanding of their use within specific social, cultural, and historical contexts.

Lewis argues that virgin-martyrs' lives were useful tools in the training of young women, because these saints were held up as exemplars of appropriate female behaviour and bearing; as 'model girls', in courtesy texts such as that written by the Knight of the Tour Landry. These texts provided a means by which mothers, fathers and elders could instil correct moral, social and religious values in young women, thus rendering them attractive and suitable as prospective wives. Lewis illustrates this point by examining the function of the life of St Katherine of Alexandria within certain manuscript miscellanies that were read and used by members of the gentry and lesser nobility for education and edification within the household. Drawing on documentary, literary and visual evidence for patterns of women's learning and education, she also explores the ways in which St Katherine may have been appropriated as a model by women themselves, both before and after marriage.

Joanna L. Chamberlayne turns to consider the relevance of the vocabulary of maidenhood for women of the highest social status: late-medieval English queens. Drawing on a variety of documentary, literary and visual sources, Chamberlayne explores the tensions between the ideals and reality of queenmaking in fifteenth-century England. In this period the traditional concept of the ideal potential queen came under threat. For generations English kings and their heirs had married young virgins of foreign royal blood, but this pattern was broken in the fourteenth century by Joan of Kent, then in the fifteenth by Joan of Navarre, and especially by Elizabeth Woodville. All of these women were widows and two of them were English. Chamberlayne explores the ways in which the imagery and authority of queenship was inseparably bound up with the quasi-magical powers of virginity and shows that queens were constructed as a type of the Virgin Mary not just at their coronation, and in liturgy, but in secular discourse as well. She shows that they are represented in visual and literary texts as displaying all of the identifiable properties of maidenhood outlined by Phillips. This ideology of queenship was challenged during the fifteenth century, notably by Joan of Navarre, wife of Henry IV. Notwithstanding, Edward IV's choice of Elizabeth Woodville for his queen appeared rather extraordinary to his contemporaries. At twenty-seven she was five years his senior and already had two children. However Chamberlayne uses surviving representations of this queen to illustrate the ways in which she was nevertheless publicly constructed in Marian terms, in order that she should fulfil a role that was traditionally the preserve of young women.

Kristina E. Gourlay's contribution is also concerned with visual representations of youthful womanhood, in its close examination and analysis of the early fourteenth-century 'Malterer Embroidery' from Germany. Her study raises the issue of young women's sexuality and sexual appeal to men – a problematic issue both for medieval commentators and their modern readers. Most of the scenes depicted within the embroidery belong to what Susan Smith has labelled the 'Power of Woman' *topos* – an iconographic theme traditionally seen as an expression of conservative, even misogynistic, views of women's sexual appeal as dangerous and negative, so much so that it could cause the humiliation even of such august and rational male figures of authority as Aristotle and Virgil. Gourlay, however, through a careful and detailed analysis of the embroidery alongside its literary sources and what can be gleaned about its historical context, comes to an original and refreshing conclusion. By considering seriously the presence of scenes from *Iwein* and of a virgin with a unicorn – aspects of the embroidery not previously satisfactorily incorporated into analyses by other art historians – she argues that the embroidery presents a view of young women's sexuality which is neither fearful nor misogynistic, but rather playful, irreverent and humorous, and which presents youthful female sexuality in a warm and positive light. Such an upbeat reinterpretation offers wider possibilities for understanding the varied and complex nature of medieval views of female sexuality, and serves to counteract the emphasis on medieval anti-feminism which is common among modern interpretations.

Isabelle Mast's study of the representation of rape in Gower's *Confessio Amantis* also involves a rethinking of medieval views of female sexuality, both from the point of view of an author and his audience. Unlike his contemporary, Chaucer, Gower's work has remained relatively unexplored by scholars interested in medieval women or gender issues. However, the *Confessio Amantis* is a rich source of ideas about and representations of women. Mast's study is of value both in drawing this to our attention and in indicating some of the ways in which the text can be read and understood. Through a close textual analysis of Gower's portrayal of the rape of several young women in comparison both to the sources upon which he drew, and to other contemporary accounts of the same stories, Mast argues that Gower makes an attempt to dramatize the pain and humiliation felt by the victims realistically. In undertaking to write about this crime in a meaningful and non-repetitive way Gower deliberately departs from his sources and provides some sensitive interpretation and insight. In describing the rapes of Philomena and Lucrece, Gower tackles the guilt and complicity which victims of rape frequently suffer. He also reveals the impact that rape has on their identity as women; in the case of Philomena through her transformation into a nightingale, in the case of Lucrece through suicide. These are standard motifs in the stories, but in both cases Gower takes a unique stance in which he attempts to compensate both women for their fate. Above all, Mast argues that Gower does not blame the victims, or criticize their behaviour. Thus, unlike many of his contemporaries he does not use the theme of rape to illustrate the fickleness of young, sexually desirable women, who say 'no' with their mouths but 'yes' with their bodies. Gower directs the attention of his readers; they are forced into a recognition of the terrible consequences of rape, both physical and mental.

Lilas G. Edwards' article utilizes new methods of historical and textual analysis to cast light on perhaps the best-known, yet ultimately elusive, young woman of the later Middle Ages: Joan of Arc. Edwards focuses specifically on the text from the first of Joan's two trials, the Trial of Condemnation of 1431 (the second, posthumous, trial being the Trial of Rehabilitation). The aim of Edwards' article, however, is not to uncover the 'true' identity or character of this fascinating figure. Rather, she recognizes that the text of the *Trial of Condemnation* presents a portrait of Joan which is simultaneously fashioned by her English condemners and by Joan herself, each for their own purposes. Edwards analyses each of the aspects of identity constructed by and for Joan – 'daughter of God', virgin, mystic, heretic, and androgyne – and examines each within the broader cultural and discursive contexts of the day, as a way of discussing the forms of authority available to Joan and those which, ultimately, had the power to bring about her downfall.

Joan is thus represented neither as a freak nor a paragon within her own cultural context, but rather as a young woman for whom certain roles and aspects of identity were available, and for whom these had the power either to exalt or condemn her. Edwards' portrayal of Joan is of a young woman who knew that her only possible escape from condemnation was to emphasize those aspects of her identity which set her apart in a sacred context and could make aspects of her behaviour, notably her flouting of gender roles, acceptable. But it was also these very aspects of her character which were the most dangerous to emphasize. Ultimately, in part though not entirely for political reasons, the power lay with her judges, who decreed that far from being blessed and exalted by God she was indeed a heretic.

The influence of interdisciplinary methodology comes to the fore in Noël James Menuge's study of wardship and marriage in later medieval England. As Menuge points out, although wardship has attracted substantial attention from historians – particularly those whose focus is on English legal history – the value of literary representations of the theme is rarely acknowledged. In Menuge's analysis, which centres on two Middle English romances paired with actual cases brought before the York consistory court in the fourteenth century, both the 'historical' and 'literary' accounts of disputes concerning female wards are treated as both textual constructions and as valid representations of issues of genuine concern within their social context. Indeed, she suggests that the literary versions, being more fully rounded-out in their narrative structures than the historical versions, might actually be able to tell us more about key concerns regarding wardship than legal cases can. The issue on which Menuge places her focus is the vexed question of consent. Despite canon-legal provisions to the contrary, marriages of young female wards often seem to have taken little account of their wishes. Menuge argues that both the romances and the records of the cases can teach us to question the meaning of 'consent', and caution us not confuse the concept with 'free choice' or 'autonomy' for the young women concerned.

P.J.P. Goldberg's study of regional prostitution argues that English prostitution in the fourteenth and fifteenth centuries comprised mainly street-walking, rather than the use of institutionalized brothels. He considers that the full-time prostitute is an elusive phenomenon, and that most women employed to some measure within the sex industry of late-medieval England would have instead been supplementing incomes from other trades, chiefly those to do with food and ale. Here he differs from historians such as Ruth Karras, who consider institutionalized prostitution to have been the norm.[15] The exceptions Goldberg considers here are towns with a regular influx of non-native males who sought the southern European type institution of the regulated brothel, including the ports of Southampton and Sandwich, and Southwark, close to the port of London. In this sense Goldberg considers these brothels to act as a means of protection for native females in such places, including young women, who might otherwise have been considered 'available'.

Goldberg considers evidence from act books, poll tax returns, and those city ordinances which sought to control the movements of these streetwalkers, and builds up a demographic picture of likely age and occupation of such women. While showing that age is a difficult factor to determine from such information, he suggests that younger women were more likely to engage in active prostitution, while older prostitutes were more likely to move into the role of procuress. He notes that some women acting as prostitutes were recorded as servants in the households of recognized procuresses, and, by analogy with other life-cycle servants, may be reasonably assumed to be in their teens or early twenties. Few of these women, it seems, were married. Thus Goldberg demonstrates that prostitution held a life- and work-cycle pattern of its own, which may have presented a limited alternative to young women with few other prospects.

Through the medium of these individual studies this collection illustrates some of the different ways in which young womanhood was represented, defined and understood. It also suggests how young women, and others, may have responded to and exploited these images and concepts. To give some idea of the connections and conclusions which arise from the collection as a whole: Phillips and Lewis demonstrate that the ideals of female beauty and behaviour were instilled in young women who were likely to be married well. Taking similar ideas further Gourlay considers the importance of sexual attractiveness in the lives of young women. Mast and Menuge show that young womanhood did not necessarily end with marriage and consider the ways in which young women were constructed as property or possessions. Chamberlayne and Edwards explore the ways in which the characteristics of young womanhood could be assumed as a mantle or even as armour to lend authority to a public role. Goldberg reminds us that not all medieval young women could afford to consider virginity, marriage, or appropriate behaviour as viable options.

The experience of young women drawn from different backgrounds and places is likely to vary. Evidently representing oneself as a paragon of maidenhood, or attempting to live up to its exacting standards also rested on the possession of a certain measure of wealth and/or social status. It was by no means a straightforward undertaking. Joan of Arc provides an example of the enmity that could be aroused by a young woman who sought to appropriate qualities and emulate conduct which was perceived to be unsuitable for her.

The above observations serve to illustrate the ways in which young womanhood, both as concept and life-cycle stage was ideologically constructed and underpinned. This collection does not seek to provide all the answers about young medieval women, but in demonstrating the ways in which this ideology operated and influenced the lives and representations of some of them, it hopes to pose questions which others will feel motivated to answer.

Notes

1. The debate over 'essentialism' (as its critics label it) and ' difference' consists of a wide literature within the field of feminist theory generally. One particularly useful contribution is Denise Riley, *'Am I That Name?' Feminism and the Category of 'Woman' in History* (Houndmills, 1988).

2. Joan Wallach Scott, 'Introduction' to Joan Wallach Scott (ed.), *Feminism and History* (Oxford and New York, 1996). While Scott thinks that this tension, though difficult, 'is one of those useful and productive tensions worth living with', p. 5, the intensity, and sometimes acrimony, which can be generated by this 'productive' tension is apparent in Mary Hawkesworth's essay 'Confounding Gender' and its accompanying responses in *Signs* 22 (1997), 649–713.

3. Louise Mirrer (ed.), *Upon My Husband's Death: Widows in the History and Literature of Medieval Europe* (Ann Arbor, 1992); Sue Sheridan Walker (ed.), *Wife and Widow in Medieval England* (Ann Arbor, 1993); Caroline M. Barron and Anne F. Sutton (eds.), *Medieval London Widows, 1300–1500* (London, 1994).

4. A full length study of the meanings of youth for young English secular women is available in Kim M. Phillips, 'The Medieval Maiden: Young Womanhood in Late Medieval England' (unpublished D.Phil. thesis, University of York, 1997).

5. P.J.P. Goldberg, esp. 'Female Labour, Service and Marriage in the Late Medieval Urban North', *Northern History* 22 (1986), 18–38; *Women, Work and Life Cycle in a Medieval Economy: Women in York and Yorkshire* c. *1300–1520* (Oxford, 1992); 'Girls Growing Up in Later Medieval England', *History Today* (June, 1995), 25–32.

6. Caroline M. Barron, 'The Education and Training of Girls in Fifteenth-Century London' in Diana E.S. Dunn (ed.), *Courts, Counties and the Capital in the Later Middle Ages* (Stroud, 1996); Judith M. Bennett, *Women in the Medieval English Countryside: Gender and Household in Brigstock Before the Plague* (New York and Oxford, 1987), ch. 4; Barbara A. Hanawalt, *The Ties That Bound: Peasant Families in Medieval England* (New York and Oxford, 1986), ch. 12; Barbara A. Hanawalt, *Growing Up in Medieval London: The Experience of Childhood in History* (New York and Oxford, 1993).

7. Richard M. Smith, e.g. 'Geographical Diversity in the Resort to Marriage in Late Medieval Europe: Work, Reputation, and Unmarried Females in the Household Formation Systems of Northern and Southern Europe' in P.J.P. Goldberg (ed.), *Woman is a Worthy Wight: Women in English Society* c. *1200–1500* (Stroud, 1992); Christiane Klapisch-Zuber, 'Women Servants in Florence During the Fourteenth and Fifteenth Centuries' in Barbara A. Hanawalt (ed.), *Women and Work in Preindustrial Europe* (Bloomington, 1986).

8. Felicity Riddy, 'Mother Knows Best: Reading Social Change in a Courtesy Text', *Speculum* 71 (1996), 66–86.

9. Philippe Ariès, *L'Enfant et la Familiale sous l'Ancien Régime* (Paris, 1960). Thoughtful summaries of the ensuing debate are available in Hugh Cunningham, *Children and Childhood in Western Society since 1500* (London, 1995), and James A. Schultz, *The Knowledge of Childhood in the German Middle Ages 1100–1350* (Philadelphia, 1995). On medieval youth or adolescence generally, see Barbara A.

Hanawalt, 'Historical Descriptions and Prescriptions for Adolescence', *Journal of Family History* 17 (1992), 341–51.

10. Hanawalt, *Growing Up*, p. 16.

11. James A Schultz, 'Medieval Adolescence: The Claims of History and the Silence of German Narrative', *Speculum* 1991, 519–37; Kathryn L. Reyerson, 'The Adolescent Apprentice/Worker in Medieval Montpellier', *Journal of Family History* 17 (1992), 353–70.

12. Christiane Marchello-Nizia, 'Courtly Chivalry', Elisabeth Crouzet-Pavan, 'A Flower of Evil: Young Men in Medieval Italy', and Michel Pastoureau, 'Emblems of Youth: Young People in Medieval Imagery' in Giovanni Levi and Jean-Claude Schmitt (eds), *A History of Young People in the West* (2 vols, Cambridge MA, and London, England, 1997), vol. 1, *Ancient and Medieval Rites of Passage.* Elliott Horowitz's essay on youth among European Jews from 1300 to 1800 treats female and male youth more equally, but most of his examples are drawn from the seventeenth and eighteenth centuries.

13. Schultz, *Knowledge of Childhood*; Stanley Chojnacki, 'Measuring Adulthood: Adolescence and Gender in Renaissance Venice', *Journal of Family History* 17 (1992), 371–95.

14. Penny Schine Gold, *The Lady and the Virgin: Image, Attitude and Experience in Twelfth-Century France* (Chicago, 1985), remains an important paradigm for this approach to medieval women. See, in particular, the preface in which she outlines her methodological approach, pp. xv–xxi.

15. See for example her *Common Women: Prostitution and Sexuality in Medieval England* (New York, 1996).

1

MAIDENHOOD AS THE PERFECT AGE OF WOMAN'S LIFE

Kim M. Phillips

In the medieval pantheon of saints an exalted position is reserved for a group of saintly women who might best be described as maidenly.[1] They are maidenly, that is, in many of the senses which the word implies. They are young, yet they are not children. They are beautiful (and the focus of male desire), yet are virgins, untouched by the episodes of marriage, sex and motherhood which mark the lives and bodies of adult women.[2] These are the virgin martyrs, whose popularity was at its height in late-medieval English culture.[3] Their popularity, their virginity, their potential as positive role models both for women and men, even their potentially pornographic function, have been remarked upon.[4] What has not, to my knowledge, attracted much interest is the life-cycle stage which these young women saints occupy. Here I shall argue that, firstly, they are all young women in the 'maidenhood' phase of their life cycle – that is, the transitional phase between childhood and fully fledged adulthood – and secondly, that they help to demonstrate that this life-cycle phase is a strong contender for the title of the 'perfect age of woman's life'.

It is not only the virgin martyrs who stand out as representative of this life-cycle phase, and also as support for the contention that it is maidenhood which, in certain discourses, represents the perfect age of woman's life. Late-medieval English representations of the Blessed Virgin Mary at her assumption and coronation, both in visual and textual sources, frequently depict a 'maidenly' figure. That is, a tender, delicate young woman of marriageable age.[5] Such images of the woman who held the highest place of any female figure add significantly to the suggestion that maidenhood as a life-cycle phase held a special place in late-medieval English ideals of femininity. A third and final example, this one from secular literature, also supports this point of view. The figure who has become known as the 'Pearl Maiden', from the late fourteenth-century poem which has been given the same name, may also be said to occupy the maidenhood phase of her life.[6] The significance of her change of age in death – from infant to, I suggest, 'maiden' – holds an important clue to the puzzle of what may have constituted the perfect age of woman's life. In death, as bride of Christ, she exists in the body of a youthful, sexually mature yet virginal young woman. She has reached the peak of her femininity.

This essay will explore these contentions through a number of stages. First, through discussion of the medieval literary, philosophical and iconographic model of the 'ages of man', and of the view of many commentators that it is *iuventus*, or middle age, which represented the perfect age of man. Their discussions, with one honourable exception, generally leave unexamined the question of whether the ages of man also constituted the ages of woman, and whether therefore middle age represented the perfect age of woman's life. This question, rarely asked and not yet answered, is explored within the remainder of the essay. The notion that 'maidenhood' existed as a distinct phase in women's life cycle is discussed briefly, before the three examples described above are examined. Maidenhood emerges as a strong candidate for the age which represented the perfected state of femininity. Let it not be thought, however, that other discourses did not present other points of view. In those, wifehood, or motherhood, or perhaps even widowhood, represented alternative ideals of femininity. What is suggested here is that maidenhood stands specifically as a corollary to the perfect age of man within the elite discourses which constituted the ages of man literature and the theology of bodily resurrection. The kinds of interests which directed those discourses (male, elite and often clerical) seem to have viewed maidenhood as representing the peak of femininity, within the English culture of the late-thirteenth to the end of the fifteenth centuries.

THE 'AGES OF MAN', THE 'AGES OF WOMAN'?

As many scholars of medieval literature, art, philosophy and science have noted, the theme of the 'ages of man', marking and describing the different characteristics of each life-cycle stage, was a popular motif within such disciplines.[7] Many versions of this topos existed, though with broadly similar outlines. Some describe three main phases in the life cycle of man, others four, still others five, six or seven, from birth to death. While the names for the different stages varied from scheme to scheme, and the complexity of the schemes differed one from another, each broadly mapped out a life cycle of man similar to Aristotle's conception of life as a curve, from *augmentum* to *status* to *decrementum*. 'Every thing generated must grow, maintain itself and then decay' he wrote, and associated this cycle with the stages of human life.[8]

For Aristotle, and for late-medieval writers who took up this theme, the middle stage represented the peak, the prime, the *acme* of a man's life.[9] This middle age, sometimes identified with *iuventus*, sometimes *maturitas* depending on the nomenclature employed in a particular age scheme, was held up by many medieval authors as the age at which a man reached a perfect balance of physical strength and mental powers.[10] This prime or peak age has a variable span in years, depending on the individual account, but in general covers the years ranging from a man's mid-twenties to his mid-forties.

Though each of the major commentators on the ages of man scheme notes that this middle age represents a peak in the idealized life cycle, only Mary

Dove's account takes this theme as its focus. More importantly for this study, it is only Dove's account which notes a firmly gendered element to the theme. Where Burrow includes feminine figures such as the Pearl Maiden, Emily of 'The Knight's Tale' and St Agnes as illustrative of points of his discussion,[11] and Sears makes little of possible differences in conceptions of the ages of man and of woman,[12] Dove notices that authors who illustrate the ages of man theme are not particularly interested in what might constitute the ages of woman. '(W)e need to remind ourselves that "man" in the Ages of Man is not normally an inclusive term, and that when I talk about "man's life" I am not being inclusive, either'.[13] Dove, along with Sears and Burrow, does note that a handful of literary and visual representations of the ages scheme used feminine imagery. Notable examples of this include the pseudo-Aristotelian *Secretum Secretorum*, where in some of the Middle English versions the four seasons are described by analogy with a woman's life, and Dante's *Il Convivio*, where the ages of the soul are also described using feminine imagery.[14] It should be noted, however, that it is not woman's life as such which is being described in these instances, but rather the seasons and the soul. The use of feminine imagery in Dante's poem may have been influenced by the grammatical gender of the concept described, rather than by a sense of the importance of mapping the stages of a woman's life. Certainly, these few exceptions to the rule are not sufficient to constitute a complete tradition on the 'ages of woman'. This essay thus picks up Dove's term 'perfect age', and the question which her study does not have space to address: what constituted the perfect age of woman's life?[15]

A similar question is opened up, though inadvertently, by those who have examined the idea of the perfect age of the body in the theology of the resurrection. Medieval commentators from St Augustine, through Ælfric to Peter Lombard were fascinated by the question of the form of the body at the resurrection, and wondered what age the body would possess in this final, perfected form.[16] They took inspiration from St Paul's words in Ephesians, 'until we all meet into the unity of faith and of the knowledge of the Son of God, unto a perfect man, unto the measure of the age of the fulness of Christ'.[17] The passage seems often to have been interpreted in literal fashion and these commentators argued that the body at the resurrection, which would be the perfect body, would take on the perfect age of Christ. Some, such as Augustine held that this would be thirty, as that was the age at which Christ began his ministry. Others, including Ælfric and Peter Lombard, argued that it would be thirty-two or three, as this was the age of Christ at his crucifixion. Either way, the perfect age of Christ, and therefore the age of the human body at resurrection, fell neatly within the 'prime' age within the ages of man scheme.

But neither the medieval commentators nor their modern historians have addressed the question of whether women, as well as men, would be resurrected in 'the age of the fulness of Christ', that is, in a 30- or 33-year-old body. Here I shall argue that the Pearl Maiden, the virgin martyrs, and the Virgin Mary at her assumption and coronation, all represented in later medieval English visual and textual imagery in the bodies which they would possess in heaven, are depicted within the 'maidenhood' phase of their life cycle, and that this indicates that for some interested parties maidenhood represented the 'perfect age of woman's life'.

Maidenhood

One cannot begin to examine the question of what constituted the perfect age of woman until one has a sense of the stages which were perceived to make up a woman's life. As the ages of man scheme seems largely uninterested in women, it is not valid simply to apply the stages named there, such as *puericia*, *adolescencia*, *iuventus*, *senectus* and so on, and to associate the qualities linked to the different stages of a man's life to a woman's life. Sketching an alternative scheme to the ages of man for women is beyond the scope of this essay, but it is important to note here that late-medieval English culture did recognize a phase in young women's life cycle intervening between childhood and fully fledged adulthood.[18]

The beginning and end points of this phase are blurry, and it would be rather artificial to set them too precisely. However, it seems reasonable to state that this stage was perceived to begin in a young woman's early to mid-teens, and to end sometime between her late teens and mid-twenties. Medieval canon law set a girl's age of consent at twelve (while for boys it was fourteen), arguing that at that age she became sufficiently physically developed to engage in procreation, and sufficiently intellectually and morally developed to understand the nature of the bond into which she was entering.[19] It does not seem possible to determine the age at which girls reached physical maturity in practice, but medical and scientific literature traditionally placed a girl's age at menarche at between twelve and fifteen.[20] Common and borough legal traditions placed women's age at majority (i.e., at which they could leave wardship), and also their age of criminal and civil responsibility, within an age range in the middle teens.[21] All these markers of development indicate a belief that women moved from the incapacities and physical immaturity of childhood into a state more closely resembling adult womanhood in the early to mid-teens.

That they did not usually, however, accomplish full transition to adulthood at this stage is suggested by a number of factors. Marriage for English girls in the later Middle Ages did not usually take place soon after legal age of puberty, but more often some time from the later teens to mid-twenties.[22] While marriage soon after or even before canonical age did occur for some girls of the gentry class and higher, this does not seem to have been the norm. Even where such early marriage did occur, anxieties expressed about the youth of the girls concerned indicates that early marriage does not necessarily indicate the absence of a notion of a phase intervening between childhood and adulthood for girls, but rather that family, political or economic interests could sometimes override that notion.[23] In addition to the evidence on age of marriage or consummation of marriage, the existence of the institution of service and its association particularly with young single women in their mid-teens to mid-twenties indicates that this life-cycle phase was recognized and accommodated within English culture.[24]

Some might label this phase 'female adolescence', and while I do not have an especially strong quarrel with the use of the phrase, I do not feel it is the most useful term available.[25] My preference is for 'maidenhood', as 'maiden' is the term more commonly used in the England of the late thirteenth, fourteenth and fifteenth centuries to refer to young unmarried women than, say, the Latin *adolescentula*.[26] Moreover, it usefully points to two key aspects of the identity of the woman at this stage: she is both young, and virginal.[27] The medieval maiden, therefore, is a woman past childhood but not yet a fully fledged adult, and one whose identity is bound to a certain tension. That is, she is at once sexually and psychologically mature (as the legal codes recognize), but she must also hold onto the virginity required by her pre-marital state. This tension, between sexual maturity and chastity, is the key to the identity of the maiden in late-medieval English culture. I shall argue here that this tension, though in other contexts problematic, could act as a focus for desire. The at-once sexual and chaste maiden was an object of desire for certain groups, and thus she could represent an ideal state of femininity.

PARAGONS OF FEMININITY

When Paul imagined Corinthian confusion on the subject of the bodies of the resurrected, 'With what manner of body shall they come?', he may or may not have had gender distinctions in mind. But we may pose the same question on more specific grounds: 'With what manner of body shall the women come?' By what bodies might the souls of saved women be known? Three examples from late-medieval English culture may give us some idea: the Virgin Mary, who by her assumption was transferred in her body direct from death to Christ's side in heaven;[28] the virgin martyrs, who in achieving sanctity were able to bypass the purgatory reserved for ordinary sinners and go straight to Christ; and the Pearl Maiden, who is also seen to have bypassed purgatory in her innocence, and is shown on her way to join her bridegroom in the Heavenly City. Do these female figures receive representation in the bodies of 30- or 33-year-old women?

Several commentators have linked the Pearl Maiden's physical state to the theology of the resurrection.[29] The poet could not represent her strictly speaking in resurrected form, as that would imply that the raising from the dead had already occurred, but still 'it is appropriate that this body should have the appearance of the one which, according to the highest patristic authority, she will assume after the General Resurrection'.[30] What no critic seems to have taken into account is that the Pearl Maiden is not represented in the body of a woman in her mid-thirties. While her age is not stated, it may be deduced from her representation, as will be discussed below. Her age might also be suggested by comparison with Boccaccio's *Olympia*. This poem bears a striking similarity to *Pearl*, in that it is a dream vision in which a father sees and speaks to his daughter, who had died at five-and-a-half but appears to her father as a girl of marriageable age.[31] Thirty or thirty-three was *not* the most desirable marriageable age for women, particularly in Tuscany. We might expect her to appear, rather, in the body of a young woman in her late teens.[32]

Pearl describes a dream vision, in which a male speaker is confronted by a vision of his daughter, his 'pearl', who had died at the age of two, but who appears to him as a beautiful and courtly young woman: a 'maiden', as he calls her.[33] The Pearl Maiden is interesting to me because she has two ages: she is a 'faunt' (161) or small child, but in death she has taken on the body of a 'maiden of menske' (162), or 'damyselle' (361). Her physical appearance is described at length (197-228). Her dress is in the style of a fashionable young woman of the late fourteenth century, and her dress is all white and covered in pearls (197-204).[34] Her skin is the purest white – whiter than whale bone, or passing the fleur de lys (212, 753). She wears a crown of pearls and flowers: 'A pyȝt coroune ȝet wer þat gyrle/ Of marjorys and non oþer ston,/ Hiȝe pynakled of cler quyt perle,/ Wyth flurted flowrez perfet vpon' ('That girl also wore a decorated crown of pearls and no other stone, with high pinnacles of clear white pearl, with perfect flowers figured on it') (205–8). Her hair is golden and hangs unbound around her face and on her shoulders: 'As schorne golde schyr her fax þenne schon,/ On schyldereȝ þat leghe vnlapped lyȝte' ('her hair, that lay lightly on her shoulders, unbound, then shone like bright cut gold') (213–14). She has grey eyes, and likens herself to a rose (254, 269). The dreamer marvels at her 'fayre figure' and dazzling beauty (747–53).

These physical characteristics – white skin, long loose golden hair, grey eyes, the likeness to a rose, marvellous beauty and fairness of figure – are all aspects of the courtly ideal of feminine beauty, which can be found in almost any youthful heroine of late-medieval English romance or courtly lyric, and will be examined in a moment. That the Pearl Maiden's appearance is meant to represent her physical state on entering heaven is made clear near the end of the poem when she joins a procession of a hundred thousand 'vergynez', all, as she is, crowned, dressed in white and covered with pearls, and goes in with this merry band to meet their bridegroom (1095–152). At that moment her childish age – a mere two years old – and her maidenly body seem combined, as the dreamer is moved to see his 'lyttel quene', making merry with her friends (1147–50). Her childish state is symbolic of her innocence, as is made clear during her debate with the dreamer over the parable of the vineyard (481–660), but she appears in a young woman's body.

There are three elements of her representation which she shares with the iconography of the virgin martyrs and the Virgin Mary at assumption and coronation, and which indicate that she was meant to be imagined as a maiden rather than an older woman. Those elements are her courtly beauty, her loose golden hair, and her crown. The conventions concerning feminine beauty were remarkably consistent in the period under discussion. The beautiful woman almost always, in both literary and visual media, has long golden hair, very fair skin, fine features, sparkling eyes, curved dark eyebrows, red lips, and a long and slender body with small breasts but a protruding belly. She often has grey eyes, though at other times they are blue, a cleft chin, and delicately rosy cheeks.[35] Matthew of Vendôme and Geoffrey of Vinsauf supply sample descriptions of the beautiful woman in their guides to poetical writing,[36] and the convention is also prominent within romances and lyrics.[37] A key aspect of the feminine ideal is her slenderness and delicacy:

> Let the upper arms, as long as they are slender, be enchanting. Let the fingers be soft and slim in substance, smooth and milk-white in appearance, long and straight in shape . . . Let the snowy bosom present both breasts like virginal gems set side by side. Let the waist be slim, a mere handful . . . let the leg show itself graceful; let the remarkably dainty foot wanton with its own daintiness.[38]

This description strongly implies that beauty was associated with the slenderness of youth and virginity.

For my purposes it is most significant that youthfulness was a key element of this ubiquitous ideal of feminine beauty. The ages of some Middle English literary heroines who are described as beautiful are stated, and they are always in their teens. Freine is twelve when men begin to notice her beauty, and Goldboru, 'the fairest wuman on live' is an heiress waiting to come of age.[39] Chaucer's Alison, whose beauty is conventional yet slightly satirized, is eighteen, and his Virginia – a 'mayde of excellent beauty' who is described in conventional terms – is fourteen.[40] Where the age of the beautiful woman is not stated, her youth is implicit in her figure, with its slender limbs, small high breasts, narrow waist and smooth white skin. An ugly woman, in contrast, is often old, with loose skin, a forest of wrinkles and breasts like deflated bladders.[41]

Some of those who have discussed the subject of beauty in history have argued that feminine beauty is ahistorical, eternal and unchanging.[42] Authors such as Kenneth Clark and Arthur Marwick seem profoundly unaware of their own subjectivities as white, middle class or higher, heterosexual males of the mid- or later twentieth century, and the effect of such subjectivities on their interpretations.[43] Others have argued that tastes have altered across time, and that representations of women must be read within their cultural and political contexts. For example, Anne Hollander argues that the notions of physical beauty present in any given period depend on the fashions of the day, as bodies represented in visual form can be said to have been shaped by the 'ghosts' of their clothing.[44] Margaret Miles discusses the appeal of the Virgin's naked breast, and argues that the attraction lay in the breast's association with food and nurture in a time of threatened nutrition (the mid-fourteenth century).[45] Similarly, the representation of the idealized beautiful woman as a slender teenage girl should not be seen as a constant across history or cultures. It should be read within the historical context of its production. I see this ideal as an aspect of the wider ideal of maidenhood as the age of consummate femininity.

The conventional beauty of the Pearl Maiden is one aspect of her representation as a youthful, idealized maiden. Her hair is another aspect. It is golden, long, and hangs loose on her shoulders.[46] Such hair is an element of conventional beauty, but it stands for more than that. Long, uncovered and loose hair had a variety of meanings in late-medieval English culture. It could be a sign of uncivilized or anti-social nature, as it is in the images of the hairy wild men and women who sometimes appear in manuscript illuminations.[47] That sign of wildness could be combined with loose hair as a sign of penitence, as it was in the *vitae* and visual representations of Mary Magdalene in the desert and Mary of Egypt.[48] Hair long enough to cover the body could provide modesty, as it does in the life of St Agnes, whose hair grows to cover her nakedness when she is stripped and thrown into a brothel, and in the legend of Lady Godiva.[49]

Perhaps paradoxically, long, loose hair was also a sign of sexual attractiveness and availability, and it was for this reason that early Christian writers demanded that a woman hide her hair under a veil.[50] The London *Liber Albus* required that the cutting of a prostitute's hair be one aspect of her punishment on a third conviction, and thus of the taming of her sexuality.[51] For professed virgins of the Middle Ages, 'taking the veil' was an event within the ritual of consecration, along with the adoption of monastic clothes and the ring by which they were wed to Christ.[52] This ceremony was ritually linked with the secular wedding ceremony, during which a bride would often wear her hair loose and uncovered, and would signal her movement from maidenhood to wifehood by tying up her hair and covering it with a headdress or wimple.[53] While young unmarried women may have often worn their hair bound or covered in practice, as is indicated in some illustrations and tomb brasses, loose uncovered hair remained an instantly recognizable symbol of the state of virginity. Loose hair also played a symbolic role in the coronation of queens – a ritual which bears many similarities to the rituals of consecration and marriage – and was probably meant as a sign of their chastity.[54]

Loose unbound hair signified an apparently contradictory state: the state of sexual attractiveness and availability, and the state of virginity. It therefore stands as the sign *par excellence* of maidenhood, an age in which sexual desirability and the fact of virginity are intermingled. There is a tension, rather than a contradiction within the state of maidenhood. Sexuality and chastity there exist simultaneously. The unbound golden hair of the Pearl Maiden is meant as a sign that she is not meant to be imagined as a sober, respectable woman in her mid-thirties, but rather as a perfectly chaste and gloriously desirable maiden, of an age probably somewhere in her mid- or late teens.

The crown of pearls and flowers which the Maiden wears is another key to her maidenly state. The author of the thirteenth-century exhortation to chastity, *Hali Meiðhad*, was stating little more than was conventional in his image of virgins in heaven. They all wear 'a circlet shining brighter than the sun, called *aureola* in Latin'.[55] The crown may stand as a symbol of spinsterhood, and thus of permanent virginity in the secular life, as it does in *The Good Wyfe Wold a Pylgremage*: 'Yfe þou wylt no hosbonde have, but wher thy mayden croun',[56] or of the permanent virginity of the woman professed to the religious life: 'Your virginity . . .will be radiant in a golden diadem'.[57] The crown or circlet is an ancient and extremely widespread symbol, whose origins cannot be established here. Suffice to say that its primary modern association, with royalty, was not its first meaning. It is possible that its later medieval associations with virginity derived from two separate traditions: one of the circlet, crown or wreath as a symbol of marriage, and the other as a symbol of victory.

The crown as both a religious and secular symbol of victory and triumph in the Middle Ages seems derived from the Greek and Roman wreath, which symbolized the victory of athletes and of military leaders, and became part of the imperial regalia.[58] The symbol passed into Christian religious use before secular, with its adoption as a symbol of victory over death, particularly for martyrs.[59] Coronation became part of royal inauguration in the West in ninth-century Carolingian rituals, and Hincmar of Rheims in the second half of the ninth century was instrumental in the development of the symbolic association of crowns with king-making.[60] The wreath of flowers as a symbol of marriage is, if anything, of much older and more obscure origin, and is perhaps associated primarily with fertility.[61] The association of flower garlands with fertility perhaps persisted in the later Middle Ages with May Day games, which involved gathering flowers and crowning of a May King and Queen, as well as with the custom of brides wearing garlands or circlets on their wedding day.[62]

The crown of virgins may have been linked to both traditions. It symbolised victory over death through the promise of eternal life, and it signified virginity through its association with marriage and fertility, and thus through the image of the virgin as the bride of Christ.[63] The Pearl Maiden's crown consists of both flowers and pearls. The latter were a well-established symbol of purity and virginity by the later Middle Ages, a symbol played upon by Jacobus de Voragine in his introduction to the life of St Margaret, as the Latin for pearl is *margarita*.[64] The Maiden's white garments also contribute to her representation as pure, innocent and virginal. White garments were associated with both the innocence of the child undergoing baptism, and professed virginity.[65] To sum up, the pearls, the crown, the loose hair and the white garments combine with the Pearl Maiden's conventional beauty to present a complex yet harmonious image of a woman who combines most admirable feminine traits: chastity, and sexual desirability.

Her appearance in many ways matches that of the virgin martyrs. The virgin martyrs, who were the most popular type of female saint in late-medieval England, include SS Katherine, Margaret, Lucy, Christina, Cecilia, Dorothy, Agnes, Barbara and Agatha.[66] Their *vitae* show individual variants, but have several main themes in common. The maiden is usually of noble and wealthy background, and is Christian in a predominantly pagan late-classical world. Upon reaching puberty her extraordinary natural beauty becomes apparent, and she is sought after by a powerful pagan suitor. Having pledged both faith and virginity to God, she rejects the advances of the pagan suitor, and is thrown into prison. She undergoes a series of horrible tortures, designed to make her renounce both faith and chastity, but refuses to give up either. Finally she is martyred, usually by beheading. While the virgin martyrs have received increasing attention from scholars in recent years, their age has been little mentioned. I see this, however, as central to their identity as ideal representations of womanhood.

Of those whose actual ages are given in their lives all are in their teens: Agnes is thirteen, Margaret is fifteen, Katherine is eighteen, and Christina is twelve when her torments begin, though she is tortured for fifteen years before her eventual martyrdom.[67] Though we are not told the ages of the others, it seems clear that they too occupy this age of post-pubertal youthful virginity. They must all be of *aetas nubiles* – the legal or actual age of puberty and capacity to marry – because the plot of each virgin martyr's life hinges on her sexual attractiveness and the efforts of her suitor/tormentor to make her marry him. We are not, therefore, dealing with child saints. The upper limit of their age may also be suggested by their eligibility – they are not spinster saints who have gone beyond the expected age of marriage – and also by the language used to describe them. In the Middle English of Osbern Bokenham's collection they are called 'maidens', and the corresponding Latin term in the *Legenda Aurea* is *puella*, not a term likely to be used of a mature woman.[68] Moreover, the lives frequently describe the martyrs as 'young' or of 'tender age', or as *tenerae puellae* – tender girls. Lucy is 'a maydyn yung and delycate',[69] Agatha is a 'damysel ying',[70] Faith is 'in hir tendir age'.[71] There can be little doubt that all the virgin martyrs would have been perceived to be young women occupying the maidenhood stage of their life cycle.

According to medieval authors on the resurrection, Christ died at thirty-three because he had reached the peak of his life, and it would not have been appropriate for Christ to experience physical decline.[72] Is it possible that the virgin martyrs died in their teens because that was the peak of the lives of their feminine bodies? It seems relevant to note that, in regard to healthy reproduction, Aristotle had argued that the perfect age for women at marriage was eighteen, while for men it was thirty-six, and Giles of Rome's *De Regimine Principium* kept Aristotle's perfect age for women, though it lowered that of men.[73] The idea that a woman's later teenage years represented a feminine physical ideal went beyond natural philosophy and eugenics, and entered the widely disseminated representations of women saints.

The late-medieval rewriting of the life of St Apollonia may be singled out as illustrative of my theory that youthfulness is a key attribute of feminine perfection. In earlier lives, including the thirteenth-century *Legenda Aurea*, she is an aging deaconess, whom Jacobus de Voragine calls 'an admirable virgin, well along in years'.[74] But by the later Middle Ages in England she is represented visually as a young maiden, alongside youthful martyrs such as Agnes.[75] Increasingly, youth was becoming a necessary element of ideal femininity.

The virgin martyrs do not generally wear the white clothes of the Pearl Maiden, but in visual representations they all share her conventional beauty, her long, loose, golden hair, and, in many cases, her crown or garland.[76] Bokenham's description of the beauty of Margaret when first seen by the prefect Olibrius is particularly notable for its engagement with courtly ideals of feminine beauty:

> And whan he sey hyr forheed lely-whyht,
> Hyr bent browys blake, & hyr grey eyne,
> Hyr chyry Chekys, hyr nose streyt & ryht,
> Hyr lyppys rody, hyr chyn, wych as pleyne
> Pulshyd marbyl shoon, & clovyn in tweyne.[77]

This matches perfectly the courtly literary ideal of feminine beauty described above. It seems apparent from Bokenham's allusions to both Geoffrey of Vinsauf and Matthew of Vendôme elsewhere within the life that his appeal to secular courtly ideals is quite consciously made, and that the reader was meant to imagine Margaret on the same terms as the sexually desirable secular ideal.[78] The conventional beauty of the virgin martyrs is significant as it clearly indicates that these saints were not meant to be conceived of in sexually neutral terms, nor that through their virginity they had 'become men'. Not only were they represented in uncompromisingly female form, they fit the image of the desirable ideal.[79]

The unbound hair of the virgin martyrs in visual representations takes on the same meanings as it does for the Pearl Maiden, of the woman who is both desired and untouched. The symbolism of the crowns which they often wear is a little more complex. As with the Pearl Maiden, they symbolize virginity and dedication to Christ, as shown by the example of Cecilia and her chaste husband

Valerian, to whom angels offer crowns of roses as signs of their chastity.[80] But they are also crowns of martyrdom – a significant aspect of the early Christian iconographic meanings of the crown.[81] Peter Abelard in the twelfth century had written of the double crown of the virgin martyrs: of lilies for virginity, and of roses for martyrdom.[82] In the case of St Katherine, a royal princess, the crown also points to regal status. Yet the significance of the crown or wreath as a symbol of virginity which is youthful and potentially fertile remains, and is appropriate to the virgin martyrs' life-cycle stage.

Representations of the Virgin Mary in English visual sources of our period also hint at the identification of women's youth with their perfect age. In contrast to her son, tradition had it that she lived on well into old age, and thus well past the perfect age of the body according to the theology of the resurrection.[83] Voragine's account of the Assumption of the Virgin says that she was fourteen when she conceived Christ and fifteen when she gave birth to him (that is, at the perfect age of woman) then after his death at thirty-three she survived him by twenty-four years, thus dying at the age of seventy-two. He says another account gives her age at death as sixty.[84] In either case, at the assumption she is, in human years, an elderly woman.

Turning to visual representation of the Virgin's assumption and coronation, one might expect to find her represented as an old woman, if the artists concerned took a naturalistic course. Alternatively, given the theology of perfect age and the resurrection of the body, one might expect to find her in a 33-year-old body. How would a married woman of that age be represented in this late-medieval English context? She would almost certainly be wimpled, with her hair bound up, and perhaps would have a slightly matronly figure; in short, perhaps she would look like traditional representations of St Anne.[85] Representations of Mary during the assumption and the coronation do not depict any such a matronly figure. Rather, like the Pearl Maiden and virgin martyrs, she is a maiden, who as queen of heaven has the unbound hair and crown of a maiden on her wedding day.[86] Scenes of the death, assumption and coronation of the Virgin in the late thirteenth-century Ramsey Psalter depict just such a youthful figure (Fig. 1). Depictions of the coronation are particularly illustrative of my theme, as they depict a mother who looks considerably younger than her son. The bearded, stately and sombre figure of Christ from the early fourteenth-century De Lisle Psalter is representative of the perfect age of man, and the demure, pretty, youthful and maidenly figure of Mary at his side is representative of the perfect age of woman (Fig. 2, p. 14).

Mary's representation is slightly more complex than those of the Pearl Maiden or virgin martyrs. Thus, for example, while she too is a conventional beauty with flowing golden hair,[87] she is often depicted with a light veil over her hair. This may be meant to signify her state as both virgin and wife, with the unbound hair of the former and the seemly, concealing veil of the latter. She is not, however,

Figure 1: The death, assumption and coronation of the Virgin, late thirteenth century. From *The Ramsey Psalter*, The Pierpont Morgan Library, New York. M. 302, f. 4. Reproduced by permission of the Pierpont Morgan Library.

Figure 2: The coronation of the Virgin, early fourteenth century. From *The De Lisle Psalter*, The British Library. MS Arundel 83 PT 2 F134v. Reproduced by permission of The British Library.

shown wimpled, as one would expect an older married woman to be. Also, her crown and the theme of her coronation hold slightly different meanings than those of the others. While the theme of 'Maria Regina', or the Virgin as queen, dates to the sixth century, the theme of the act of the coronation of the virgin dates only from the twelfth and thirteenth centuries.[88] It is argued that through this iconography the Virgin is represented in her primary late-medieval role as royal intercessor, who shared in Christ's power over heaven and earth and could be called upon by believers to intercede in earthly affairs.[89]

Yet, as with the virgin martyrs, the multi-layered meanings of the representations of the Virgin do not detract from the observation that she is, in English art of the later Middle Ages, regularly depicted in the body of a conventionally desirable young maiden at the moments of her bodily ascension and her crowning. At these moments, it seems reasonable to assume, it would have been thought appropriate to represent her in the ideal feminine form. That this ideal contrasts so strongly with the ideal of masculinity represented by her son suggests a clear distinction in notions of the perfect age of man and of woman.

CONCLUSION

In taking up the question opened up by Dove's analysis of the perfect age of man, this article has sought representations of feminine figures which might suggest an answer to that question. The female figures chosen to provide that answer were not selected at random, but rather because they provide images of the perfected female body in death. Representations of women in funerary monuments and tomb brasses sometimes also depict similarly maidenly figures, the example of the tomb and crosses of Eleanor of Castile perhaps providing the most obvious example.[90] A broad study of such monuments, their representations of women, and their variation (over time, for example), might also hold clues to this puzzle.

It might be objected that it is not valid to seek too hard for a single definitive answer to the question posed. If late-medieval English culture had held a firm, fixed and single notion of a perfect age of woman, surely it would have expressed this in clearer ways. For example, a complete alternative tradition to the ages of man scheme – and a notion of the prime age within that – could have been established for women. This would be a fair objection, and I do not suggest that there existed any comparably conscious and thought-through notion of the perfect age of woman as of man. Moreover, it may be said that there was more than one perfect age of woman, and that the age was determined differently by the interests of those who directed particular discourses. In the 'real world' of medieval society, at all social levels, it was not at all desirable that a young woman die in her mid- to late teens. Rather, she should become a wife and a mother, thus fulfilling her obligations to her family and culture and becoming, in another sense, 'perfected'. In terms of economic or legal capacity, one might argue that a woman was only 'perfected', or made whole and complete, in widowhood, when she could own and control property, businesses and chattels in a way which was greatly limited for women at other stages.

Yet the power of the images discussed cannot be overlooked. As paragons of femininity, the Virgin Mary and the virgin martyrs were present in media which permeated late-medieval English culture. They were visible not only in the books of hours, hagiographic collections and art treasures of the elite, but in the sermons addressed to the laity all the way down the social scale, and in the panel paintings, carvings and stained glass which adorned the simplest parish church. No such broad audience can be envisaged for *Pearl*, but it may be that the Pearl Poet was responding to and borrowing from this well-established and popular image of femininity in constructing the image of the Pearl Maiden. And in death, in their heavenly bodies, these familiar female figures do not resemble wives, matrons or dowagers.

Given the breadth of the image's popularity, it becomes difficult to answer precisely the question, 'For whom was the maiden "perfect"?' Questions of who produced these images, and for whom, are too lengthy and complex to be explored here. But, leaving aside the minutiae of production and reception, it seems reasonable to assert that these ideals of femininity were, ultimately, the product of clerical culture, in which the social values of wifehood, motherhood, or economic and legal capacity, were pushed aside in favour of the spiritual value of chastity. The physical maturity of the maiden makes her chastity all the more valuable, and desirable, to the male clerical elite for whom women were (or were supposed to be) untouchable. It was the power of this group within medieval culture which ensured that representations of the virgin martyrs and Virgin Mary as maidens became ubiquitous, and dominant. In the end, although the perfect age of woman was never as clearly or uniformly expressed as that of man, the most powerful image of ideal femininity available was that of the maiden.

Notes

1. I would like to thank several individuals whose ideas and insights have contributed much to the argument as it is presented in this essay, in particular Jeremy Goldberg, Felicity Riddy, Katherine Lewis, Chris Given-Wilson, Alastair Minnis, and the audience at the 1995 Leeds International Medieval Congress, where an earlier version was delivered.

2. Hans Kurath, Sherman Kuhn and Robert E. Lewis (eds), *Middle English Dictionary* (Ann Arbor, 1956–ongoing), s.v. 'maidenli': 'Like a virgin or maiden'; 'maiden': 1.(a) 'An unmarried woman, usually young', 2.(a) 'A virgin'; 'mai': (a) 'A woman; esp. a young attractive woman (married or single)'.

3. On the popularity of virgin martyrs' lives in general and St Katherine in particular see Katherine J. Lewis, '"Rule of lyf alle folk to sewe": Lay Responses to the Cult of St Katherine of Alexandria in Late-Medieval England, 1300–1530', (unpublished D.Phil. thesis, University of York,

1996), esp. pp. 71–7. See also Jocelyn Wogan-Browne, 'Saints' Lives and the Female Reader', *Forum for Modern Language Studies* 27 (1991), 314–32; Wogan-Browne, 'The Virgin's Tale' in Ruth Evans and Lesley Johnson (eds), *Feminist Readings in Middle English Literature: The Wife of Bath and All Her Sect* (London, 1994), pp. 165–94; Eamon Duffy, 'Holy Maydens, Holy Wyfes: The Cult of Women Saints in Fifteenth- and Sixteenth-Century England' in W.J. Sheils and Diana Wood (eds), *Women in the Church*, Studies in Church History 27 (Oxford, 1990), 175–96.

4. On their popularity see Lewis, 'Rule of lyf', pp. 71–7; Duffy, 'Holy Maydens, Holy Wyfes', pp. 180–90. On their virginity see Wogan-Browne, 'Virgin's Tale', pp. 172–81. On their potential as role models see Lewis, 'Rule of lyf', esp pp. 218–57. On their possible use as pornographic figures see Kathryn Gravdal, *Ravishing Maidens: Writing Rape in Medieval French Literature and Law* (Philadelphia, 1991), pp. 21–5.

5. See Figs 1 and 2.

6. For background information on the date, authorship and manuscript of the poem see E.V. Gordon (ed.), *Pearl* (Oxford, 1953), introduction; Malcolm Andrew and Ronald Waldron (eds), *The Poems of the Pearl Manuscript* (Exeter, 1987), introduction; Derek Brewer and Jonathan Gibson (eds), *A Companion to the Gawain-Poet* (Cambridge, 1997). References in the text and notes are to the Andrew and Waldron edition, unless otherwise stated.

7. Three authors provide extensive studies of the ages schemes: J.A. Burrow, *The Ages of Man: A Study in Medieval Writing and Thought* (Oxford, 1986); Mary Dove, *The Perfect Age of Man's Life* (Cambridge, 1986); Elizabeth Sears, *The Ages of Man: Medieval Interpretations of the Life Cycle* (Princeton, 1986). See also Michael E. Goodich, *From Birth to Old Age: The Human Life Cycle in Medieval Thought* (Lanham MD, 1989).

8. *De Anima* Bk III, ch. 12, cited in Burrow, *Ages of Man*, p. 6. See also Aristotle, *On Rhetoric: A Theory of Civic Discourse*, ed. and tr. George A. Kennedy (New York, 1991), pp. 168–9.

9. Burrow, *Ages of Man* pp. 6–11; Dove, *Perfect Age*, esp. pp. 26–36; Sears, *Ages of Man*, pp. 45, 56, 119.

10. See for example M.C. Seymour et al. (eds), *On the Properties of Things. John Trevisa's Translation of Bartholomaeus Anglicus'* De Proprietatibus Rerum. *A Critical Text* (2 vols, Oxford, 1975), vol. 1, lib. 6, cap. 1, p. 292: 'Aftir þis *adholescencia* "striplynges age" comeþ þe age þat hatte *iuventus*, and þis age is in þe middil amonges ages, and þerfore it is strengest.'

11. Burrow, *Ages of Man*, pp. 64–6, 69, 102, 104–5, 112; J.A. Burrow, 'Chaucer's *Knight's Tale* and the Three Ages of Man' in J.A. Burrow, *Essays on Medieval Literature* (Oxford, 1984), pp. 27–48.

12. She does, however, note that representations of women within the ages schemes were generally exceptional, Sears, *Ages of Man*, p. 24, and points to some visual examples where the lives of men and women are represented side by side, pp. 110–13. These, however, do not mark out middle age as a particularly notable phase in a woman's life cycle.

13. Dove, *Perfect Age*, p. 25.

14. Burrow, *Ages of Man*, p. 30; Dove, *Perfect Age*, pp. 22–3; Sears, *Ages of Man*, pp. 99–113. M.A. Manzaloui (ed.), *Secretum Secretorum: Nine English Versions*, Early English Text Society, Original Series 276 (Oxford, 1977), pp. 55–8, 153–5, 346–9, 572–4; Dante, *Il Convivio* in K. Foster and P. Boyde (eds and tr.), *Dante's Lyric Poetry* (2 vols, Oxford, 1967), vol. 1, pp. 137–9.

15. In this essay, as in Dove's work, the term 'perfect age' is used to refer to a sense of the prime of

life in a broad, cultural sense, rather than in the strictly legal sense (where it could refer to age of consent or majority): see Dove, *Perfect Age*, pp. 13–14. Though the two concepts overlapped, the aim here is to present a view of the phase of life which represented woman's perfect femininity, and this had meanings beyond the purely legal.

16. Caroline Walker Bynum, *The Resurrection of the Body in Western Christianity, 200–1336* (New York, 1995), esp. pp. 98, 122; Jackie Tasioulas, 'Seeds of Perfection: The Childlike Soul and the Resurrection of the Body' in P.J.P. Goldberg and Felicity Riddy (eds), *Youth in the Middle Ages* (Woodbridge, forthcoming); Burrow, *Ages of Man*, pp. 104–5, 135–44.

17. Ephesians 4:13.

18. For more on this subject see Kim M. Phillips, 'The Medieval Maiden: Young Womanhood in Late Medieval England' (unpublished D.Phil. thesis, University of York, 1997), esp. pp. 29–66.

19. Gratian, *Decretum*, sec. pars, c.30, q.2, c.un, and *Decretales Gregorii IX (Liber Extra)*, lib. 4, tit. 2, caps. 1–14, in A.L. Richter and A. Friedberg (eds), *Corpus Iuris Canonici*, 2nd edn (2 vols, Leipzig, 1922); A. Esmein, *Le Mariage en Droit Canonique*, 2nd edn (2 vols, New York, 1968), vol. 1, pp. 211–16; W. Onclin, 'L'Âge Requis pour le Mariage dans la Doctrine Canonique Médiévale' in Stephan Kuttner and J. Joseph Ryan (eds), *Proceedings of the Second International Congress of Medieval Canon Law* (Vatican City, 1965), pp. 237–47; R.H. Helmholz, *Marriage Litigation in Medieval England* (Cambridge, 1974), p. 98.

20. See J.B. Post, 'Ages at Menarche and Menopause: Some Mediaeval Authorities', *Population Studies* 25 (1971), 83–7, but also Peter Laslett, 'Age at Sexual Maturity in Europe Since the Middle Ages' in Peter Laslett, *Family Life and Illicit Love in Earlier Generations: Essays in Historical Sociology* (Cambridge, 1977), pp. 214–32; and Darrel W. Amundsen and Carol Jean Diers, 'The Age at Menarche in Medieval Europe', *Human Biology* 45 (1973), 363–9.

21. On wardship and majority see Henry de Bracton, *Bracton on the Laws and Customs of England*, ed. G.E. Woodbine, tr. Samuel E. Thorne (4 vols, Cambridge, MA, 1968), vol. 2, p. 251; Sue Sheridan Walker, 'Proof of Age of Feudal Heirs in Medieval England', *Mediaeval Studies* 35 (1973), 306–23; F. Pollock and F.W. Maitland, *The History of English Law Before the Time of Edward I*, 2nd edn (2 vols, Cambridge, 1968), vol. 1, p. 320, vol. 2, pp. 438–40. On age of criminal responsibility see William Holdsworth, *A History of English Law* (16 vols, London, 1942), vol. 3, p. 372.

22. See esp. P.J.P. Goldberg, 'Marriage, Migration and Servanthood: The York Cause Paper Evidence', and Richard M. Smith, 'Geographical Diversity in the Resort to Marriage in Late Medieval Europe: Work, Reputation, and Unmarried Females in the Household Formation Systems of Northern and Southern Europe', both in P.J.P. Goldberg (ed.), *Women in Medieval English Society*, 2nd edn (Stroud, 1997), pp. 1–15, 16–59.

23. Phillips, 'Medieval Maiden', pp. 60–6; T.H. Hollingsworth, 'A Demographic Study of the British Ducal Families' in D.V. Glass and D.E.V. Eversley (eds), *Population in History: Essays in Historical Demography* (London, 1965), pp. 364–5. John Carmi Parsons' study of marriage among the Plantagenets, Mortimers and Hollands from 1150 to 1500 shows that even in instances where aristocratic girls were married off soon after puberty, consummation of the match was often delayed by a few years. See his chapter 'Mothers, Daughters, Marriage, Power: Some Plantagenet Evidence, 1150–1500' in John Carmi Parsons (ed.), *Medieval Queenship* (Stroud, 1994), pp. 66–7. His findings strongly suggest that even where marriage took place early in a girl's life, it was not necessarily

considered appropriate that she take on the fully adult roles of sexual partner and mother until she had gained a few more years' maturity.

24. See works by P.J.P. Goldberg, esp. *Women, Work, and Life Cycle in a Medieval Economy: Women in York and Yorkshire* c. *1300–1520* (Oxford, 1992), pp. 158–86.

25. Other historians dealing with the subject of medieval youth have preferred 'adolescence', for example Barbara A. Hanawalt, *Growing Up in Medieval London: The Experience of Childhood in History* (Oxford, 1993), p. 8.

26. For late-medieval English uses of *adolescentula* see R.E. Latham (ed.), *Dictionary of Medieval Latin from British Sources* (London, 1975-ongoing), s.v. *'adolescentula'*. For more on the issue of terminology see Phillips, 'Medieval Maiden', pp. 21–5.

27. In their translation of thirteenth-century English texts on virginity, Bella Millett and Jocelyn Wogan-Browne say that while they sought modern equivalents for Middle English words where possible, they made an exception for 'maiden', as there is no current English word which similarly suggests both 'girl' and 'virgin': *Medieval English Prose for Women: Selections from the Katherine Group and Ancrene Wisse* (Oxford, 1990), p. xliii.

28. For an overview of the history of the theology of Mary's assumption see Marina Warner, *Alone of all Her Sex: The Myth and Cult of the Virgin Mary* (London, 1976), ch. 6.

29. See for example Burrow, *Ages of Man*, pp. 104–5; Ian Bishop, *'Pearl' in its Setting* (Oxford, 1968), p. 101.

30. Bishop, ibid., p. 101.

31. Giovanni Boccaccio, *Eclogues*, tr. Janet Levarie Smarr (New York, 1987), pp. 156–69. The similarities between *Pearl* and *Olympia* have been noted by scholars since early this century, but it has not proved possible to confirm whether the Pearl Poet was influenced by the latter. *Olympia* survives in a manuscript copy from about 1367–8, and may have been composed earlier, and thus in terms of timing it is possible that the Pearl Poet saw Boccaccio's poem. Gordon suggests *Pearl* may be dated to between 1360 and 1395, and belongs more probably to the latter part of this period, Gordon, *Pearl*, introduction, p. xliv. The fact that *Olympia* is in Latin rather than Italian would have made it more accessible to readers outside Italy. But, in short, no firm connections may be drawn. See Richard Newhauser, 'Sources II: Scriptural and Devotional Sources' in Brewer and Gibson (eds), *Companion to the Gawain-Poet*, p. 268. I am indebted to Felicity Riddy and Nick Havely for their communications regarding this subject.

32. Christiane Klapisch-Zuber and David Herlihy have postulated a Tuscan model of marriage in the later Middle Ages in which girls in their mid- to late teens married men around ten years older than themselves: *The Tuscans and their Families: A Study of the Florentine Catasto of 1427* (New Haven, 1985), pp. 87, 210–11, 215; Herlihy, *Medieval Households* (Cambridge MA, 1985), pp.103–11. Richard Smith, along with Jeremy Goldberg, has suggested that this model should be seen as distinctively 'Mediterranean' rather than 'European', and that English girls, for example, can be shown to have married at a later age to men more nearly their contemporaries. See for example R. Smith, 'The People of Tuscany and their Families in the Fifteenth Century: Medieval or Mediterranean?', *Journal of Family History* 6 (1981), 107–28; R. Smith, 'Some Reflections on the Evidence for the Origins of the "European Marriage Pattern" in England' in C.C. Harris (ed.), *The Sociology of the Family: New Directions for Britain*, Sociological Review Monograph 28, (Keele, 1979); and see n. 23, above.

33. The Maiden's age at the time of her death is stated: 'þow lyfed not two ȝer in oure þede' (483), while the relationship between dreamer and maiden is implied when the former says 'Ho watȝ me nerre þen aunte or nece' (233). There has been debate over the interpretation of the poem since early this century. Some have read it as pure allegory, with the Pearl Maiden representing some abstract concept such as purity, while others have taken a more literal approach, seeing her as the daughter of the dreamer. A useful approach seems to be to see that the Pearl Maiden combines realistic and symbolic qualtities. See Andrew and Waldron (eds), *Pearl MS*, p. 32, n. 7; P.M. Kean, *The Pearl: An Interpretation* (London, 1967), pp. 115–20; Bishop, *'Pearl'*, p. 15; John Conley (ed.), *The Middle English Pearl: Critical Essays* (Notre Dame, 1970); and more recently, David Aers, 'The Self Mourning: Reflections on Pearl' in *Speculum* 68 (1993), 54–73, pp. 55–6.

34. Gordon notes that the Maiden's dress is 'a very simple form of the aristocratic dress of the second half of the fourteenth century', with the very long sleeves – 'lappeȝ large' (201) – characteristic of aristocratic dress, *Pearl*, p. 56, n. 228.

35. D.S. Brewer, 'The Ideal of Feminine Beauty in Medieval Literature, Especially "Harley Lyrics", Chaucer, and Some Elizabethans', *Modern Language Review* 50 (1955), 257–69; Walter Clyde Curry, *The Middle English Ideal of Personal Beauty; As Found in the Metrical Romances, Chronicles, and Legends of the XIII, XIV, and XV Centuries* (Baltimore, 1916); Kim M. Phillips, 'The Medieval Beauty Myth: An Aesthetics of Virginity', *Medieval Life* 5 (1996), 10–13.

36. Matthew of Vendôme, *The Art of Versification*, tr. Aubrey E. Galyon (Ames, 1980), p. 43; Geoffrey of Vinsauf, *The Poetria Nova*, tr. in Ernest Gallo, *The Poetria Nova and its Sources in Early Rhetorical Doctrine* (The Hague, 1971), pp. 45–7.

37. See for example the description of Felice in *The Romance of Guy of Warwick*, ed. Julius Zupitza, Early English Text Society, extra series 42, 49 and 59 (Oxford, 1883, 1887, and 1891, reprinted in one volume 1966), ll. 65–74, p. 7. See also descriptions of courtly beauties in Rossell Hope Robbins (ed.), *Secular Lyrics of the XIVth and XVth Centuries* (Oxford, 1955), pp. 120–8, 144–5, 183, 223; and G.L. Brook (ed.), *The Harley Lyrics: The Middle English Lyrics of MS Harley 2253* (Manchester, 1968), pp. 33–4, 37–41.

38. Geoffrey of Vinsauf, *Poetria Nova*, p. 45.

39. 'Lay le Freine', ll. 238–40, 257–70; 'Havelok the Dane', ll. 258–9, both in Donald B. Sands (ed.), *Middle English Verse Romances* (University of Exeter Press, 1986), pp. 241–2, 65.

40. 'The Miller's Tale', ll. 3221–70, 'The Physician's Tale', ll. 7–8, 30–8, from Geoffrey Chaucer, *The Canterbury Tales* in Larry D. Benson (ed.), *The Riverside Chaucer* (Oxford, 1987), pp. 68–70, 190.

41. Matthew of Vendôme *Versification*, p. 44. The female grotesque found literary expression in the Loathly Lady: see for example 'The Wedding of Sir Gawain and Dame Ragnell', ll. 231–43, in Sands (ed.), *ME Verse Romances*, pp. 331–2.

42. Kenneth Clark, *The Nude: A Study of Ideal Art* (London, 1956), p. 11 and *passim*; Kenneth Clark, *Feminine Beauty* (London, 1980); Arthur Marwick, *Beauty in History: Society, Politics and Personal Appearance* c. *1500 to the Present* (London, 1988).

43. Marwick fervently denies any political element to perceptions of beauty, and presents his views as natural or self-evident: 'All the complicated talk of politics and power struggles and male conspiracy and oppression seem to me to miss the simple heart of the matter: the sheer uncomplicated joy of going to bed with a beautiful woman', p. 21. Angela Carter suggests an

alternative title for Marwick's book as 'Women I have fancied throughout the ages with additional notes on some of the men I think I might have fancied if I were a woman' in her review, 'I Could Have Fancied Her', *London Review of Books* 11 (February 1989), p. 8.

44. Anne Hollander *Seeing Through Clothes* (New York, 1975).

45. Margaret Miles, 'The Virgin's One Bare Breast: Female Nakedness and Religious Meaning in Tuscan Early Renaissance Culture' in Susan Rubin Suleiman (ed.), *The Female Body in Western Culture: Contemporary Perspectives* (Cambridge MA, 1986).

46. The artist who produced the four drawings contained in the manuscript did not precisely follow the description of the Pearl Maiden supplied in the text. In the two illustrations depicting the Pearl Maiden she is shown to have her hair done in plaits and bound up on either side of her head; see *Pearl, Cleanness, Patience and Sir Gawain, Reproduced in Facsimile from the Unique MS Cotton Nero A.x. in the British Museum*, introduction by I. Gollancz, Early English Text Society, Original Series 162 (Oxford, 1923), ff. 38r and 38v. This style may have been meant as a more realistic than symbolic representation of a maiden, as young unmarried women seem often to have worn their hair up or covered in their daily lives. Loose hair was a recognizable symbol of maidenhood, but that does not mean that all maidens wore their hair down day-to-day.

47. Timothy Husband with Gloria Gilmore, *The Wild Man: Medieval Myth and Symbolism* (New York, 1980).

48. For the *vitae* of Mary Magdalene and Mary of Egypt see Jacobus de Voragine, *The Golden Legend: Readings on the Saints*, tr. William Granger Ryan (2 vols, Princeton, 1993), vol. 1, pp. 227–9, 374–83. On loose hair as a sign of penitence see Margaret R. Miles, *Carnal Knowing: Female Nakedness and Religious Meaning in the Christian West* (Boston, 1989), pp. 48–51. On the hair of Mary Magdalene see Katherine L. French, 'The Legend of Lady Godiva and the Image of the Female Body', *Journal of Medieval History* 18 (1992), 3–19, pp. 15–16.

49. For St Agnes see *The Golden Legend* vol. 1, pp. 101–4; For Lady Godiva see French, 'Lady Godiva', and Marina Warner, *Monuments and Maidens: The Allegory of the Female Form* (London, 1985), pp. 307–10.

50. 'Every woman that prayeth or prophesieth with her head uncovered dishonoureth her head', 1 Corinthians 11:5. 'Judge in yourselves: is it comely that a woman pray unto God uncovered?: Doth not even nature itself teach you, that if a man have long hair it is a shame unto him? But if a woman have long hair, it is a glory to her: for *her* hair is given to her for a covering', 1 Cor. 11:13–15. The Apostle seems oblivious to the self-contradiction of his statement – that hair must be covered, and that it is in itself a covering. Herein lies a central meaning of women's hair in Christian thought, as at once unseemly and glorious. Tertullian, 'On the Veiling of Virgins' in S. Thelwall (ed. and tr.), *The Writings of Tertullian*, Ante-Nicene Christian Library 18 (3 vols, Edinburgh, 1870), vol. 3, pp. 154–80. See Miles, *Carnal Knowing*, pp. 49–50, and Mary Rose D'Angelo, 'Veils, Virgins, and the Tongues of Men and Angels: Women's Heads in Early Christianity' in Howard Eilberg-Schwartz and Wendy Doniger (eds), *Off with Her Head: The Denial of Women's Identity in Myth, Religion, and Culture* (University of California Press, Berkeley, 1995). The latter volume also contains interpretations of the meanings of loose, bound, covered or cut hair across a number of cultures.

51. Henry Thomas Riley (ed.), *Liber Albus in Munimenta Gildhallae Londoniensis*, Rolls Series 12 (3 vols, London, 1859–62), vol. 1, p. 459.

52. See the orders for the consecration of nuns in J.B.L. Tolhurst (ed.), *The Ordinale and Customary of the Benedictine Nuns of Barking Abbey*, Henry Bradshaw Society 65–6 (2 vols, London, 1927–28), vol. 2, pp. 353–5: 'Et postea ponat uelaman super caput uirginis dicens. *Accipe uirgo christi uelamen uirginitatis*', p. 354. See also the order of consecration of nuns in William Maskell (ed.), *Monumenta Ritualia Ecclesiae Anglicanae* (3 vols, London, 1846–7), vol. 2, pp. 308–31: 'And then shall the bisshop delyver or put uppon yche of theym theyr veyle: saying to every of theym, severally: Accipe, Christi virgo, velamen virginitatis et continentiae indicium', p. 319.

53. Chaucer's Griselda, on her wedding day, has her hair 'kembed, that lay untressed/ Ful rudely', 'The Clerk's Tale', ll. 379–80, p. 142. See Phillis Cunnington and Catherine Lucas, *Costumes for Births, Marriages and Deaths* (London, 1972), pp. 92–3. Lyndal Roper shows that brides in Reformation Augsburg often wore their hair loose until after their weddings, and then adopted wimples, '"Going to Church and Street": Weddings in Reformation Augsburg', *Past and Present* 106 (1985), 62–101, p. 88. Arnold van Gennep claims that the cutting of hair on the day of marriage symbolizes a girl's movement from one age group to another, *The Rites of Passage*, tr. Monika B. Vizedom and Gabriel L. Caffee (Chicago, 1960), p. 167, and it is possible that the medieval practice is a variant of an ancient one shared by many cultures.

54. Elizabeth Danbury, 'Images of English Queens in the Later Middle Ages', *The Historian* 46 (1995), 3–9; John Carmi Parsons, 'Ritual and Symbol in English Medieval Queenship to 1500' in Louise Olga Fradenburg (ed.), *Women and Sovereignty* (Edinburgh, 1992), p. 62; Joanna Chamberlayne, 'Queenship in the Fifteenth Century' (unpublished D.Phil. thesis, University of York) and her article in the present volume.

55. Millett and Wogan-Browne (eds and tr.), 'A Letter on Virginity' in *Medieval English Prose for Women*, p. 21.

56. *The Good Wyfe Wold a Pylgremage*, l. 67, in Tauno F. Mustanoja (ed.), *The Good Wife Taught Her Daughter, The Good Wyfe Wold a Pylgremage, The Thewis of Gud Women* (Helsinki, 1948), p. 175.

57. Osbert of Clare, writing to his niece Cecilia, quoted in Barbara Newman, 'Flaws in the Golden Bowl: Gender and Spiritual Formation in the Twelfth Century', *Traditio* 45 (1989–90), 111–46, p. 127.

58. The wreath as a victor's crown at the ancient Olympic games features in mythology. See Robert Graves, *The Greek Myths* (2 vols, Harmondsworth, 1960), vol. 1, pp. 185–7.

59. Gertrud Schiller, *Iconography of Christian Art*, tr. Janet Seligman (2 vols, London, 1972), vol. 1, pp. 100–1, 133–4; vol. 2, pp. 5, 106, 108; André Grabar, *Christian Iconography: A Study of its Origins* (London, 1969), p. 41.

60. Janet L. Nelson, 'Inauguration Rituals' in her *Politics and Ritual in Early Medieval Europe* (London, 1986), p. 295, reprinted from P.H. Sawyer and I.N. Wood (eds), *Early Medieval Kingship* (Leeds, 1977). I owe this reference to Joel Burden.

61. Graves, *Greek Myths* vol. 1, pp. 224, 237, 271. Note that men as well as women could wear garlands. On the use of crowns or wreaths of flowers during Roman and early medieval marriage rituals see René Metz, 'La Couronne et l'Anneau dans la Consécration des Vierges, *Revue des Sciences Religieuses* 28 (1954), 113–32, pp. 116–19, reprinted in R. Metz, *La Femme et l'Enfant dans le Droit Canonique Médiéval* (London, 1985).

62. Ronald Hutton, *The Rise and Fall of Merry England: The Ritual Year 1400–1700* (Oxford, 1994), pp. 27–31, 115–17; Roper, 'Church and Street', p. 88; Cunnington and Lucas, *Costumes*, p. 92.

63. Metz, 'La Couronne et l'Anneau', argues that the consecration of nuns borrowed symbolism, including that of the wedding crown or wreath, from the Roman and early-medieval ritual of marriage.

64. *The Golden Legend*, vol. 1, 368; C.A. Lutrell, 'The Medieval Tradition of the Pearl Virginity', *Medium Ævum* 31 (1962), 194–200; James W. Earl, 'Saint Margaret and the Pearl Maiden', *Modern Philology* 70 (1972), 1–8.

65. On baptism see Cunnington and Lucas, *Costumes*, p. 41; Bishop, *'Pearl'*, pp. 114–21. On white clothes as appropriate for professed virgins see Tolhurst (ed.), *Ordinale . . . Barking Abbey*, p. 353; Margery Kempe's adoption of white clothes, and the Archbishop of York's puzzlement: 'Why gost þu in white? Art þu a mayden?', S.B. Meech and H.E. Allen, (eds), *The Book of Margery Kempe*, Early English Text Society, Original Series 212 (Oxford, 1940), pp. 32, 124; Mary C. Erler, 'Margery Kempe's White Clothes', *Medium Ævum* 62 (1993), 78–83; Dyan Elliott, 'Dress as Mediator Between Inner and Outer Self: The Pious Matron of the High and Later Middle Ages', *Mediaeval Studies* 53 (1991), 279–308, pp. 294–5.

66. Unless otherwise stated, references to the lives of the virgin martyrs are taken from Ryan's translation of *The Golden Legend*. The lives of Margaret, Christina, Ursula and the eleven-thousand virgins, Faith, Agnes, Dorothy, Katherine, Cecilia, Agatha and Lucy are also contained in Osbern Bokenham's mid-fifteenth-century Middle English *Legendys of Hooly Wummen*, ed. Mary S. Serjeantson, Early English Text Society, Original Series 206 (Oxford, 1938).

67. *The Golden Legend*, vol. 1, pp. 102, 368; vol. 2, p. 334; Bokenham, *Legendys*, pp. 12, 58, 85, 113, 175.

68. *Jacobi a Voragine, Legenda Aurea Vulgo Historia Lombardica Dicta*, ed. Thomas Graesse (Osnabrück, 1969), e.g. pp. 31, 178, 402, 621, 633, 635, 776, 791.

69. Bokenham, *Legendys*, p. 254.

70. Ibid., p. 232.

71. Ibid., p. 99.

72. See Burrow, *Ages of Man*, p. 143.

73. Aristotle, *Politics*, ed. H. Rackham (Cambridge MA, 1932), pp. 617–9; *The Governance of Kings and Princes. John Trevisa's Middle English Translation of the* De Regimine Principum *of Aegedius Romanus*, tr. David C. Fowler, Charles F. Briggs, and Paul G. Remley (New York, 1997), bk 2, pt 1, ch. 16, p. 196; Peter Biller, '"Demographic Thought" around 1300 and Dante's Florence' in John C. Barnes and Cormac Ó Cuilleanáin (eds), *Dante and the Middle Ages: Literary and Historical Essays* (Dublin, 1995), p. 67.

74. *The Golden Legend*, vol. 1, p. 268.

75. David Hugh Farmer (ed.), *The Oxford Dictionary of Saints* (Oxford, 1992), p. 28. For a visual example of St Apollonia represented alongside and resembling the other virgin martyrs see the reproduction of the south rood screen at Westhall Church, East Anglia in Duffy, 'Holy Maydens, Holy Wyfes', p. 183, pl. 2. I owe the example of Apollonia to Katherine Lewis.

76. For visual examples from later medieval English manuscript illustrations, see J.J.G. Alexander (ed.), *A Survey of Manuscripts Illuminated in the British Isles* (6 vols, London, 1975–1996): vol. 5, Lucy Freeman Sandler, *Gothic Manuscripts 1285–1385* (2 parts, London, 1986), pt 1, no. 168; and vol. 6, Kathleen L. Scott, *Later Gothic Manuscripts 1390–1490* (2 parts, London, 1996), pt 1, nos 92, 231, 460, 461. For examples from panel paintings see Duffy, 'Holy Maydens, Holy Wyfes', pls 1–3.

77. Bokenham, *Legendys*, p. 13.

78. Ibid., pp. 12, 32.

79. Miles, *Carnal Knowing*, argues that feminine beauty was always problematic within medieval Christianity because of its threat to male chastity, and that the mutilation experienced by the virgin martyrs before martyrdom may be read as part of the discourse of the grotesque, pp. 70–1, 156. I feel this is something of a simplification, and that Miles is too quick to dismiss the significance of the appeal of the virgin martyrs to the heterosexual male viewer. It must be significant that the mutilations which they experience are not the cause of their martyrdoms, but instead are miraculously healed. Their beauty is thus not diminished before death, which usually takes place by beheading. Veronica Sekules notes the convention of representing holy women as beautiful, and suggests that this, along with their riches, is meant to convey to the viewer an idea of their sanctity which is conveyed through earthly notions of superiority, 'Women and Art in England in the Thirteenth and Fourteenth Centuries' in Jonathan Alexander and Paul Binksi (eds), *Age of Chivalry: Art in Plantagenet England 1200–1400* (London, 1987), p. 43.

80. *The Golden Legend*, vol. 2, p. 319.

81. Grabar, *Christian Iconography*, p. 41.

82. Cited in Newman, 'Golden Bowl', p. 123.

83. *The Golden Legend*, vol. 2, p. 78 provides an account of the Virgin's biography. For a Middle English version see Peter Meredith (ed.), *The Mary Play from the N Town Manuscript* (London, 1987).

84. *The Golden Legend*, vol. 2, p. 78.

85. For examples from manuscript illuminations see Sandler, *Gothic MSS*, pt 1, nos 2 and 388; Scott, *Later Gothic MSS*, pt 1, nos 95 and 198.

86. For late thirteenth- to late fifteenth-century English representations of a maidenly Virgin Mary during her assumption see Sandler, *Gothic MSS*, pt 1, nos 147 and 372; Scott, *Later Gothic MSS*, pt 1, nos. 51 and 156. For a maidenly Virgin Mary during the act of her coronation see Sandler, pt 1, nos 39, 111, 167, 169, 194, 281; Scott, pt 1, nos 6, 51, 381, 408.

87. On the virgin's later-medieval resemblance to courtly beauties see Michael Camille, *The Gothic Idol: Ideology and Image-Making in Medieval Art* (Cambridge, 1989), pp. 220–41.

88. On the iconography of the Virgin as Queen see Rosemary Muir Wright, 'The Virgin in the Sun and in the Tree' in Fradenburg (ed.), *Women and Sovereignty*; Warner, *Alone of all Her Sex*, pp. 81–117; Engelbert Kirschbaum, Lexikon der Christlichen Ikonographie (Rome, 1970), cols 671–5, s.v. *'Krönung Mariens'*. Bruce Bernard, *The Queen of Heaven: A Selection of Paintings of the Virgin Mary from the Twelfth to the Eighteenth Centuries* (London, 1987), pls 160–4 provide late-medieval (non-English) examples of the youthful, blonde, crowned Virgin.

89. See Elizabeth A. Johnson, 'Marian Devotion in the Western Church' in Jill Raitt (ed.), *Christian Spirituality: High Middle Ages and Reformation*, World Spirituality: An Encyclopedia of the Religious Quest 17 (New York, 1987), pp. 405–10.

90. David Parsons (ed.), *Eleanor of Castile 1290–1990: Essays to Commemorate the 700th Anniversary of Her Death: 28 November, 1290* (Stamford, 1991), pls 10–11, 13–16.

2

MODEL GIRLS? VIRGIN-MARTYRS AND THE TRAINING OF YOUNG WOMEN IN LATE MEDIEVAL ENGLAND[1]

Katherine J. Lewis

This article forms part of an attempt to understand the meaning and value of virgin-martyr cults for women in late medieval England.[2] By considering the hagiographic narratives of their lives within their social and cultural settings, we can suggest some of the ways in which they may have been read and understood by those who had access to them. The article will begin by discussing some of the ways in which virgin-martyrs were explicitly presented as behavioural role-models for young women in conduct literature. It will then turn to consider how virgin-martyrs may have been perceived and appropriated as models by women themselves, examining the place of their lives within some late-medieval manuscript miscellanies. This investigation will establish that virgin-martyrs were perceived as model girls, in both presentation and reception, and that their lives were useful tools in the training of young women.[3]

Within the discourse of courtesy literature directed at young women, St Katherine and other virgin-martyrs were put to a variety of paradigmatic uses.[4] Certainly their words and conduct within the legends provide examples of faith and fortitude, but more than this they are also presented as the epitome of young womanhood. Kim Phillips' article in this collection argues that their beauty, youth and chastity make them the ideal representatives of the perfect age of a woman's life: maidenhood. Although virgin-martyrs were presented as models to women by men (with the single verifiable exception of Christine de Pisan), we know that women commissioned and read virgin-martyr lives. Indeed, virgin-martyr lives are among the only texts that we know for sure were commissioned by or written for married women. For example, Anne, Lady March requested a life of St Margaret from John Lydgate in the 1420s.[5] Osbern Bokenham composed thirteen female saints' lives in the mid-fifteenth century, six of which were dedicated to named female patrons.[6] The lives of the virgin-martyrs St Katherine, St Dorothy and St Agatha are dedicated to named female patrons. In the case of SS Katherine and Agatha to women who share the saint's name: Katherine Denston and Katherine Howard and Agatha Flegge.[7] It is therefore valid to suggest that virgin-martyrs are much more than an example of what men think women should be like, or how they should behave, but are, in part at least, representative of women's ideal of maidenhood.[8]

This argument should be borne in mind throughout the following analysis. Virgin-martyrs were presented as models to women, but that does not mean that they internalized her example in uncomplicated and unresponsive ways.[9] It seems reasonable to suggest that virgin-martyrs were so popular among lay women because they felt that these saints provided a relevant and validating example. Devotion to virgin-martyrs could help them enhance not only the quality of their inner spiritual lives, but also their social and cultural standing as women.[10]

Before turning to examine virgin-martyrs' appearance as models within courtesy literature, we shall look at an example of the ways in which the texts of their lives present them as exemplary in this respect. The best example is provided by a life of the most popular virgin-martyr: St Katherine of Alexandria. The early fifteenth-century life of the saint contained in the 'Red Book of Bath' presents the saint very explicitly as a model young lady. It was probably written for a chapel of St Katherine in Bath to be read out on her feast day and perhaps on other occasions as well.[11] It injects a distinctly didactic and moral tenor to the narrative. The text begins by constructing St Katherine as 'a lesson of helth' which will teach the audience 'how þat ȝe schall heuene wynne'. The opening description of St Katherine reads as follows:

> of vanyte & pryde heo sette full lyte
> Of felyttys in þe forheed noþer of hornes
> Of gay gownes & furres noþer reuersse
> he sette hyt & well myght as gyle & (as) skornes
> and put heore herte to vertyweȝ busynesse
> Noþer daunced ne trypped as doþ many mon
> þat ys a werk of pryde & rancour & of synne
> And butteþ at helle doore: brekyng har schoon
> huppyng & skyppyng at þey wer þer inne
> þut was þere heore non lyke in any place
> Of connynge of wytt of sadnesse & beawte
> Amyable of chere wommanly of face
> Comfort to gode men: to loky & to see
> Louely to loky on wyþ chere & spech sad
> fetures full fayre werkes deuowte
> heore presence made fooleȝ a drad
> for grace & vertyw þat were hure abowte.

It is plain that St Katherine is indeed the perfect young lady; beautiful, yet soberly dressed, not affected by worldly vanities such as dancing; intelligent, yet reserved and demure. Her excellence puts others to shame. This portrait of Katherine accords well with the perfect femininity constructed in conduct books for women, and it is for this reason that her example, along with that of other virgin-martyrs, was included within them.

There are very few extant examples of conduct books written for girls or women in England.[12] An important example is provided by *The Book of the Knight of the Tour Landry*. In the late fourteenth century the eponymous Knight compiled a handbook of moral, religious and social advice for his daughters, all of whom were evidently destined for marriage at some future date.[13] This popular text was translated into English twice in the fifteenth century, Caxton printing his version in 1484.[14] In the prologue the Knight explains that he decided to:

> make a book and an examplayre for my doughters to lerne to rede and vnderstonde how they ought to gouerne them self/and to kepe them from euylle.[15]

In order to describe correct conduct to his daughters and prepare them for their future as dutiful wives he decided to include in the book:

> . . . the good maners and good dedes of good ladyes and wymmen and of theyr lyues soo that for theyr vertues and bountees they ben honoured And that after theyr dethe ben renommed and preysed and shal be vnto the ende of the worlde *for to take of them good ensample and countenance* [my italics].[16]

Virgin-martyrs are included in this band of 'good ladyes' and appear several times in the course of the book as exemplars of virginity, charity and education.

In fact virgin-martyrs are used as exemplars of sexual abstinence rather than virginity per se, as chapter 62 demonstrates. This chapter, entitled 'Of the roper or maker of cordes and kables and of the fat Pryour' tells the salutary tale of the rope maker's wife, who has an unbridled affair with the fat prior.[17] The guilty couple are eventually killed by the rope maker who is thoroughly exempted from any blame, driven to it as he was by the behaviour of his wife. The wife is clearly damned by her inability to say no to the prior. In order that his daughters should learn how to deal with the enticements of extramarital suitors the Knight exhorts his daughters to remember the legends of:

> saynt katheryn/saynt margaryte/of saynte Crystyn/the enleuen thowsand vyrgyns and of many other/of whiche the grete constaunce and feruente courage of them/were to longe to be recounted/For they surmounted many grete temptacions and vanquysshed many tyraunts/wherby they gate & conquered the grete reame of blysse and glorye/where as they shalle euer be in perdurable ioye.[18]

The daughters are to remember that these saints, through their courage and constancy, overcame temptation. A standard motif in all virgin-martyr lives is the offer of worldly wealth, power and even love made by a pagan persecutor, on the condition that she renounce her Christianity.[19] The saint's unequivocal refusal to exchange a heavenly crown and bridegroom for their earthly equivalents signals the beginning of her martyrdom. She undergoes ferocious tortures and eventually execution, unswerving in her rejection of all tempting offers that would mean a betrayal of her faith. Execution marks her final victory in withstanding all threats to her physical and spiritual purity.[20]

Katherine and the other virgin-martyrs are concerned to preserve their virginity that has already been dedicated to Christ. Their virginity in fact becomes a tangible signifier of their faith and miraculous fortitude. However, the Knight uses these saints as examples of virginity that will become, in the case of his daughters, wifely chastity. He warns them that:

> many grete and euylle [presumably sexual] temptacions shall befyght and assaylle yow/Be ye thenne stronge and valyaunt to resiste & ouercome them/And loke and behold the place wheroute ye be come of/and what dishonour and shame myght come to yow therof.[21]

Virgin-martyrs provide a very fitting conclusion to this chapter because from them the Knight's daughters can learn to be staunch in their resistance and also preserve the good reputation both of themselves and of their family, a concern which lies behind the Knight's closing remarks.

Chastity is not the only virtue that the virgin-martyrs are used to exemplify. Chapters 51 to 53 tell 'Of the good knyght that had thre wyues and of their lyues'.[22] After the death of each wife the distraught Knight visits his uncle, a hermit, who is able, through visions, to describe the afterlife fate of each woman. The Knight is told that his first wife 'for her pryde and for the grete quantite of gownes and Iewelles that she hadde was loste and dampned for euer'.[23] The Knight of the Tower warns his daughters:

> And therfore euery good woman after she is of estate and degree she ought to hold and behaue her symply and honestly in her clothyng/and in the quantite of hit/And gyue a parte to god/to thende she may in the other world be clothed of all ioye and glorye/as dyde the hooly ladyes and hooly vyrgyns as in their legende is redercyd/As of seynt Elyzabeth/of saynt Katheryn and of seynt Agathe and other mo that gaue their gownes to the poure folke for the loue of god And soo ought to doo euery good woman.[24]

Chapter 110 'How the wymmen ought to be charytable after the exemplary of our lady' includes the example of other virgin-martyrs:

> And at thexample of her [the Virgin Mary] dyd saynt Elyzabeth/saynte Lucye/saynt Cecylle and many other holy ladyes/whiche were so charitable that they gaf to the poure & Indygent the most parte of theyr reuenues/As reherced is playnly in theyr legendes.[25]

The Elizabeth in question is presumably Elizabeth of Hungary whose legend contains many instances of her concern for the needy, Bokenham explaining that she became known as 'Modyr of pore men'.[26] The legend of St Cecilia recounts that during the three day period between receiving three fatal blows to the neck and her actual death Cecilia preached to the people:

> Amoung whom also wyth hert glade
> She departyd swych thyngys as she had
> In almes-dede. . . . [27]

St Lucy, having vowed herself to Christ, asks her mother for her dowry to be distributed amongst the poor, which the two of them do, much to the chagrin of the man who was expecting to marry Lucy.[28]

However, no extant version of the lives of St Katherine or St Agatha include an account of them distributing their gowns in this way. The prose life of St Katherine does contain descriptions of more general charitable behaviour. This dates from the four year period between her mystical marriage and her martyrdom during which she is seen governing her palace and its inhabitants: 'of all þe substaunce of hir faders lyflode she kept bot a lytell to hir self and alle the remenaunt wyth al hir faders tresour she disposed to þe sustenance of þe pore puple'.[29] This sort of description may have provided the foundation for her inclusion in the Knight's list of charitable saints. As we have seen, charity does form an explicit part of other virgin-martyr lives. A further example is provided by St Christina who smashed the gold and silver idols that her father ordered her to worship and gave the precious metals to the poor.[30] It may be, therefore, that the Knight felt that this behaviour was appropriate to both Katherine and Agatha, even if it was not precisely described in their legends.[31] This is testament to the power of virgin-martyrs as role models.

In chapter 89 'How men oughte to sette and put theyr children to scole' the Knight specifically holds up St Katherine as a model of the benefits which can accrue from having one's daughters educated:

> . . . saynt katheryn whiche thurgh her wysedome and by her clergye with the grace of the holy ghoost surmounted & vaynquysshed the wysest men of al grece/And by her hooly clergye and sure feythe god gaf her the vyctorye of her martirdome/& made her body to be borne by his angels xiiij dayes Iourney for the place where as she suffred her martirdome vnto the Mount of

> Synay/& her holy body rendrid holy oyle And the begynnyng and fundament of the knowledge of god she had thurgh the clergye where as she knewe the trouthe/& the sauement of her self.[32]

The Knight is concerned that his daughters should be armed with the ability to recognize good from evil and thus to be responsible for their own salvation. He is not interested in education per se divorced from its religious and moral uses. However, this does not lessen the importance of St Katherine's example as a model of the educated and knowledgeable woman. Nor was she the only virgin-martyr to be held up as an example of learning to young women. Humbert of Romans' mid-thirteenth century sermon entitled 'For girls or maidens who are in the world', shares the opinion of the Knight that education is necessary for the spiritual welfare of girls and observes:

> Of this knowledge you have an example in Blessed Agnes who went to school, in Blessed Cecilia, Catharine, Lucy, Agatha, who were all learned as their legends bear witness.[33]

The origin of Humbert's remark about St Agnes is to be found in her legend. She is described as being on her way home from school when the prefect's son sees and falls in love with her.[34]

It is therefore evident that by learning of the behaviour and beliefs of virgin-martyrs (among other women) and imitating it, the Knight's daughters can conduct themselves according to the criteria of ideal femininity that these saints represent. St Katherine appears as the model of models, the Knight mentioning her three times in all, as opposed to the one or two mentions enjoyed by the other virgin-martyrs. The implication is that reading and utilizing St Katherine's life and demeanour is part of a strategy by which the Knight's daughters can construct themselves as ideally suited for marriage.

This is a point that is made explicit by Christine de Pisan in her *The Treasure of the City of Ladies*. In the chapter entitled 'Of the instruction for both girls and older women in the state of virginity' de Pisan is not really concerned with nuns, or women who will be nuns, but with those who will be married.[35] Girls are instructed to be 'in their countenances, conduct and speech moderate and chaste' just as St Katherine is said to be in the Bath life.[36] Having offered various prescriptions as to appearance and conduct at mixed gatherings de Pisan then says 'A young girl should also especially venerate Our Lady, St Catherine, and all virgins, and if she can read, eagerly read their biographies'. Thus St Katherine, and other virgin-martyrs, become part of a training programme for the would-be wife. De Pisan is quite explicit on this point, saying 'Young girls taught and brought up in this way are much sought after by men looking for wives'.[37]

That the Knight and Christine de Pisan both single St Katherine out as worthy of the particular attention of young women is related to her status as the most popular of the virgin-martyr saints. She was arguably the most popular saint in late-medieval England. This statement is born out by the sheer amount of extant documentary, literary and visual evidence relating to her cult.[38] In part this popularity is clearly attributable to her status as a powerful and effective intercessor.[39] But the explanation also lies in the ways that her life was read and used as an exemplary text, with respect to both religious and cultural practices.[40]

There are fourteen extant versions of the life of St Katherine in Middle English to be found in a great number of manuscripts.[41] But the popularity of her life is not simply to be measured in quantity. A further measure of it is revealed by the fact that it did not remain a static text in this period but was elaborated throughout the course of the fourteenth and fifteenth centuries.[42] The *Legenda Aurea* version of the narrative, written in the mid-thirteenth century was based on an eleventh-century text of her life known as the Vulgate. The *Legenda Aurea* provided the basis for all of the Middle English lives of St Katherine.[43] This contains the more familiar elements of her life, or more accurately her passion: the debate with the fifty philosophers, the smashing of the spiked wheels, her decapitation and burial on Mount Sinai. Examples of Middle English versions are to be found in the *South English Legendary*, Mirk's *Festial*, and as an individual item in manuscripts such as Edinburgh, National Library of Scotland, MS Advocates 19.2.1 and Cambridge, University Library MS Ff.2.38.[44]

During the fifteenth century an account of Katherine's birth, early life, education and mystical marriage became a standard part of the narrative of her life, prefixing her passion.[45] The life written by Capgrave in the 1440s follows this expanded narrative pattern.[46] The early fifteenth-century prose life provided the medium by which the additional elements noted above were conveyed to a wide audience. The prose life survives in four redactions in twenty-four manuscripts.[47] This narrative development can be related to St Katherine's exemplary potential. In considering the presentation or adoption of St Katherine as a model we need to examine the conceptualization of her as one; a process which involves the selection and emphasis of certain features of her person and her life which best suited current interests.[48] Within the context of household manuscripts it seems no coincidence that versions of St Katherine's life which highlight her upbringing and education should be deemed particularly suitable for inclusion. It appears that the elaboration of these episodes had a direct bearing on her status as a model for young women experiencing the same stage in their life cycle.

Conduct literature therefore demonstrates the ways in which virgin-martyrs, and in particular St Katherine, were presented as models to young women. It is now necessary to turn from the theory of training young women, to the practice. Is there any way of ascertaining whether virgin-martyrs were actually used in the training and socialization of young women in late-medieval England? Were the lives of virgin-martyrs used as behavioural blueprints to produce model girls? By identifying and examining the values and practices of those who actually owned copies of virgin-martyr lives we can provide answers to these questions. We shall therefore be examining a specific group, defined by certain identifiable social and cultural characteristics, who may have read the life of St Katherine as an authorization of women's educational practices. This is not to suggest that the life can be used as direct evidence for aspects of female behaviour and training in late-medieval England. But because there are so many texts of the life of St Katherine extant, we can investigate the kinds of social purpose to which she was put. In order to undertake this it is necessary to locate both culturally and chronologically the written versions of her life found in household manuscripts. These are manuscripts apparently written for, and read within a lay domestic milieu, rather than that of the parish church, the monastery or the convent.[49]

There are at least seven manuscripts, containing the life of St Katherine, whose format and contents suggest that they were created for and read within lay households. These are Edinburgh, National Library of Scotland MS Advocates 19.2.1 (The Auchinleck Manuscript, 1330s); British Library, MS Arundel 168 (fifteenth century); Aberystwyth, National Library of Wales MS Porkington 10 (mid-fifteenth century); Edinburgh, National Library of Scotland MS Advocates 19.3.1 (second half of the fifteenth century); Manchester, Cheetham's Library MS 8009 (late fifteenth century); Cambridge, University Library Ff.2.38 (late fifteenth century); British Library, MS Cotton Titus A. xxvi (early sixteenth century).[50] These manuscripts date from the early fourteenth to the early sixteenth centuries, with the majority of examples coming from the mid- to late fifteenth century. The Auchinleck Manuscript and Ff.2.38 both contain verse 'passion' lives of St Katherine.[51] Arundel 168 contains Capgrave's lengthy verse life. The remaining four manuscripts contain the earliest version of the prose life, orginally written before 1420.[52] The owners were drawn from the ranks of the aristocracy, gentry and, increasingly during the fifteenth century, from wealthy urban mercantile families.[53] The contents of all seven manuscripts have been surveyed in order to uncover some common thematic concerns and interests. This indicates the contextual similarities of these manuscripts, which can help us to identify what functions were performed and interests served by the life of St Katherine within them.[54]

These seven manuscripts contain a fairly similar selection of texts, including saints' lives, romances, homiletic and monitory pieces, poems and treatises of religious and moral instruction, chronicles, humorous tales, and so on.[55] Household manuscripts provided their owners with comprehensive collections of texts for education, edification and entertainment. The lives of St Katherine considered here could have been read privately, or aloud, both to members of the family and to the wider household. The life of St Katherine evidently served the twin purposes of education and entertainment admirably, for it appears far more frequently in such manuscripts than that of any other saint.[56]

It would seem that, on the whole, the presence of a saint's life in such manuscripts, or its existence as an independent text, was due to the devotional initiative of an individual. Its presence was also dependent on its availability to scribes as an exemplar. This is not to say that one could not buy 'off the peg' copies of saints' lives, but this trend seems to have become more prevalent towards the end of the period, with the advent of printing. Some of these manuscripts may have been made speculatively for sale, rather than at the behest of specific patrons. If this is the case it would suggest that the life of St Katherine was regarded as part of the standard contents of such books by scribes and compilers. On the whole, however, it would appear that most of these books were originally designed for use in specific households. Many of them obviously passed through several different readers, men and women who have left marks of ownership upon them in the form of names and signatures. They also passed through different households and this indicates the utility of their contents.

Even if a book was owned or used by different families during this period, it would be likely to remain within a broadly similar social and cultural milieu. The defining characteristics of the three social groups for whom the books were produced (that is, aristocracy, gentry and urban mercantile families) often became blurred and indistinct in later medieval England. Families of gentry or mercantile background sought to adopt the life style of the nobility. Reading the life of St Katherine could even have been bound up with the cultivation of an aristocratic identity, especially as the contents of these household books often suggest a training programme of required knowledge and conduct for the well-born.[57] The possession of books was a measure of social status, partly because of their cost, partly because of the assumption of literacy that it entailed.[58] Medieval authors frequently vilify members of the mercantile elite for flaunting their books of hours in an attempt to appear socially 'better' than they really were.[59]

If the ownership of books could be used to construct or affirm social and cultural identities, then similar factors may well have been at work in the reading and possession of a life of St Katherine. The cult of St Katherine appears to be bound to an identity of power and status. All virgin-martyrs are of implicitly high status; St Katherine alone is described as a sovereign queen. When her cult first appeared in England it apparently found favour with the royal family and spread from the court to the rest of the country.[60] Depending on one's background, the choice of St Katherine as a patron could be about the self-affirmation of status for a member of the nobility, or about an assumption of an aristocratic identity for someone a few rungs down the social ladder.

Related to this issue is the observation that women seem to have had a central ideological place within the household, fulfilling a variety of representational functions and allowing the home to act as a theatre for the staging of a family's social position.[61] This observation accords with women's apparent responsibility for education within the domestic sphere and the fundamentally aspirant nature of many of these manuscripts, with their apparent goal of consolidating social and cultural status. These concerns provide a further context for the value and utility of virgin-martyrs, and especially St Katherine, to women as household managers and educators.

It seems that the education and training of children and young people were part of the responsibilities of motherhood and that women may therefore have been responsible for the provision of education in the household.[62] There is no firm evidence to support this suggestion; indeed, the phenomenon of domestic education is unlikely, by its very nature, to leave any such evidence. However, it is a suggestion that appears to be borne out by a variety of literary, historical and art historical sources. Indeed, it has been argued that the image of St Anne teaching the Virgin to read, which apparently originated in fourteenth-century England, performed the cultural function of recording and communicating the fact that children's literacy was a mother's responsibility.[63]

The mother herself, or in higher status households, governesses to whom she delegated responsibility, appears to have been held to be primarily responsible, for the upbringing and training of children and young women. They would learn correct behaviour, deportment, dancing and embroidery, as well as reading and religious tenets and observances.[64] This training encompassed all the social, cultural and practical skills which girls would need to fit them for adult life as wives and mothers, and which they could, in turn, pass on to others. Children often spent part of their childhood in households other than their own: such an arrangement offered them the chance to widen their experience and training and forge valuable connections with other families.[65] Mothers may therefore, on occasion have found themselves responsible for the upbringing of several girls, not just their own. These patterns of domestic education provide an intrinsic context for the use of household manuscripts, which, in some respects at least, may have been particularly useful to women as educators.

Michael Clanchy believes that there is a direct connection between women's ownership of books and the growth of literacy in fourteenth- and fifteenth-century Europe.[66] The recent body of scholarship investigating women's literacy and book ownership gives an idea of the range of texts which were being read and used by them, illuminating patterns of female book ownership and the existence of book reading, giving and lending networks among women.[67] Books sometimes bear the inscriptions of a whole succession of female owners or readers.[68]

Two of the household manuscripts containing lives of St Katherine have women's names or signatures written in them. Chetham 8009 has the name 'Elysabet' written in it, which may be the name and signature of an actual woman.[69] Advocates 19.3.1 contains the name 'elsabet Bradshaw', written by the scribe, Richard Heege, on f. 45 at the top of a page of the life of St Katherine. Other contemporary names have possibly been cut off, as the book has been shaved. Jaime Araujo argues that Elizabeth's name may have been written in the pamphlet before the life of St Katherine, and suggests that this booklet was written at her behest, or with her in mind.[70] This is not to suggest that men did not have access to, or make use of such books, indeed Advocates 19.3.1 also contains the names of several men. If women were held to be responsible for the education and training of the household, such collections would perhaps have been of particular use and value to them.

The educational attainments of St Katherine thus appear to be of prime importance to the frequency with which she appears in these manuscripts. The *Legenda Aurea* account of her life tells us that Katherine received an academic education, she was 'fully instructed in all the liberal studies'.[71] All of the Middle English lives of St Katherine, except one, describe her as learned not simply through divine illumination, but through study.[72] The prose life expands considerably upon this motif, telling us that her father, King Costus, built her a large tower in which she could study uninterrupted and employed 'vij the beste maystres and hyest of konnynge that myghte be found in that end of the worlde of all the vij artes'.[73] Subsequently Katherine 'encressid soo marvelusly in wysdoom' that she ends up teaching the masters who came to instruct her.[74] It is perhaps in keeping with the educative concerns of household manuscripts that five of the seven containing a life of St Katherine have a version which gives the most depth and detail to her education.[75]

But would the highly educated St Katherine have been a figure with whom the women, owning, reading and using these manuscripts could identify and perceive as a model? We have seen that the education of girls and young women did not match up to the specifically academic standards of St Katherine's. However, it is possible that the construction of St Katherine as educated and educator performed an authorizing cultural function, regardless of whether, or how far, it reflected the realities of women's education. In exploring this issue we must remember that the prose life of St Katherine describes her not just receiving an education, but also performing the role of household manager: 'And iiii ȝere aftyr þis [her mystical marriage to Christ] sche helde here housholde in here paleys whit full crystyn governaunce'.[76] Ultimate authority, in the households with which we are concerned, was seen to reside in the male figure of husband/father. But such households were frequently governed by women during the absence of their husbands, due to the demands of business that had to be conducted away from home.[77] St Katherine is seen to perform the role of household manager in the absence of her husband, Christ.[78] This can help us to understand further the ways in which women may have appropriated her as a model for their own domestic experiences.

We have seen that the life of St Katherine appears to have been the most popular for inclusion in household manuscripts. This is not to say that other saints' lives are not to be found within them. There is an apparent interest in female saints throughout this corpus. This is particularly marked in Chetham 8009, which also contains the lives of saints Dorothy and Anne and an account of the Assumption of the Virgin. Similarly Arundel 168 also has a life of St Dorothy and special prayers to her, a life of St Christine and Lydgate's *Life of Our Lady*. The life of Mary Magdalene occurs in three of the manuscripts (the Auchinleck, Ff.2.38 and Cotton Titus A. xxvi), St Margaret in two (Auchinleck and Ff.2.38) and the Auchinleck Manuscript also has a life of St Anne. Male saints do appear; St Thomas à Becket, St Martin, St Alexis, St Julian and the Seven Sleepers, but only once each. Several of the manuscripts also contain Marian texts; the Auchinleck Manuscript, Ff.2.38 and Chetham 8009 contain accounts of the Assumption. Advocates 19.3.1 contains extracts from Lydgate's *Life of Our Lady* and 'Ave Regina Coelorum', as does Porkington 10. This may indicate that these manuscripts are catering for female, or feminized readers and owners.[79] Given the ways in which virgin-martyr saints were used in courtesy texts it seems valid to suggest that their frequent inclusion in household manuscripts indicate that they were being used for purposes of training young women.[80] In order to explore this supposition and put the lives of St Katherine and other virgin-martyrs into context as a tool of education and socialization, we need to look at the contents of the manuscripts that contained it. This will bear out the above contention that they were particularly concerned with various sorts of teaching and learning.[81]

Household manuscripts frequently contain texts that are specifically concerned with the training of children or young people, and the maintenance of their health.[82] Two of the manuscripts, Chetham 8009 (f. 48) and Arundel 168 (f. 7), contain the translation of the *Distichs of Cato*. This is a Latin school poem, made by Benedict Burgh, who subequently became archdeacon of Colchester. This translation was undertaken in the 1440s or 1450s for William, son of Henry Viscount Bourchier, and was published by Caxton in 1483.[83] In its original form the poem would only have been suitable for the education of boys. Its translation into English, albeit originally for a boy, opens up the possibility that it was used in the education of girls. It does appear that in the later fifteenth century the education of girls of noble status, at least, came to mirror that of their brothers much more closely.[84] The text in this form would also be available to mothers educating their sons. Whether or not that education would then be taken over by clerics or professional masters would depend on the wealth and status of the individual household. Many of these educational texts would have been intended to inform both mother and son of the moral and social expectations and accomplishments of a young gentleman. The possible use of such texts in the training of girls must not be precluded, although this supposition is almost impossible to prove.

Advocates 19.3.1 contains two well known educational texts: *Stans Puer ad Mensam* (f. 28) and *The Lytlle Childrenes Lytil Boke* (f. 84), both of which catalogue appropriate moral and social conduct for gentry children.[85] Again, the focus is on male children but much of the behavioural 'map' thus laid out would have been appropriate to girls as well. For example, Arundel 168 contains a poem of seven stanzas upon 'Prudence, Justice, Temperance, Descrecione, Resone, Plesaunce and GodeWylle, and Curtesye and Norture' (f. 14), which would presumably provide guidance for the requsite social skills of genteel young persons. Porkington 10 contains texts such as 'Be trewe and holde þat ȝe have hyȝt' (f. 130) and 'Ever say well or hold thee still' (f. 150). British Library, MS Cotton Titus A. xxvi contains a short poem warning how important it is not to lose good (perhaps suitable) friends, and not to waste time (f. 173). These all seem to be concerned with inculcating 'proper' values in the young.

Many of the texts contained in these manuscripts are clearly concerned with the deportment of children aimed at training them in the bearing fitting to their station, or indeed a higher station. These texts could thus be used in the construction of a pseudo-aristocratic identity; the adoption of signifying practices which would distance oneself and one's behaviour from lower status individuals.[86] Porkington 10 (f. 184, ff. 187–188), Chetham 8009 (f. 337) and Advocates 19.3.1 (f. 1, f. 62, f. 63) include texts explaining the terms of hunting and carving game. The acquisition of such knowledge was much about correct table manners and etiquette as it was about the chase itself. It was an essential part of the upbringing of a noble child, or of one who was educated in the ways of the aristocracy, that she or he might emulate them in manner and demeanour.[87] One of these texts is thought to have been written by a woman, Juliana Berners, for her child – 'My dere chylde . . . lystyn to yowre dame and she shall yow lere'.[88] This further underlines the role of woman as teacher and transmitter of essential knowledge to children, and others within her household.

Both Advocates 19.3.1 (f. 64, f. 86) and Porkington 10 (f. 89) contain medical recipes. The latter manuscript also contains such practical texts as a treatise on grafting and planting trees and astronomical tables (f. 27, ff. 5–11). Advocates 19.3.1 contains a text on predicting the weather (f. 212). This lends further weight to the idea that such manuscripts could function as comprehensive hand books for women as household managers. Women of middle to high status were apparently expected to have a certain proficiency in a whole range of matters that could be bolstered by professionals when necessary. It was important for women to be repositories of advice and information, able to intervene in any issue of import to the running of all domestic affairs. This was true even if they did not have a direct involvement in them.

A household manuscript gave women access to a range of texts that allowed them to ensure the physical, moral and spiritual welfare of their household and its inhabitants. That the education of the whole household was also provided for is demonstrated by the inclusion in Porkington 10 of two courtesy texts; 'The gode wyf wolde a pilgremage' (f. 135) followed by 'The friar and the boy' (f. 139).

Ff.2.38 contains 'How the goode man taught hys sone' (f. 53). These texts would probably be used by women to instruct and train the lower status men and women, servants and/or apprentices, living within the household.[89] Their conduct would have a bearing on the reputation of the household and thus needed guidance and regulation. These manuscripts with their aspirant tastes and interests seem to describe what has been identified as an ethos of respectability.[90] This was apparently expressed equally in the children being well versed in 'noble' etiquette, as well as the female servants being told not to behave like tarts.[91]

This factor of respectability also enlarges our understanding of the inclusion of a variety of religious and devotional texts in these manuscripts. In running her household St Katherine is very concerned that it should have an overtly Christian identity: 'she helde here housholde . . . whit full crystyn governaunce'.[92] She converts many people to Christianity and lives an exemplary life of service and charity in her palace.[93] Maintaining the Christian identity and unity of the household would have also been of great importance to the women owning and using these manuscripts.[94] Religious education is provided for in the manuscripts by formulaic catechetical texts; lists and expositions of the Ten Commandments, the Seven Deadly Sins, The Nine Virtues, the Seven Works of Mercy and so on.[95] These works form part of the late-medieval pastoral initiative that sought to improve the level of religious education among both clergy and laity.[96] Such texts are patently not just about religious knowledge, but also moral and social conduct, which again fits with wider concerns.

The manuscript setting of these lives of St Katherine thus suggests a more than haphazard connection between context and content; explicable in terms of the overtly educational and aspirant nature of household manuscripts. The life of St Katherine provides a useful socializing tool for those concerned with the training of young women. Her demeanour and conduct identify her as a paradigm of maidenhood, one wholly suitable for emulation by fledgling young ladies as they learn the behaviour that will present them as ideal and desirable wives. Once they have achieved that goal the life continues to be of use to them, as they become managers of their own households and assume responsibility for the upbringing of a new generation of young women. This helps us to understand some of the ways in which virgin-martyr narratives held a positive value for women and why Christine de Pisan should write of these saints as 'women . . . whose fair lives serve as excellent examples for every woman above all other wisdom'.[97]

Notes

1. In exploring the issue of women's training and wider ideas about education and the household I am particularly grateful to Felicity Riddy, Jeremy Goldberg, Anne Dutton, Kim Phillips and Jaime Araujo for their ideas, advice and criticism.

2. Much recent scholarship on virgin-martyrs has moved away from simplistic readings of their lives as displaced rape narratives which can only have immasculated the female reader. A more sophisticated approach is exemplified by the work of Jocelyn Wogan-Browne which explores the possibility of resistant readings of these narratives, which in particular contexts may constitute relative empowerment or recuperation: see her article 'The Virgin's Tale', in Ruth Evans and Lesley Johnson (eds), *Feminist Readings in Middle English Literature: The Wife of Bath and All Her Sect* (London and New York, 1994), pp. 165–94.

3. 'Training' is used here to refer to the various sorts of education that a girl of middle to high social status would receive within the household. This encompasses a learning programme that was above all concerned with the acquisition of social and religious mores and cultural accomplishments in order to prepare a girl for marriage. More strictly 'educational' attainments such as literacy did play a role in this but were not necessarily seen as essential for young women per se. For an alternative definition and exploration of training which focuses on apprenticeship, schooling and literacy see Caroline M. Barron, 'The Education and Training of Girls in Fifteenth-Century London', in Diana E.S. Dunn (ed.), *Courts, Counties and the Capital in the Later Middle Ages* (Stroud, 1996), pp. 139–53. For more on women's education see later in text.

4. Kathleen Ashley, 'Medieval Courtesy Literature and Mirrors of Dramatic Conduct', in Nancy Armstrong and Leonard Tennenhouse (eds), *The Ideology of Conduct: Essays in Literature and the History of Sexuality* (New York and London, 1987), pp. 25–38, explores the ways in which the Virgin Mary was used as a model of moral and behavioural prudence for young women in both courtesy literature and cycle drama. For a definition of 'courtesy' and 'courteous behaviour' see Jonathan Nicholls, *The Matter of Courtesy: Medieval Courtesy Books and the Gawain Poet* (Woodbridge, 1985), pp. 7–21.

5. For Lydgate and his female patrons see Carol M. Meale, '". . . alle the bokes that I haue of Latyn, englisch and frensch": Laywomen and their Books in Late Medieval England', in Carol M. Meale (ed.), *Women and Literature in Britain 1150–1500* (Cambridge, 1993), pp. 128–58, pp. 137–8. For the text of his life of St Margaret and its dedication to Lady March see Henry Noble MacCracken (ed.), *The Minor Poems of John Lydgate*, Early English Text Society, Extra Series 107, 192 (2 vols, London, 1911 and 1934), vol. 1, pp. 173–92.

6. Mary S. Serjeantson (ed.), *Legendys of Hooly Wummen* by Osbern Bokenham, Early English Text Society, Original Series 206 (Oxford, 1938). The lives dedicated to female patrons are those of SS Katherine, Dorothy, Anne, Agatha, Mary Magdelene and Elizabeth of Hungary. For a discussion of Bokenham and his patrons see A.S.G. Edwards, 'The Transmission and Audience of Osbern Bokenham's *Legendys of Hooly Wummen*', in A.J. Minnis (ed.), *Late-Medieval Religious Texts and their Transmission: Essays in Honour of A.I. Doyle* (Cambridge, 1994), pp. 157–67; Samuel Moore, 'Patrons of Letters in Norfolk and Suffolk, *c.* 1450, 2', *Publications of the Modern Language Association of America*, 28 (1913), 79–105.

7. Serjeantson (ed.), *Legendys of Hooly Wummen*, pp. 174, 227. All three of these women were married, see Moore, 'Patrons of Letters', pp. 83, 85, 91. The life of St Dorothy is dedicated jointly to Isabel Hunt and her husband John; Serjeantson (ed.), *Legendys of Hooly Wummen*, p. 136.

8. For a more detailed articulation of this argument see Kim M. Phillips, 'Medieval Maidenhood: What Old Men Say About Young Girls', in P.J.P. Goldberg and Felicity Riddy (eds), *Youth in the Middle Ages* (Woodbridge, forthcoming).

9. For an exploration of this issue in relation to the presentation of female saints as preachers see Alcuin Blamires, 'Women and Preaching in Medieval Orthodoxy, Heresy and Saints' Lives', *Viator*, 26 (1995), 135–52.

10. This is not to suggest that virgin-martyrs did not appeal to men. Testamentary evidence provides ample proof of male devotion to these saints. But there does seem to have been a marked association between women and virgin-martyrs, both as models and intercessors. For an exploration of this issue see Katherine J. Lewis, '"Rule of lyf alle folk to sewe": Lay Responses to the Cult of St Katherine of Alexandria in Late-Medieval England, 1300–1530' (unpublished D.Phil. thesis, Centre for Medieval Studies, University of York, 1996), pp. 219–22.

11. For a discussion of this life see Jennifer Relvyn Bray, 'The Legend of St Katherine in Later Middle English Literature' (unpublished Ph.D thesis, Birkbeck College, University of London, 1984), pp. 134–40. The most recent study of this life is provided by Jacqueline Jenkins in '"Such peple as be not letterd in Scripture": Popular devotion and the legend of St Katherine of Alexandria in Late-Medieval England' (unpublished Ph.D. thesis, University of Western Ontario, 1996). I am very grateful to her for sharing her findings and allowing me to quote from her unpublished transcription of the text, which forms Appendix 2 of her thesis. The transcription itself is taken from the 'Red Book of Bath': Longleat House MS 62.55, f. 55v, and the quotation from this manuscript is included by permission of the Marquess of Bath, Longleat House, Warminster, Wiltshire. For a description of this manuscript see Gisela Guddat-Figge, *Catalogue of Manuscripts containing Middle English Romances* (Munich, 1976), pp. 232–5.

12. For a survey of medieval courtesy literature directed at women see Diane Bornstein, *The Lady in the Tower: Medieval Courtesy Literature for Women* (Hamden, CONN, 1983).

13. William Caxton, *The Book of the Knight of the Tower*, ed. M.Y. Offord, Early English Text Society, Special Series 2 (London, 1971), on the Knight and his daughters see pp. xviii–xix, and xxxv–xxxix.

14. Ibid., p. xiv.

15. Ibid., p. 13.

16. Ibid., p. 12. The Knight also includes bad women as negative examples.

17. Ibid., pp. 87–92.

18. Ibid., p. 91.

19. For example St Katherine of Alexandria is tempted three times with such promises by Maxentius, inviting obvious comparisons with Christ and the Devil in the Wilderness, see Serjeantson (ed.), *Legendys of Hooly Wummen*, pp. 187, 192, 197.

20. For a discussion of the virgin-martyr narrative blueprint see Jocelyn Wogan-Browne, 'Saints' Lives and the Female Reader', *Forum for Modern Language Studies*, 37 (1991).

21. Caxton, *Book of the Knight of the Tower*, p. 92.

22. Ibid., pp. 74–8.

23. Ibid., p. 76.

24. Ibid., p. 75.

25. Ibid., p. 147.

26. Serjeantson (ed.), *Legendys of Hooly Wummen*, p. 270.

27. Ibid., p. 224.

28. Ibid., p. 248.

29. H.H. Gibbs (ed.), *The Life and Martyrdom of Saint Katherine of Alexandria, Virgin and Martyr* (London, 1884), p. 22.

30. Serjeantson (ed.), *Legendys of Hooly Wummen*, p. 64.

31. For more on the association between women and charity see P.H. Cullum, '"And hir name was charite": Charitable Giving by and for Women in Late-Medieval Yorkshire', in P.J.P. Goldberg (ed.) *Woman is a Worthy Wight: Women in English Society* c. *1200–1500* (Stroud, 1992), pp. 182–211.

32. Caxton, *Book of the Knight of the Tower*, p. 121.

33. Rosemary Barton Tobin, *Vincent of Beauvais' 'De Eruditione Filiorum Nobilium' and the Education of Women* (New York, Berne, Frankfurt, 1984), pp. 32–3.

34. Serjeantson (ed.), *Legendys of Hooly Wummen*, p. 113.

35. Christine de Pisan, *The Treasure of the City of Ladies, or The Book of the Three Virtues*, tr. Sarah Lawson (Harmondsworth, 1985), pp. 160–2.

36. Ibid., p. 161.

37. Ibid., p. 162.

38. For a fuller exploration of St Katherine's popularity in relation to other virgin-martyrs see Lewis, 'Rule of lyf', pp. 52–95.

39. For a discussion of virgin-martyrs explaining their popularity almost exclusively in terms of their intercessory function see Eamon Duffy, 'Holy maydens, holy wyfes: The Cult of Women Saints in Fifteenth- and Sixteenth-Century England', *Studies in Church History*, 23 (1990).

40. Again, despite the current focus on women it should be noted that St Katherine could also function as a wider model of lay affective piety, of relevance to men as well as women. This will be discussed in my study of the cult of St Katherine in late medieval England (Woodbridge, forthcoming).

41. For a comparison of extant numbers of Middle English saints' lives see Charlotte D'Evelyn and Frances A. Foster's survey in J. Burke Severs (ed.), *A Manual of Writings in Middle English: 1050–1500* (8 vols, Connecticut, 1970), pp. 561–635. Lives of St Katherine are listed on pp. 599–602.

42. Magdalena Carrasco, 'Spirituality and Historicity in Pictorial Hagiography: Two Miracles by St Albinus of Angers', *Art History*, 12 (1989), 1–21, for the ramifications of change and development in a hagiographic text.

43. The text of the Vulgate has been edited by S.R.T.O. d'Ardenne and E.J. Dobson and is to be found in their *Seinte Katerine: Re-edited from MS Bodley 34 and the Other Manuscripts*, Early English Text Society, Special Series 7 (Oxford, 1981), pp. 144–203. For a discussion of the text see Bray, 'Legend of St Katherine', pp. 23–34. For the *Legenda Aurea* life of St Katherine see Jacobus de Voragine, *The Golden Legend: Readings on the Saints*, tr. William Granger Ryan (2 vols, Princeton, 1993), vol. 2, pp. 334–41. Ryan's translation is based on the Latin text edited by Thomas Graesse, *Jacobi a Voragine, Legenda Aurea* (orginally published Leipzig, 1850; reprinted Osnabruck, 1969), pp. 789–97. See Bray, 'Legend of St Katherine', pp. 87–90.

44. For editions of the Middle English 'passion' life of St Katherine: Charlotte D'Evelyn and Anna J. Mill, *The South English Legendary*, Early English Text Society, Original Series 235–6, 244 (3 vols, London, 1956–59), vol. 2, pp. 533–43; John Mirk, *Festial*, ed. Theodor Erbe, Early English Text Society, Extra Series 96 (London, 1905), pp. 275–7; , E.H. Weatherly (ed.), *Speculum Sacerdotale*, Early English Text Society, Original Series 200 (Oxford, 1935), pp. 243–4; W.M. Metcalf (ed.), *The Legends*

of the Saints in the Scottish Dialect of the Fourteenth Century, Scottish Text Society 22–25 (4 vols, 1888–91), vol. 4, pp. 442–7; three other versions of the life of St Katherine were edited by Carl Horstmann, see his *Altenglische Legenden, Neue Folge* (Heilbronn, 1881), pp. 165–71, 242–59, 260–4. Bokenham's version belongs to this group, Serjeantson (ed.), *Legendys of Hooly Wummen*, pp. 172–201.

45. The most complete account of this development is that provided by Auvo Kurvinen, 'The Life of St Catharine of Alexandria in Middle English Prose' (unpublished D.Phil. thesis, University of Oxford, 1960), pp. 189–211. See also Bray, 'Legend of St Katherine', pp. 257–70.

46. This lengthy life is extant in four manuscripts. For an edition see John Capgrave, *Life of St Katherine*, ed. Carl Horstmann, Early English Text Society, Original Series 100 (London, 1893).

47. The most recent list of prose life manuscripts is provided by Saara Nevalinna and Irma Taavitsainen, *St Katherine of Alexandria: The Late Middle English Prose Legend in Southwell Minster MS 7* (Cambridge, 1993), pp. xi–xii. This work also provides the only modern published edition of the prose life.

48. See Berenice Fisher, 'Wandering in the Wilderness: The Search for Women Role Models', *Signs*, 13 (1988), 219–221.

49. For a discussion of household manuscripts, their owners and the place of such miscellanies within wider patterns of lay domestic religious practices and lay literacy see Frances McSparran and P.R. Robinson (eds), *Cambridge University Library MS Ff.2.38* (London, 1979), pp. vii–xii. See also Julia Boffey and John J. Thompson, 'Anthologies and Miscellanies: Production and Choice of Texts', in Jeremy Griffiths and Derek Pearsall (eds), *Book Production and Publishing in Britain: 1375–1475* (Cambridge, 1989), pp. 279–315; Carol M. Meale, 'Patrons, Buyers and Owners: Book Production and Social Status', in ibid., pp. 201–238; Carol M. Meale, '"godemen/Wiues maydnes and alle men": Romance and its Audiences', in Carol M. Meale (ed.), *Readings in Medieval English Romances* (Cambridge, 1994), pp. 209–25; Felicity Riddy, *Sir Thomas Malory* (Leiden, New York etc., 1987), pp. 16–23; Philippa Hardman, 'A mediaeval "Library *in Parvo*"', *Medium Aevum* 47 (1978), 262–73.

50. The following works provide descriptions of each manuscript and its appearance: a facsimile of Advocates 19.2.1 has been published; Derek Pearsall and I.C. Cunningham, *The Auchinleck Manuscript: National Library of Scotland Advocates MS 19.2.1* (London, 1979); see McSparren and Robinson, *Ms Ff.2.38*, for a facsimile of Ff.2.38. For a description of Arundel 168 see J. Forshall, *Catalogue of Manuscripts in the British Museum. New Series 1, part 1: The Arundel Manuscripts* (London, 1834), pp. 46-7. This manuscript does not precisely fit the contents pattern of other household manuscripts but it does contain female saints' lives alongside courtesy texts, hence its inclusion here. For Cotton Titus A. xxvi see J. Planta, *A Catalogue of Manuscripts in the Cottonian Library Deposited in the British Museum* (London, 1802), pp. 515–16). This manuscript consists of three originally separate sections now bound together; the contents of the middle section suggest that it once functioned as a household book. For the remaining manuscripts see Guddat-Figge, *Catalogue of Manuscripts*, pp. 73–8 (Porkington 10), pp. 127–30 (Advocates 19.3.1), pp. 238–40 (Chetham 8009).

51. For the Auchinleck life see Horstmann, *Altenenglische Legenden*, pp. 242–58, for the life in Ff.2.38 see ibid., pp. 260–64.

52. For a discussion of the four prose life recensions see Kurvinen, 'Life of St Catharine', pp. 1–6. This earliest version, 'a' as Kurvinen calls it, is also found in two other manuscripts: Oxford Corpus Christi MS 237 (second half of the fifteenth century) and British Library, Harleian MS 5259 (mid-fifteenth century).

53. See the works cited in note 49 above. See also Nicholls, *The Matter of Courtesy*, especially the chapter 'Courtesy books in secular society and fiction', pp. 45–56.

54. This approach has been influenced by Felicity Riddy's work on the courtesy text, 'How the Good Wijf Tauȝte hir Douȝtir', in her article 'Mother Knows Best: Reading Social Change in a Courtesy Text', *Speculum* (1996), 66–86, although Riddy's focus is on lower status urban households. Jaime K. Araujo's comparison of Advocates 19.3.1 with six other household books also provided a useful paradigm, see her 'MS Advocates 19.3.1: A Woman's Book in a Woman's Context?' (unpublished MA dissertation, Centre for Medieval Studies, University of York, 1993), pp. 21–30. The present survey focuses on the social and cultural value of saints' lives. This is not intended to convey the impression that this was their only or most important function, but to uncover a dimension which has remained relatively unexplored in accounts of the popularity of saints and their cults in the later Middle Ages.

55. Although this broad definition of household manuscripts serves for the present study, as it allows comparisons to be drawn between different manuscripts, it should be stressed that there is no established 'blueprint' for identifying household manuscripts. By their very nature they resist simplistic categorization. Much more work needs to be done on the nature and provenance of such manuscripts and their place within domestic devotional life.

56. This can be seen, for example, by examining the contents of the various household manuscripts catalogued by Guddat-Figge, *Catalogue of Manuscripts*, *passim*.

57. For household manuscripts as educating and socializing tools see Riddy, *Thomas Malory*, pp. 69–74. See also Araujo, 'Advocates 19.3.1', pp. 14–20.

58. H.E. Bell, 'The Price of Books in Medieval England', *The Library*, 4th Series 17 (1936–7), 312–32.

59. Lawrence R. Poos, 'Social History and the Book of Hours', in Roger S. Wieck (ed.), *Time Sanctified: The Book of Hours in Medieval Art and Life* (New York, 1988), pp. 33–8.

60. Lewis, 'Rule of lyf', pp. 69–71.

61. This approach to the question of the household as a religious and ideological unit has been influenced in particular by the work of Lyndal Roper on the early Reformation household in Germany, *The Holy Household: Women and Morals in Reformation Augsburg* (Oxford, 1989). Many of the observations made by Elizabeth Langland on women's place within the middle-class Victorian household have also been applicable, *Nobody's Angels: Middle-Class Women and Domestic Ideology* (Ithaca and London, 1995), in particular the idea of the home as a theatre and the signifying practices that are staged within it, p. 9.

62. Nicholas Orme, *Education and Society in Medieval and Renaissance England* (London and Ronceverte, 1989), pp. 158, 161, 223–4.

63. See S.J.E. Riches, ' "The Pot of Oure Hope": Images of St Anne in the Late Medieval World' (unpublished MA dissertation, Centre for Medieval Studies, University of York, 1991), pp. 65–8; also Pamela Sheingorn, ' "The Wise Mother": the Image of St Anne teaching the Virgin Mary', Gesta, 32/3 (1993), 69–80; Wendy Scase, 'St Anne and the Education of the Virgin: Literary and Artistic Traditions and their Implications', in Nicholas Rogers (ed.), *England in the Fourteenth Century: Proceedings of the 1991 Harlaxton Symposium* (Stamford, 1993), pp. 81–96.

64. For the education of medieval women see Orme, *Education and Society*, pp. 161–75 and Nicholas Orme, *From Childhood to Chivalry: The Education of the English Kings and Aristocracy, 1066–1530* (London

and New York, 1984), pp. 106–9, pp. 156–63. See also Barron, 'Education and Training of Girls', in Dunn (ed.) *Courts, Counties and the Capital, passim*; Henrietta Leyser, *Medieval Women: A Social History of Women in England, 450–1500* (London, 1995), pp. 133–41, provides a useful introductory survey.

65. Orme, *Childhood to Chivalry*, pp. 59–60. See also Jennifer C. Ward, *English Noblewomen in the Later Middle Ages* (London, 1992), pp. 93–7.

66. M.T. Clanchy, *From Memory to Written Record: England 1066–1307* (Oxford, 1993), p. 252.

67. Anne M. Dutton, 'Women's Use of Religious Literature in Late Medieval England' (unpublished D.Phil. dissertation, Centre for Medieval Studies, University of York, 1995); Felicity Riddy, '"Women Talking About the Things of God": A Late Medieval Sub-Culture', in Meale, *Women and Literature*, pp. 104–27; Meale, '. . . alle the bokes that I haue', *passim*.

68. A particularly good example is provided by Oxford, Bodleian Library MS Hatton 73. See Josephine Koster Tarvers, '"Thys ys my mystrys boke": English Women as Readers and Writers in Late-Medieval England', in Charlotte Cook Moore, Penelope Reed Doob, Marjorie Curry Woods (eds), *The Uses of Manuscripts in Literacy Studies: Essays in Honour of Judson Boyce Allen* (Michigan, 1992), pp. 305–27, 317. Further examples are to be found on p. 318.

69. Rhiannon Purdie argued that this was the signature of an actual woman in her paper, 'Sexing the Manuscript: MS Chetham 8009 and the Identification of Women's Books Through Internal Evidence', given at the Gender and Medieval Studies conference 'Gender and Community in the Middle Ages', Gregynog, University of Wales, January 1995. I am very grateful to Rhiannon Purdie for giving me a copy of this paper to consult.

70. Araujo, 'Advocates 19.3.1', p. 12. A scribe called John Hawghton also worked on parts of this manuscript.

71. *The Golden Legend*, p. 334.

72. The exception to this rule is the life in the *Northern Homily Cycle*. For a possible explanation see Lewis, 'Rule of lyf', pp. 121–3.

73. I quote from Kurvinen's transcription of the 'a' version of the prose life. Her main source was the text contained in Oxford, Corpus Christi MS 237. This manuscript does not fall into our corpus but the texts of the life contained in the four manuscripts which do are not substantially different. This is apparent from Kurvinen's inclusion of textual variations from all six manuscripts. Kurvinen, 'Life of St Catharine', p. 229.

74. Ibid.

75. Capgrave's life affords even more space to Katherine's education, *Life of St Katherine*, pp. 31–42. Although the verse lives in the Auchinleck Manuscript and Ff.2.38 do not describe her education in such detail, she is still clearly presented as highly educated and extremely intelligent.

76. Kurvinen, 'Life of St Catharine', p. 291.

77. For an exploration of this phenomenon see Rowena Archer, '"How Ladies Who Live on Their Manors Ought to Manage Their Households and Estates": Women as Landholders and Administrators in the Later Middle Ages', in Goldberg, *Woman is a Worthy Wight*, pp. 144–81.

78. No sooner is the marriage ceremony complete than Christ returns to Heaven. Katherine must wait another four years until her martyrdom reunites them. See Kurvinen, 'Life of St Catharine', pp. 287–93.

79. Lydgate composed the *Invocation to St Anne*, for Anne, Countess of Stafford, the mother of Anne, Lady March, another patron of his mentioned earlier. He also wrote 'The Fifteen Joys of Our Lady'

for Isabella Despencer. A copy of this text is to be found in Cotton Titus A. xxvi. See Meale, '. . . alle the bokes that I haue', pp. 137–8 for more on Lydgate, Bokenham, female saints and female readers. See also Riddy, 'Women Talking About the Things of God', pp. 104–6. However, we must beware of assuming an absolute correlation between female saints and female readers; Osbern Bokenham wrote his life of St Margaret for his close friend Thomas Burgh: Serjeantson (ed.), *Legendys of Hooly Wummen*, p. 7. Equally women display devotion to male saints. Capgrave wrote a life of St Augustine for 'a gentill woman' who was born on his feast day: Samuel Moore, 'Patrons of Letters in Norfolk and Suffolk, c. 1450', 98.

80. There are also examples of household manuscripts which do not contain a life of St Katherine, e.g. Oxford, Bodleian Library MS Ashmole 61 (see Guddat-Figge, *Catalogue of Manuscripts*, pp. 249–52) and British Library, MS Cotton Caligula A. ii (Ibid., pp. 169–72).

81. St Margaret is presented as an educated woman, but unlike St Katherine, who receives a male education from masters, she receives a more typically female upbringing from a nurse. See Katherine J. Lewis, 'The Life of St Margaret of Antioch in Late Medieval England: A Gendered Reading', *Studies in Church History* (forthcoming 1998). Given the status of Mary Magdalene as repentant prostitute, and St Anne as mother, it may be that their lives would become of value to our young women once they had married, become sexually active and given birth. Further exploration of this question is beyond the scope of the present article. See Gail MacMurray Gibson, 'Saint Anne and the Religion of Childbed: Some East Anglian Texts and Talismans', in Kathleen Ashley and Pamela Sheingorn (eds), *Interpreting Cultural Symbols: Saint Anne in Late Medieval Society* (Athens and London, 1990), pp. 95–110. Noël James Menuge suggests that Mary Magdalene was a popular role-model for non virgins, and may have been a more accessible role model than the Virgin Mary, due to the Magdalene's sexual (and yet redeemed) past. See Noël James Menuge, '"Body and sowle damdpned perpetuall!": An Exploration of the Representation of the Conflated Sexuality and Persona of Mary Magdalen in the Late Medieval Digby *Mary Magdalen* Play' (unpublished MA dissertation, University of York, 1993), pp. 3–6. See also Susan Haskins, *Mary Magdalene* (Hammersmith, 1993), esp. chapter 5, 'Beata Peccatrix', *passim*, for further explanation of why this may have been so.

82. For the purposes of this article the focus is on texts of a broadly educational nature. The ensuing survey is not intended to be exhaustive, but to point out some key texts and themes that the manuscripts have in common. Five of these manuscripts also contain verse romances. These texts, like the saints' lives, probably provided entertainment, edification and models of courteous behaviour, but there is not space to give proper consideration to this issue here. See Stephen Knight, 'The Social Function of the Middle English Romance', in David Aers (ed.), *Medieval Literature: Criticism, Ideology and History* (Sussex, 1986), pp. 99–122; Nicholls, *The Matter of Courtesy*, pp. 47–56; Orme, *Education and Society*, p. 155.

83. Orme, *Childhood to Chivalry*, p. 104.

84. Ibid., p. 158; Orme, *Education and Society*, p. 171.

85. Orme, *Education and Society*, pp. 160–1. According to Philippa Hardman the version of 'Stans Puer ad Mensam' is not the version attributed to Lydgate, but one by the anonymous *Urbanitas* poet. I am grateful to her for sharing this information with me.

86. This argument was influenced by Langland's discussion of the ways in which middle-class Victorian women 'policed the social borders', *Nobody's Angels*, pp. 24–61. For an example of the use of

a text in the construction, indeed imposition, of an identity see Riddy, 'Mother knows best', pp. 6–13. Riddy has also discussed the condition of social uncertainty in which vernacular courtesy texts and household manuscripts have their significance, *Thomas Malory*, pp. 60–83.

87. Orme, *Childhood to Chivalry*, pp. 195–6.

88. Alexandra Barratt, *Women's Writing in Middle English* (London and New York, 1992), p. 234. For information on Berners' possible identity see pp. 232–3.

89. The fiction of a father or mother giving advice seems clearly intended for use by those acting *in loco parentis* to such young people. Riddy, 'Mother Knows Best', *passim*, for a detailed discussion of the intended audience for such texts and the kinds of social conduct which they attempt to inculcate. For the texts of 'The good wyfe wold a pylgrymage', 'The gode wif tauȝhte hire douȝtir', and 'The thewis of gud women', see Tauno F. Mustanoja (ed.), *The Good Wife Taught Her Daughter, The Good Wyfe Wold A Pylgremage, The Thewis of Gud Wuman* (Helsinki, 1948). For the text of 'How the goode man taught hys sone', see F.J. Furnivall (ed.), *Queene Elizabethes Achademy, A Boke of Precedence, Etc*, Early English Text Society, Extra Series 8 (1869), pp. 52–5.

90. Riddy, 'Mother Knows Best', pp. 66–7. Here Riddy discusses a specifically bourgeois ethos, located within an urban setting. Similar concerns would have been important to gentry and lesser noble families, as well as to rich mercantile ones.

91. In 'The good wyfe wold a pylgremage', the goodwife tells her daughter to 'hyde thy legys whyte' and not to run about the town like 'an Antyny gryce', or she may be mistaken for a 'callot'; Mustanoja, *The Good Wife*, p. 173.

92. Kurvinen, 'Life of St Catharine', p. 291.

93. Ibid., p. 292.

94. For discussions of the Christian identity of noble and gentry households and the kinds of religious observances which were practised within them see Kate Mertes, *The English Noble Household 1250–1600: Good Governance and Politic Rule* (Oxford, 1988), chapter 5, 'The Household as Religious Community', pp. 139–60. Her article 'The Household as a Religious Community', in Joel Rosenthal and Colin Richmond (eds), *People, Politics and Community in the Later Middle Ages* (Gloucester, 1987), pp. 123–39, widens the discussion to include gentry families.

95. This is especially marked in the Auchinleck Manuscript and Ff.2.38.

96. Leonard Boyle, *Pastoral Care, Clerical Education and Canon Law, 1200–1400* (London, 1981); W.A. Pantin, *The English Church in the Fourteenth Century* (Cambridge, 1955), pp. 189–243; Judith Shaw, 'The Influence of Canonical and Episcopal Reform on Popular Books of Instruction', in Thomas J. Heffernan (ed.), *The Popular Literature of Medieval England* (Knoxville, 1985), pp. 44–60. For the religious education of children see Nicholas Orme, 'Children and the Church in Medieval England', *Journal of English History*, 45 (1994), 563–87.

97. de Pisan, *Treasure of the City of Ladies*, p. 219. Karen A. Winstead, *Virgin Martyrs: Legends of Sainthood in Late Medieval England* (Ithaca NY and London, 1997) was published too late for consideration within this article.

3

CROWNS AND VIRGINS: QUEENMAKING DURING THE WARS OF THE ROSES[1]

Joanna L. Chamberlayne

'Although the coronation in England demands that a king should marry a virgin whoever she may be, legitimately born and not a widow, yet the king took this one against the will of all his lords.'[2]

Thus wrote the Danzig chronicler, Caspar Weinreich, commenting upon the announcement in September 1464 of Edward IV's marriage to Elizabeth Woodville. Since 1066 the women chosen to be queens of England had all been young virgins of noble, usually royal, blood, with only three exceptions: Eleanor of Aquitaine, whose lands made her the most eligible bride in Europe in spite of her marital history; Joan of Kent, a lady of English royal blood who never actually became queen; and Joan of Navarre, whose second husband was himself a widower. No such mitigating circumstances applied to Elizabeth Woodville, the 27-year-old mother of two, daughter and widow of Lancastrian knights, who married a king five years her junior. It is the purpose of this paper to explore the ideologies implied in Weinreich's observation regarding the preference for virgins as queens. It will first consider the literary 'queenmaking' of chronicles, romances, pageants and liturgies as they constructed their notion of the ideal queen, and her function in the monarchy. The challenges to this ideology in the practice of queenmaking during the Wars of the Roses will then be discussed, before we return to Elizabeth Woodville and the propaganda by which she was made to fit a role traditionally the preserve of young virgins.

LITERARY QUEENMAKING

A Potential Mother

A practical and obvious motive for desiring a young woman as queen was her potential to provide her king with heirs. Even in romances the connection between a queen and childbearing was often immediately assumed by certain characters: when the hero of the anonymous fifteenth-century dream romance

The Isle of Ladies announced his success in finding a queen after seven years of searching, his lords expressed their delight 'For faste desyred they an heyer.' Similarly, John Hardyng, in a chronicle successively dedicated to Henry VI, Richard Duke of York and his wife Cecily, and Edward IV, maintained that in choosing among the Count of Hainault's daughters for a bride, the future Edward III was advised to choose

> hir with good hippis I mene
> For she will bere good soones at myne entent.[3]

It is probably an apocryphal tale, but may have been a not so subtle hint to Hardyng's first dedicatee who produced but a single child. Moreover, Hardyng recorded that, before making the choice, the prince was first assured that all three of the count's daughters were virgins.[4] In his history of Richard III, half a century later, Thomas More drew attention to the risk of acquiring a barren wife inherent in such a process, attributing to Edward IV the following response to his mother's supposed objections regarding his marriage:

> she is a widow & hath alredy children, by god's blessed Ladye, I am a batcheler & have some to: & so eche of vs hath a profe yt neither of vs is lyke to be barain.[5]

It was a common complaint of misogynistic discourse that women could not be 'tried out' prior to acquisition as other purchases could, notably in Jerome's *Adversus Joviniam*.[6] None the less, as the context for More's account implies, the preference for virginity prevailed.[7] This was possibly in part due to the desire to ensure true hereditary succession. A virgin bride ensured that it would not be the child of a previous marriage who inherited her new husband's possessions. More generally applicable was the argument of fourteenth- and fifteenth-century canonists that second marriages were motivated primarily by a desire for continued sex, which implied that a remarried widow could be less trusted to maintain chastity within marriage.[8] The Domincan author of the fourteenth-century treatise *The Solace of the Game of Chess* asserted that chastity was one of the two principal responsibilities of a queen in order to ensure unquestioned hereditary succession.[9]

Childbearing had not always been considered essential to queenship. Edward the Confessor's lack of offspring gave rise to the story of his vow of virginity. According to *La Estoire de Seint Aedward le Rei*, given to Eleanor of Provence, this vow was shared by the Confessor's wife Edith; but in spite of this, Edith was portrayed as an ideal queen, deserving of this role by virtue of her goodness, sense, learning and beauty.[10] Five centuries before that translation was made, Bede had celebrated the achievement of St Etheldreda, who succeeded in maintaining her virginity during two marriages to English kings.[11] However, in the centuries following the Norman Conquest, primogeniture, rather than election, very slowly became the accepted criterion for kingship, thereby making the production of heirs of greater importance to kings, both for maintaining stability and for revealing God's approval of their sovereignty. Consequently, there was greater criticism of later queens who failed in this duty, notably Margaret of Anjou: in 1448 a farm labourer was accused of declaring that

> Oure Quene was none abyl to be Quene of Inglond, but and he were a pere of or a lord of this ream . . . he would be on of thaym that schuld helpe to putte her a doun, for because that sche bereth no child, and because that we have no pryns in this land.[12]

However, even in the later middle ages, an absence of offspring did not necessarily mean that a woman was not considered a true queen. In a literary context, Guinevere's failure to produce an heir was never a matter for discussion in Malory or his sources, and she remained an integral part of the court beside her husband. Historically, a queen was not always necessary for the continuation of a king's line; most notably in Henry IV's situation, for he already had four adult sons on his accession to the throne. In spite of the considerable expense involved in acquiring a queen, and the risk to the stability of court life regularly occasioned by a queen's unpopular foreign companions, Henry still chose to remarry.[13] Such a decision strongly implies that queens were necessary to kings for reasons besides producing heirs. At the point of choosing a new queen, these reasons almost invariably impinged upon the validity and nature of the king's authority. For example, the origins of a potential queen might serve to affirm the king's position in intimating acceptance of his kingship by the powerful elite from which she came, or in integrating him with a conquered people through marriage to one of their own. They might also serve to consummate his sacred and chivalric kingship, providing a required feminine aspect to monarchy.

A Means of Validating Kingship

The queen's role in political affirmation appeared only rarely in romances, but commonly in the pageantry surrounding royal marriages and coronations; it was a theme which concerned those in authority – the king, his advisers and civic authorities – but was somewhat at odds with the literary concept of royal marriages for love. One possible instance in a romance context is that of Guinevere: in her mid-fifteenth century incarnation in Malory's work, it was she who brought to Arthur the Round Table of his father, complete with one hundred knights, thus forming a link between past and present legitimacy.[14] In a reversal of the priorities of Malory's story, Catherine of Valois was handed over to

Henry V along with inheritance of the kingdom of France, an emblem of the French crown's acceptance of Henry's position, and possibly a device to make the transfer more acceptable to the French people. In the messages of the subtleties at her coronation banquet it was stated that her marriage had brought an end to war: following the third course, 'a mete in paste with iiij Aungels in the fourme of seynt kateryne whele in the mydde' bore the message 'Il est escrite pur voir & dit par mariage pure, ce guerre ne dure.'[15] This twisting of political facts to represent the queen as the origin of peace served both to fit the queen into an accepted female role and to glorify the monarchy as a whole.[16]

For a king whose position was insecure, a foreign-born queen could represent the recognition of his position by important powers abroad. In 1501 Henry VII succeeded in acquiring a daughter of the Spanish royal house, Katherine of Aragon, for his eldest son, at a time when his dynasty's hold on the throne was by no means uncontested. Henry VII had rather more involvement in the arrangement of the welcome pageantry than was customary and clearly used it to affirm his own legitimacy through repeated stresses on Katherine's origins during the marriage celebrations, including a figure of her illustrious ancestor Alfonso X, the Wise, claiming to have foreseen such a union.[17] Edward IV and Richard III, or at least their ministers, probably hoped to arrange similar foreign affirmation for the shaky Yorkist kingship. Almost as soon as Edward was crowned, an embassy was despatched to Burgundy to negotiate a marriage with one of the duke's nieces, but Duke Philip was not prepared to make such a commitment.[18] Similarly, on the death of Richard III's queen, Anne Neville, overtures were made to the royal houses of Spain and Portugal with almost unseemly haste, only to be curtailed by Richard's death five months after that of his wife.[19]

An alternative means for conquering kings to connote legitimacy via marriage was to choose a bride from the elite of the conquered people. Henry I chose Edward the Confessor's great-great-niece, the Anglo-Scottish princess Eadgyth, as his bride, in a deliberate gesture of union between the English and their Norman conquerors.[20] Had Edward IV wished to make a similar gesture he could have done little better than marry Elizabeth Woodville, the eldest step-daughter of John Duke of Bedford, the most generally respected of the Lancastrians.[21] However, such a gesture might equally have undermined his claim to blood superiority over the Lancastrians, and no trace of propaganda constructed along these lines remains to suggest that his choice of bride might have been intended, as in so many earlier cases, to strengthen his position of authority. Henry VII, in contrast, had little choice but to marry Elizabeth of York, eldest daughter of the conquered Yorkist dynasty, for his power base was so small that he did not dare risk allowing an alternative faction to build up around her. Unlike Eadgyth or Elizabeth Woodville, Elizabeth of York was not merely a representative of a defeated house but could have been queen in her own right, and as such presented a challenge to notions of authority as intriguing as that raised by her mother. The second continuator of the Crowland Chronicle summed up the situation, referring to a parliamentary discussion on the king's marriage to

> the lady Elizabeth, King Edward's eldest daughter, in whose person it seemed to all, there could be found whatever appeared to be missing in the king's title elsewhere.[22]

Elizabeth of York's capacity to consummate her husband's kingship was unprecedented in its political nature. Yet to some extent all queens had the potential to make their husband's kingship more whole. This occurred on a variety of levels, often hinging upon a need for a female element in even the most male structures, be that the typical noble household, the chivalric court of romance or the medieval perception of God himself, all of which formed models for monarchy. To begin with the noble household, in which the king's household originated: K. Mertes has observed that it was virtually always centred upon a couple, a single 'conjugal unit', who served as a focus for unity. Although widows might be the heads of households, which were composed almost entirely of men, widowers almost always remarried.[23] This apparent need for a woman within a primarily male power structure may well explain Henry IV's surprising second marriage, especially since, as the Duke of Brittany's widow, Joan of Navarre could not be said to offer the kind of foreign affirmation of his kingship present in a bride like Katherine of Aragon, the young daughter of powerful parents. A woman was required in this context not just as an ornament to the king's court but to complement the king's masculine qualities with perceived feminine virtues of mercy and peacemaking. The importance of a potential queen's character was referred to in both literary and diplomatic writings in which they were almost invariably presented as specimens of ideal womanhood, and this generally included virginity. In the thirteenth century, Edward the Confessor's future wife was described in the following glowing terms:

> A daughter had [Godwin], very beautiful,
> A well-disposed damsel,
> Imbued with courtesy . . .
> Modest was she in conduct,
> As well befits a virgin;
> Eloquent was she and wise
> More than maiden of her age.[24]

In the fourteenth-century *Of Arthour and Merlin*, Guinevere, prior to her marriage, was considered 'bothe fair and wise/Of al the lond sche berth the priis'.[25]

Another politically motivated description of a queen presented a similar ideal in the fifteenth-century: an oration written to be delivered to the Pope regarding Henry VII's choice of bride described Elizabeth of York thus:

> The beauty and chastity of this lady are indeed so great that neither Lucretia nor Diana herself were ever either more beautiful or more chaste. So great is her virtue and her character so fine, that she certainly seems to have been preserved by divine will from the time of her birth right up until today to be consort and queen.[26]

Implicit in these extracts is the notion that a queen needed to be worthy of her role and her king.[27] Like any other husband, a king sought a wife who would reflect well upon him, but her character, wisdom and beauty were important for other reasons. The author of *The Solace of the Game of Chess* explained that a queen must be wise so that she would be discreet over confidential matters and would ensure the good education of her children; and she must be chaste, not only for the reasons of hereditary succession referred to above, but so that she would provide a good example to her subjects, 'for as she is above all other in estate and reverence so should she be ensaumple unto all other in her lvyng honestyle'.[28] Christine de Pisan, as a result of her observation of court life, described some of the means by which the 'good princess' could complement her husband: with concern for his spiritual welfare; encouraging him to give alms; or in making peace between him and his subjects or other rulers, because

> men are by nature more courageous and more hot-headed . . . But women are by nature more timid and also of a sweeter disposition, and for this reason . . . they can be the best means of pacifying men.[29]

De Pisan also argued that a queen's charitable deeds provided an important example for her people to follow, 'for nothing influences the common people so much as what they see their lord and lady do.'[30] The queen was not only the inspiration for charitable deeds but also, since the twelfth-century lyrics of the troubadours, for feats of chivalry.[31] The persistence of these notions is evident in the pageantry that greeted Margaret of Anjou on her 1456 entry into Coventry. Here actors, representing the Nine Worthies, offered her their service in language strongly reminiscent of the literature of courtly love. For instance, 'Joshua' promised,

> I . . . wyll abey to your plesur, princes most riall,
> As to the heghest lady that I can ymagyne ...
> To the plesure of your persone, I wyl put me to pyne,
> As a knyght for his lady boldly to fight

whereas 'Julius Caesar' said,

> Welcum you, princes most benynge & gude
> Of quenes that byn crowned so high non knowe I.[32]

But the implication of this language was not simply comparison with queens of romance, but also with the queen of Heaven. The Old Testament prophets in this pageantry made the connection rather more explicitly: 'Isaiah' maintained

> Like as mankynde was gladdid by the birght of Jhesus,
> So shall this empyre ioy the birthe of your bodye

whereas 'Jeremiah' claimed,

> Vnto the rote of Jesses rote likken you well I may.[33]

By the late Middle Ages comparison between English queens and the Virgin Mary were not uncommon, although this instance was unusually explicit. The reason for such emphatic association of Margaret with romantic and Christian ideals of queenship probably lay in the political instability of 1456, which drove Margaret to move the court from London to her own dower lands in Warwickshire. As E.F. Jacob observed, it was a move which shifted the emphasis of authority firmly onto the royal person in that the centre of government was where the king was.[34] It is thus possible that Margaret, or her advisers, influenced the pageant organizers to portray Margaret as an inspiration to her subjects whose ideal qualities reflected well upon both the king and her young son, the heir of Lancaster, both presented by implication as types of Christ.

The most striking use of a woman chosen to be queen in the discourse of royal legitimation by analogy with the sacred occurred at Katherine of Aragon's 1501 wedding. In the fifth pageant to greet her on her entry into London, a 'prelate of the church' explained that,

> . . . the moost convenient wise
> For manys Redempcion was thought to be than
> The maryage of God to the nature of man

which Jesus had explained thus,

> The Kyng of Heven is like an erthely kyng
> That to his sonne prepareth a weddyng

so, the 'prelate' continued,

And right so as oure soveraign lord, the Kyng,
May be resemblid to the Kyng Celestiall . . .
This noble Kyng doeth a mariage ordeigne
Betwene his furst begoten sonne, Prince Arthure,
And you, Dame Kateryne . . .[35]

This association of the future king's marriage with entry into the world of the saviour of mankind was developed in a poem, possibly recited on the day of the marriage ceremony and certainly written close to the occasion. This poem dwelt on the prophets who longed for Christ's coming, and on Simeon's joy at seeing him as a baby in the temple, and then drew parallels with the royal wedding:

For this bond and unyon, I trust, shall never be broke.
In Poulis many Simeons thought they had well taryed
To see thus Spayne and Englond toguyders to be married.[36]

The ideal queen thus consummated her husband's kingship by beauty, chastity and noble character that were an inspiration to good deeds, by mercy and emotion which complemented his judgement and logic, by an inclination to peace that tempered his courage, and by the flesh of the most human that complemented his spirit approaching the divine. Yet women were, and had been for centuries, so thoroughly identified with the point of separation from God, with chaos, with man's tendency to evil, that the intimations of a woman's access to power inherent in these constructions of monarchy were deeply threatening to the misogynistic philosophy of patriarchy.[37]

The Coronation and Virginity

The resolution of this conflict is evident in the process of the queenmaking ceremony itself. The coronation was a celebration of the potential of queens, opening with an orison that began, 'Almighty and everlasting God . . . who in no way abhors the frailty of the feminine sex by reproaching it, but rather chooses worthily to approve it, and who by choosing the weak things of the world does confound those that are strong,' thus drawing on the central Christian theme of God's reversal of human power structures.[38] It is a theme that has for centuries been subverted by church and state to apply to God's kingdom beyond this world, thereby leaving their structures unchallenged, so that even here the full implication of what was said was probably mentally translated to a purely spiritual context.[39] None the less, that same orison also celebrates her potential to 'honour the whole kingdom' with 'the fruit of her womb'.[40] Later in the ceremony, at the presentation of the rings, she was assigned a role complementary to the king's regarding the church; he was to protect the

Christian faith while she was to convert 'heathen nations'.[41] Most striking of all, she was anointed upon the head, as was the king, in spite of Innocent III's 1204 decretal *On Holy Unction* which stated that only bishops were permitted this privilege with its sacerdotal connotations.[42]

However, beside this empowering, sacred imagery of queenship, was another ideal: its proximity to virginity. The blessing prior to her anointing included the request that 'remaining always chaste in the compact of a royal marriage she may obtain the palm next to virginity'.[43] After the actual crowning she was enjoined to labour to be beautified with the 'gold of wisdom and the jewels of virtue' that she might meet in death 'together with the wise virgins, her husband our everlasting Lord Jesus Christ'.[44] The second-century Platonist Methodius of Olympus had explained that 'virginity's principal attraction is its ability to cancel woman's womanliness'; a concept that informed much of medieval writing on women and virginity.[45] Yet to see this association of ideal queens with virginity purely as a means of making acceptable a woman in a position of power by de-sexualizing her, is to ignore contemporary notions of virginity's empowering properties. The early fathers had argued that virginity made humans equal with angels, and even hastened the coming of God's kingdom.[46] Closer to the fifteenth century, popular legends of female martyrs such as Saints Margaret and Katherine often suggested that their supernatural strength to resist temptation and the devil was rooted in their virginity.[47] Similarly, in more secular literature, it was Sir Galahad's virginity which enabled him to succeed in the grail quest.[48] Moreover, dramatic or artistic anthropomorphic representations of almost any virtue were virgins.[49]

The quasi-magical powers of virginity also impinged upon the ideology of kingship. One aspect of this was a link between kings and angels, whose nature was to be virgins. In his *The Governance of England*, John Fortescue compared the character of the king's power with that of angels, both being of a different nature from that of ordinary human beings, somewhere between God and man.[50] This connection was illustrated by the regular use of angels in royal pageantry, notably in the welcome for a new queen according to regulations laid down by Henry VII.[51] On a more practical level, contemporaries showed concern for their king's sexual conduct; Gregory's Chronicle reported that 'men mervelyd that oure soverayne lorde [Edward IV] was so longe with owte any wyffe, and were evyr ferde that he had not be chaste of hys levynge'.[52] The virginity of kings was bound up in notions of perfect knighthood and the sacerdotal nature of kingship. A eulogy written on Edward IV's accession addressed the king,

> Thoue vergyne knight of whom we synge
> Vn-Deffiled sithe thy begynnyng
> Edwardes, Dai gracia.[53]

Half a century later, Thomas More ascribed to Edward IV's mother, Cecily Neville, the view that 'the sacre magesty of a prince . . . ought as nigh to approche priesthode in clenes as he doth in dignitie'.[54] Priests emulated Christ in their virginity; kings were meant to be types of Christ also, albeit in a more secular context, hence the value of Edward the Confessor's alleged virginity in making him an ideal of English kingship. Given the impracticality of virgin kings once primogeniture had become the accepted criteria for the royal succession, this potential source of sacred dignity could only be used symbolically.

By this period, virginity as a virtue was most often associated with women: for them chastity was the single quality by which their reputation stood or fell, besides which, because virginity enabled a woman to approach spiritual masculinity, its implications for their salvation were greater than for men who were already closer to the notion of an ideal Christian.[55] Consequently, this royal virtue came to be more associated with queens, who at least shared their gender with the prototype of virgin parenthood: Mary. As the quotation which heads this article implies, it was in the coronation ceremony that this was made most explicit. The liturgy, as we have seen, drew attention to the value of virginity, asking God to treat the newly made queen as He treated virgins. The visual imagery of the occasion made the association of queenship and virginity far more explicit. Throughout the proceedings she wore her hair loose, a symbol of virginity almost invariably used in images of the Virgin Mary herself. Her hair would be kept in place with a jewelled coronet which, presumably because it was used to keep loose hair tidy, was described in the account of Elizabeth Woodville's coronation as 'thatyre of virgins'.[56] Moreover, during the procession to Westminster on the day prior to her coronation, a queen would be dressed in white, travelling in a carriage furnished with white cloth of gold, whereas the king wore purple.[57] There were other public occasions on which women wore white, most notably in some profession rites for nuns and at their weddings, in both cases denoting the wearer's virginity.[58] The accepted connotation of this colouring is evident in Margery Kempe's experience; when she wore white clothes she was challenged by the archbishop of York, 'Why gost þu in white? Art þu a mayden?'[59]

The property of virginity, both desexualizing and mysteriously empowering, separated a woman from others of her gender and made her worthy to be a bride of Christ – or of a king, a type of Christ. Whereas other brides lost their maidenhood at marriage, a queen continued to be constructed as a type of the Virgin Mary, not just at her coronation and in liturgy, but in secular discourse also. Almost all pictures of queens painted after their coronation in which they were crowned or held their regalia continued to portray them with loose hair.[60] The reception of Margaret of Anjou after her son's birth constructed her in strikingly Marian terms, as 'Moder of mekenes, dame Margaret, princes most excellent,' and even 'Emprice, quene, princes excellent, in on person all iij'.[61] Here Margaret was figured in terms of a Marian Trinity, an accolade stronger than those used for the king himself who was commonly associated with either God the Father or Jesus as king.[62]

The fact that, in Hoccleve's words, 'A king, by wey of his office/ to god I-likened is' both impinged upon ideals of queenship and meant that a queen could be constructed to affirm the king's sacred position, as his bride. For although the Judaeo-Christian God has no consort in the manner of earlier gods, the Church is considered to be the 'bride of Christ' and from the second century this came to be associated in Christian thinking both with Mary and with the woman 'clothed with the sun' of Revelation 12.[63] The crown of twelve stars worn by the latter figure was one of the origins of Mary's queenly role, expressed in a prayer in an earlier pageant for Margaret of Anjou, on her arrival in London in 1445:

Cristes Modre, Virgyn immaculate,/God hys tabernacle to sanctifie
Of sterres xij the croune hath preparate,/Emprise, Queen and Lady Laureate
Praie for oure Queen that Crist will here gouerne
Long here on lyve in hir noble astate,/Aftirward crown here in blisse eterne.[64]

Mary the queen/bride/mother figure had become essential to the medieval understanding of God's working and purpose: as mother she proved Christ's human aspect; as intercessor she was a channel between him and his people; as bride and queen she looked forward to the coming of God's kingdom. Thus kings could draw parallels between their own position and that of God simply by mimicking the structure of the heavenly hierarchy, bringing in that female and feminine element which Mary represented. This adoption of a type of the Virgin Mary into English kingship was not new in the fifteenth century. Almost as soon as portraits of the Virgin appeared bearing a heavenly regalia of orb and floriated sceptre in the twelfth century, earthly queens too bore these items, rather than their own coronation regalia, on pictures and in seals.[65] The queen's traditional role as intercessor had also long been connected with the Virgin Mary. The notion of queen as intercessor – mercy in opposition to the king as judgement – was prevalent in literature, chronicles and civic receptions of queens.[66] P. Strohm has observed, on the basis of the story of Queen Philippa's intercession for the burghers of Calais, that this model of complementary queenship served to empower the king, enabling him to change his mind without undermining the image of his authority.[67] J.C. Parsons argues that only by interpreting this role in Marian terms could contemporaries avoid the dangerous implication that a king might be susceptible to womanly charms: the queen's intercession must be a product of her weaker gender, not her sexuality, hence identification with a virgin intercessor.[68] These then were the qualities of the ideal potential queen painted by clerics, chroniclers, romance authors, court observers and pageant writers: a young, beautiful, wise, virtuous, noble, merciful, peacemaking, Christian virgin who would bear children. Kings themselves, however, might have a different agenda.

QUEENMAKING IN PRACTICE

Historical Precedent

Between the Norman conquest and the fifteenth century, English kings almost invariably chose young virgins of foreign extraction and noble parentage to be their queens. The outstanding exception was the charismatic and wealthy divorcee, Eleanor of Aquitaine: the most sought after bride in Europe at the time because of her lands, and consequently deemed a suitable bride for Henry II in spite of her marital history. However, a precedent for later departures from tradition was set by Edward of Woodstock, the Black Prince, heir to Edward III. In the spring of 1361 the 30-year-old prince secretly married his 33-year-old, recently widowed cousin, Joan of Kent. Joan had first been married at the age of twelve to William Montague, future Earl of Salisbury. The union was dissolved nine years later when she asserted that she had been pre-contracted to Sir Thomas Holland with whom she was to have three children. Although there is no evidence that the king was as angry at her marriage to the Black Prince as French chroniclers imagined, the couple had to do penance for marrying within prohibited degrees, and chroniclers on both sides of the channel registered their disapproval: the author of the *Chronique des quatre premiers Valois* pictured Joan as a calculating *femme fatale* luring the foolish prince into marriage, whereas English chroniclers attributed to her the sarcastic epithet 'virginem Cancie' ('the Maid of Kent') and recorded the general amazement at the prince's decision to wed Joan in spite of her previous marriages.[69]

The disapproval at Joan's third marriage was not purely because the groom was expected to become a king. The argument that remarriage was motivated primarily by a desire for continued sex and was therefore unseemly has already been mentioned, and young people regularly used charivaris to harass newly married couples if one of them had previously been widowed.[70] The church and civic authorities censured the charivaris but, following a decretal by Pope Alexander III, clerics were forbidden to give the nuptial blessing to such unions, resulting in St Bonaventure's claim that second marriages were sacramentally incomplete.[71] Indeed, despite the Biblical assertion that there was no marriage in heaven, there is considerable evidence of anticipated reunion after death: death did not entirely sever that first union.[72] It is therefore not surprising that the term 'bigamy' was used in law to describe both simultaneous marriage to two spouses and remarriage after widowhood.[73] This does not mean that second marriages were uncommon, but, given the king's supposedly sacred position, such a context explains the chroniclers' criticism of the Black Prince's marriage, an issue which was further complicated by the fact that Joan of Kent's first husband, the Earl of Salisbury, was still alive. Joan, however, never actually became queen and it was only during the Wars of the Roses that the traditional ideals of queenship were seriously challenged.

Challenges to the Ideal Queen

The first Plantagenet king of England to marry a widow was Henry IV, three years after he had deposed his cousin Richard II. Although this wedding, to Joan of Navarre, was by no means as private as that of his uncle the Black Prince, Henry IV did conduct the initial negotiations in secret and his choice came as a surprise to many.[74] Henry was himself a widower, which meant that his wife's widowhood was more acceptable. Besides which, at thirty, she was some five years younger than her new husband.[75] It is possible that the circumstances of his usurpation had partly dictated his choice of an older bride than was common for kings. His propaganda criticizing Richard II characterized the previous king as a child (he was in fact only a year younger than Henry), a notion buttressed by the existence of Richard's child bride Isabel.[76] In choosing Joan as his wife, Henry made clear the greater maturity of the Lancastrian monarchy.

Both Henry IV's son and grandson reverted to the practice of marrying young foreign virgins, but his disruption to the royal line of inheritance aroused a number of would-be kingmakers who saw young English noblewomen as their route to greater power. One such adventurer was Richard, Earl of Cambridge, who attempted in 1415 to replace Henry V with Edmund Mortimer, great grandson of Lionel of Antwerp and thus of a more senior line than the king. Cambridge was motivated largely by the fact that he was himself married to Mortimer's sister and heiress, whereas Mortimer in fact wanted no part in such a rebellion and denounced his brother-in-law to the king.[77] Cambridge's son, Richard Duke of York, prior to pressing his own claim to the throne, probably hoped to make his eldest daughter, Anne, the first English-born queen since the conquest when he married her to Henry VI's heir general, Henry Holland, in 1445. The contract was made when Anne was only six years old, and York paid a dowry of 6,500 marks: the largest recorded dowry in late-medieval England.[78] Another potential heir to Henry VI at the time was his cousin Margaret Beaufort, the ward of William de la Pole, Duke of Suffolk. Suffolk was soon to be accused of planning to marry his own son John to Margaret with treasonable intentions.[79] Nine years after Henry VI's initial depostion it was the Earl of Warwick who sought to set himself up as father-in-law to the king, firstly by marrying his elder daughter Isabel to Edward IV's brother and closest male heir, the Duke of Clarence and initiating a rebellion, imprisoning the king and producing propaganda stating that Edward was not the son of Richard Duke of York so that Clarence was the true heir to the throne.[80] After this adventure failed, he turned his queenmaking attentions to his younger daughter Anne, accepting the French king's proposal of a reconciliation with Margaret of Anjou which involved Anne's marriage to Edward of Lancaster, the only son of Margaret and Henry VI. The political unrest of the period had meant that it was no longer connections on the continent but position in the English power structure which made a woman a potential queen. But this shift in the ideology of queenship could not prepare people for a queen such as Elizabeth Woodville.

Although much younger than Joan of Kent on her marriage to the Black Prince, Elizabeth Woodville, at twenty-seven, was five years the king's senior and already had two sons. There has been dispute among historians regarding the popularity of the match in 1464, but certainly in later years disparaging remarks were to be made about Elizabeth's previous marital status. Isabel of Castile, in a letter to Richard III, referred to her resentment at being rejected by Edward IV in favour of a 'widow of England'.[81] The Italian Dominic Mancini, writing in 1483, reported that, when the marriage was announced, Edward's brother, George Duke of Clarence, had declared that 'the king, who ought to have married a virgin wife, had married a widow in violation of established custom,' and thirty years later Thomas More attributed to Cecily Neville a tirade which drew on the notions of bigamy and the king's sacred position previously referred to:

> Ye only widowhed of Elizabeth Gray . . . shold yet suffice, as me semeth, to refrain you from her mariage, sith it is an vnfitting thing, & a veri blemish & highe disparagement, to the sacre magesty of a prince . . . to be defouled w[ ] bigamy in his first mariage.[82]

MAKING THE WIDOW INTO A QUEEN

Royal image makers adopted two strategems in dealing with Elizabeth's unconventional status. The first was simply to ignore the fact that she did not conform. The second was to construct her motherhood in strikingly Marian terms, so distancing her from ordinary women. Pretending that a queen did conform to stereotype was not a new device. The author of the *Encomium Emmae Reginae*, presumably with the approval of the queen herself who had commissioned the work, referred to Emma as a virgin prior to her marriage with Cnut.[83] In fact, she was the widow of Cnut's predecessor, Aethelred Unraed, and already mother of the future Edward the Confessor. Elizabeth was never actually called a virgin herself, but, as mentioned above, the records of her coronation referred to her coronet as 'thatyre of virgins'.[84] Sadly no record of her actual coronation procession exists but, given that Anne Neville and Elizabeth of York, both also already mothers, made the journey dressed in white with their hair loose, it is probable that Elizabeth Woodville did also.[85] Even the pregnant Anne Boleyn travelled from the Tower to Westminster in 'a kirtle of white cloth of tissue, and a mantle of the same furred with ermine, her hair hanging down'.[86] The public body of the queen at her coronation was virginal whatever the physical individual truth might be. For these queens the period of fictional virginity attributed to their predecessors had simply been brought forward to include that process of being made queen, traditionally performed upon genuine young virgins. Elizabeth Woodville later appeared dressed in white and gold in the royal window at Canterbury Cathedral, and on this occasion both her husband and sons were also dressed in these colours. The origin of white as the colour of virginity probably lies in New Testament references to white as the colour of heavenly clothing, but as such it could also be considered as appropriate clothing for representatives of the divine: royalty. On this occasion, Elizabeth's daughters, although they wore their hair loose in token of virginity, were not dressed in white and gold, reinforcing the implication that the spiritual superiority implied by the use of white here is not virginity but proximity to the throne. Indeed, in the description of Elizabeth of York's coronation the author explained that she was 'rially apparelde, having about her a Kyrtill of whithe Cloth of Golde of Damaske, and a Mantell of the same'.[87] This does not diminish the symbolism of virginity within the white clothing for this was, at least on the evidence of Margery Kempe's experience, the principal implication understood by a fifteenth-century audience. None the less, it reinforces the notion that in royalty there was a special sort of virginity which set the queen apart from all others of her sex, as did that of the mother of God.[88]

The construction of Elizabeth Woodville's motherhood in Marian terms was probably particularly well illustrated in the pageant which greeted her on her arrival at London Bridge on her route to the Tower prior to coronation. The 'ballads' which accompanied the pageant have not survived but according to the financial accounts of the London Bridgemasters, she was here greeted by men dressed as St Elizabeth and Mary Cleophas, the cousin and sister of the Virgin. St Elizabeth was of course the queen's namesake, but she was also the mother of John the Baptist, while Mary Cleophas, according to medieval tradition, was the mother of three apostles – Thaddeus, James the Less and Simon the Zealot – and also of Joseph Justus, one of the candidates to replace Judas Iscariot. In the fifteenth century these holy mothers were most commonly represented pictorially with the Virgin Mary herself, at the Visitation or in groupings of the Holy Family in which Mary would usually be clearly distinguishable by her crown.[89] Consequently, a queen seen beside these two women would instantly evoke comparisons with the Virgin Mary in spectators' minds. Thus the scene at London Bridge appeared to be the obvious setting for the Virgin Mary and her Son. Then, in their place, arrived Elizabeth Woodville, in white and gold, her hair virginally loose beneath its jewelled circlet.

In constructing herself in Marian terms, Elizabeth Woodville appears to have been fortunate in possessing the long blonde hair traditionally attributed to virgins, be that in paintings of the Virgin Mary or the verbal description of the Pearl Maiden. Marina Warner has drawn attention to the dual resonances of fertility and virginity in blonde hair, which result from its similarity to the colours of corn and of haloes.[90] In the fifteenth century blonde Virgins were common across Europe, and Warner argues that, 'blondeness is an index of the virgin's youth as well as innocence, for many children are fair in infancy and grow darker with age'.[91] This livery of youth and innocence was transferred to queens, even to the extent that an early fifteenth-century Bohemian image of the Queen of Sheba in full regalia, although black skinned, possessed long blonde hair.[92] It is, therefore, possible that not all the queens of late fifteenth-century England possessed the fair hair with which they were invariably depicted.

A more permanent representation of Elizabeth Woodville in stunningly Marian terms was in a full page portrait in the Records of the London Skinners marking her entry into their Fraternity of Our Lady's Assumption. Although the considerable skill of the artist would suggest that he might have been employed by the Crown and thus be familiar with royal imagery of ideal queenship, it may also indicate the terms in which this queen was seen by the merchant classes of London. The queen's hair was loose beneath a crown and not only was she carrying the Virgin's regalia, but she wore a wide blue cloak strongly reminiscent of Mary as Mother of Mercy protecting mankind, an image reinforced by the legend on the illustration:

> Oure moost goode and graciouse Quene Elisabeth Soster unto this oure Fraternitie of oure blissed Lady and Moder of Mercy Sanct Mary Virgyn Moder of God.[93]

Around the portrait are pink roses and gillyflowers or pinks. Roses were not only emblems of love, but also of virginity in the middle ages.[94] Gillyflowers traditionally represented virtuous love and marriage, but were also symbols of the Virgin's chastity and motherhood, commonly appearing in Mary's hand in pictures of the Virgin and child.[95] Elizabeth Woodville probably adopted this latter flower as her personal device for it also appears beside her in the glass of the Royal Window at Canterbury which portrays Elizabeth with her king and seven of their children. The only other flower in the picture is probably a forget-me-not, and this too was part of the re-invention of Elizabeth Woodville as an ideal queen. It was the device she and her ladies used to pin upon her brother's leg on the occasion of their challenge to him to establish a tournament to her honour. The scene, as described by Anthony Woodville in his letter to the Bastard of Burgundy, clearly originated in the literature of romance, and was designed to affirm her right to her role in romance terms just as the scene on London Bridge did in religious terms.[96]

CONCLUSION

In conclusion, the literary queenmakers of the fifteenth century, and before, assumed that women chosen to become queens would complement their king's government with their wisdom, mercy, peacemaking, fertility, chastity and inspirational beauty. By the power of their consecration as queens, they were set apart from other women, possessors of a special claim to virginal status which was rooted in their position as bride and mother of Christ's representatives in this earthly kingdom. In this context, the role of potential queen was assumed to belong to young women of high status. Most of the would-be queenmakers of the Wars of the Roses focused on similar young women, be these women the potential holders of the right to the throne themselves, the daughters of ambitious lords seeking to guarantee influence over a king who was their son-in-law, or the foreign noblewomen offered as brides to actual kings. However, the political needs of Henry IV and the passion of Edward IV served to challenge this ideal, the former emphasizing the fact that the production of heirs was not the only role for which a king needed a queen, the latter proving that even a knight's widow could be perceived as the English representative of the queen of Heaven. The clandestine wedding employed by Edward IV to secure his unconventional bride may have indicated to contemporaries a sense of his disrespect for the institution of marriage, which would later make Richard III's task of usurpation on the grounds of Edward's supposed pre-contract rather easier. None the less, the fact that Elizabeth Woodville was not a young woman at her marriage was not a major factor in denying her the role of king's mother. The surviving images of Elizabeth Woodville as queen indicate that the construction of her public image reinforced the ideology of a queen who possessed a perpetual spiritual virginity, an eternal young womanhood appropriate to the wife of a king whose own public body never died.[97]

Notes

1. This paper is a result of D. Phil. research undertaken with British Academy funding at the Centre for Medieval Studies, University of York. I would like to thank Elizabeth Shields and James Binns for correcting my Latin translations, and Mark Ormrod, Felicity Riddy, Richard Marks, Jeremy Goldberg, and especially Kim Phillips and Mark Smith for their advice and suggestions.

2. 'Wiwol die kronung in Engelandt held, das ein konig solde eine junkfer zur ehe nemen, wer sie auch sein mochte, jedoch echtgeborn, aber keine witwe nicht; diese aber nam der konig wider aller seiner herren dank.' L. Visser-Fuchs, 'English Events in Caspar Weinreich's Danzig Chronicle, 1461–1495', *The Ricardian*, 7 (December 1986), no. 95, p. 31.

3. J. Hardyng, *The Chronicle of John Hardyng*, ed. H. Ellis (London, 1812), p. 317.

4. Ibid., p. 317.

5. T. More, *The Complete Works of St Thomas More*, ed. R.S. Sylvester (15 vols. Yale University Press, 1963–87), vol. 2, p. 64.

6. C. Larrington, *Women and Writing in Medieval Europe: A Sourcebook* (London, Routledge, 1995), p. 78.

7. Ibid.

8. J.A. Brundage, *Law, Sex, and Christian Society in Medieval Europe* (University of Chicago Press, 1987), p. 514. Chaucer's portrait of the Wife of Bath is an obvious instance of this notion.

9. J. de Cessolis, *The Game of Chess* (London, 1946), p. 45.

10. H.R. Luards (ed.), *Lives of Edward the Confessor*, Rolls Series 3, (London, 1858), pp. 58–61.

11. Bede, *A History of the English Church and People*, tr. L. Sherley-Price (Harmondsworth, Penguin, 1968), p. 238.

12. Royal Commission on Historical Manuscripts, *Report 5: House of Lords* (London, HMSO, 1876), p. 455.

13. A. Crawford, 'The King's Burden: The Consequences of Royal Marriage in Fifteenth-Century England', in R.A. Griffiths (ed.), *Patronage, the Crown and the Provinces in Later Medieval England* (Gloucester, Alan Sutton, 1981), *passim.*

14. T. Malory, *Works*, ed. E.Vinaver (Oxford University Press, 1977), p. 60. Three centuries earlier, in Geoffrey of Monmouth's *History of the Kings of Britain*, Guinevere was a noble Roman lady, and thus symbolized the stability and dignity of Roman rule, lost after the Roman withdrawal but re-established by King Arthur. Geoffrey of Monmouth, *The History of the Kings of Britain*, tr. L. Thorpe (Harmondsworth, Penguin, 1966), p. 221.

15. A.H. Thomas and I.D. Thornley (eds), *The Great Chronicle of London* (London, 1938), p.118.

16. See below for Christine de Pisan's characterization of woman as peacemaker.

17. Thomas & Thornley (eds), *Great Chronicle*, p. 310. G. Kipling (ed.), *The Receyt of the Ladie Kateryne*, Early English Text Society, Original Series, 296 (Oxford University Press, 1990), pp. 17, 20, 23, 25, 27, 30.

18. C.L. Scofield, *The Life and Reign of Edward the Fourth* (2 vols, London, Frank Cass & Co, 1967), vol. 1, pp. 211–12.

19. B. Williams, 'The Portuguese Connection and the Significance of "The Holy Princess"', *The Ricardian*, 6 (1983), no. 80, p. 143.

20. C.A. Newman, *The Anglo-Norman Nobility in the Reign of Henry I: The Second Generation* (Philadelphia, University of Pennsylvania Press, 1988), p.13.

21. This connection was observed by Tim Thornton in discussion following a workshop on Medieval Queenship, University of York, June 1996.

22. '. . . dominae Elizabeth primogenitae Regis Edwardi: in cujus persona visum omnibus erat posse suppleri, quicquid aliunde ipsi Regi deesse de titulo videbatur', N. Pronay and J. Cox (eds), *The Crowland Chronicle Continuations 1459–1486* (London, Richard III and Yorkist History Trust, 1986), pp. 194–5.

23. K. Mertes, *The English Noble Household 1250–1600* (Oxford, Basil Blackwell, 1988), pp. 180, 54.

24. 'Une fille avoit mut bele,/Bein entetchée damoisele/D'afaitement endoctrinée . . . Simple est de cuntenement,/Cum a pucele ben apent . . . Eloquinée fui e sage/Plus ke pucele de sun age'. Luards (ed.), *Lives of Edward the Confessor*, pp. 58, 212.

25. O.D. MacRae-Gibson (ed.), *Of Arthour and Merlin*, Early English Text Society, Original Series, 268 (London, Oxford University Press, 1973), p. 206.

26. 'Hujus plane forma pudicitiaque tanta est, ut neque Lucretia neque Diana ipsa vel speciosor vel casta magis fuerat unquam. Tanta deinde est ei virtus ac morum elegantia, ut certe nutu quodam divino ab ipsa sua nativitate ad haec usque tempora sibi consors et regina reservata esse videatur.' J. Gairdner (ed.), *Letters and Papers Illustrative of the Reigns of Richard III and Henry VII*, Rolls Series 24 (2 vols, Wiesbaden, Kraus Reprint, 1965), vol. 1, p. 421.

27. In the tenth-century *Encomium Emae Reginae* this notion had been made explicit in a passage explaining how difficult it was to find a bride worthy of Cnut. A. Campbell (ed.), *Encomium Emmae Reginae*, Camden Society, Third Series, no. 72 (London, Royal Historical Society, 1949), pp. 32–3.

28. de Cessolis, *Game of Chess*, p. 45.

29. C. de Pisan, *The Treasure of the City of Ladies*, tr. S. Lawson (Harmondsworth, Penguin, 1985), p. 51.

30. Ibid., p. 53.

31. For example, throughout Chrétien de Troyes', *Erec and Enide*, ed. and tr. C.W. Carroll (New York, Garland Publishing, 1987).

32. M.D. Harris (ed.), *The Coventry Leet Book or Mayor's Register 1420–1555*, Early English Text Society, Original Series, 134–5 (London, Oxford University Press, 1907–13), pp. 290–1.

33. Ibid., p. 287.

34. E.F. Jacob, *The Fifteenth Century 1399–1485* (Oxford University Press, 1961), p. 513.

35. Kipling (ed.), *Receyt of the Ladie Kateryne*, p. 30.

36. Ibid., p. 41.

37. C. Bynum, *Fragmentation and Redemption: Essays on Gender and the Human Body in Medieval Religion* (New York, Zone Books, 1991), p. 151.

38. 'Omnipotens sempiterne deus . . . qui feminei sexus fragilitatem nequaquam reprobando auertis. Sed dignanter comprobando pocius eligis. et qui infirma mundi eligendo forcia queque confundere decreuisti'. L.C. Wickham Legg (ed.), *English Coronation Records* (London, Constable, 1901), p. 109.

39. R.R. Reuther, *Sexism and Godtalk: Towards Feminist Theology* (London, SCM Press, 1983), p. 30.

40. 'Fructu uteri sui fecundari seu gratulari mereatur ad decorem tocius regni,' Legg (ed.), *Coronation Records*, p. 109.

41. 'Barbaras gentes', ibid., p. 110.

42. E.H. Kantorowicz, *The King's Two Bodies: a Study in Medieval Political Theology* (Princeton University Press, 1957), pp. 319–21. P.E. Schramm, *A History of the English Coronation*, tr. L.G.W. Legg (Oxford University Press, 1937), pp. 6–7. The actual oil used was different for the queen at joint coronations, but, according to the *Liber Regalis*, a queen crowned alone would receive chrism just as a king would. Legg (ed.), *Coronation Records*, p. lviii.

43. 'ut in regalis federe coniugii semper manens pudica, proximam virginitati palmam continere queat', Legg (ed.), *Coronation Records*, p. 111.

44. 'auro sapiencie, uirtutumque gemmis'; 'cum prudentibus virginibus sponso perhenni domino nostro ihesu christo', Legg (ed.), *Coronation Records*, p. 111.

45. Quoted by M. Warner, *Monuments and Maidens: the Allegory of the Female Form* (London, Weidenfeld and Nicolson, 1985), p. 64.

46. J. Bugge, *Virginitas: an Essay in the History of the Medieval Ideal* (The Hague, Martinus Nijoff, 1975), p. 31.

47. Ibid., p. 52.

48. Malory, *Works*, pp. 600–6.

49. Warner, *Monuments and Maidens*, p. 249.

50. Kantorowicz, *King's Two Bodies*, p. 8.

51. *A Collection of Ordinances and Regulations for the Government of the Royal Household* (Society of Antiquaries of London, 1790), p. 123.

52. J. Gairdner, *The Historical Collections of a Citizen of London in the Fifteenth Century*, Camden Society, New Series, no. 17 (London, 1876), p. 226.

53. J. Furnivall, *Political, Religious and Love Poems*, Early English Text Society, Original Series 15 (London, Oxford University Press, 1930), pp. 4–5.

54. More, *Complete Works*, vol. 2, p. 62.

55. J. O'Faolain and L. Martines (eds), *Not in God's Image: Women in History*, (Glasgow, Fontana/Collins, 1974), p. 514. Warner, *Monuments and Maidens*, p. 64.

56. G. Smith, *The Coronation of Elizabeth Wydeville* (London, Ellis, 1935), p. 17. A.F. Sutton and P.W. Hammond (eds), *The Coronation of Richard III: The Extant Documents* (Gloucester, Alan Sutton, 1983), pp. 31, 33.

57. Sutton and Hammond (eds), *Coronation of Richard III*, pp. 31, 33.

58. It should be noted that the ordinal presented to Barking Abbey in 1404 allowed both virgins and widows to be dressed in white at the start of their profession ritual while other orders, such as the Bridgettines at Syon did not wear white at all, but simply their ordinary clothes. M.C. Erler, 'Margery Kempe's White Clothes', *Medium Ævum*, 62 (1993), pp. 79, 82–3.

59. S.B. Meech (ed.), *The Book of Margery Kempe*, Early English Text Society, Original Series 212 (London, Oxford University Press, 1997), p. 124.

60. For example, Anne Neville in the Rous Roll, British Library, Additional MS 48976 nos 62–3; Margaret of Anjou in the frontispiece to the collection of romances presented to her by the Earl of Shrewsbury at the time of her marriage British Library, Royal MS 15.E.VI f. 2; or Elizabeth Woodville in the London Skinners' book of the Fraternity of the Assumption of the Virgin Mary, J.J. Lambert (ed.), *Records of the Skinners of London, Edward I to James I* (London, 1933), p. 82.

61. Harris (ed.), *Coventry Leet Book*, p. 287.

62. G.L. Harris, *Henry V: the Practice of Kingship* (Oxford University Press, 1985), p. 10.

63. G. Ashe, *The Virgin* (London, Routledge & Kegan Paul, 1976), p. 128.

64. G. Kipling, 'The London Pageants for Margaret of Anjou: A Medieval Script Restored', *Medieval English Theatre*, 4 (1982), no. 1, p. 23.

65. T.A. Heslop, 'The Virgin Mary's Regalia and Twelfth-Century English Seals', in A. Borg and A. Martindale (eds), *The Vanishing Past: Studies of Medieval Art, Liturgy and Metrology presented to Christopher Hohler* (British Archaeological Reports International Series 111, 1981), p. 53. See note 60 for some images of queens holding floriated sceptres.

66. P. Strohm, *Hochon's Arrow: the Social Imagination of Fourteenth-Century Texts* (Princeton University Press, 1992), pp. 96, 105. J.C. Parsons, 'The Queen's Intercession in Thirteenth-Century England', in J. Carpenter and S-B. MacLean (eds), *Power of the Weak: Studies in Medieval Women* (Urbana and Chicago, University of Illinois Press, 1995), *passim*.

67. Strohm, ibid., pp. 103–5.

68. Parsons, 'The Queen's Intercession', pp. 158–9.

69. R. Barber, *Edward, Prince of Wales and Aquitaine* (London, Allen Lane, 1978), pp. 173, 244. J. Taylor, 'A Wigmore Chronicle, 1355–77', *Proceedings of the Leeds Philosophical and Literary Society*, 2 (1964–6), p. 88. R. Higden, *Polychronicon Ranulphi Higden*, ed. J.R. Lumby, Rolls Series 41 (9 vols, Wiesbaden, Kraus Reprint, 1964), vol. 8, p. 360.

70. This was particularly the case if a much older man was seen to be marrying a young bride and consequently denying the young men of the town a possible wife. Brundage, *Law, Sex and Christian Society*, pp. 514, 540.

71. Ibid., pp. 343, 477.

72. Larrington, *Women and Writing*, pp. 14–15.

73. Brundage, *Law, Sex and Christian Society*, p. 478.

74. J.L. Kirby, *Henry IV of England* (London, Constable, 1970), p. 136.

75. Ibid., p. 135.

76. M. Aston, 'Richard II and the Wars of the Roses', in F.R.H. du Boulay and C.M. Barron (eds), *The Reign of Richard II* (London, Athlone Press, 1971), p. 307.

77. J.G. Davies, *Henry V* (London, Arthur Baker, 1935), p. 160.

78. R.A. Griffiths, 'The Sense of Dynasty in the Reign of Henry VI', in C. Ross (ed.), *Patronage, Pedigree and Power in Later Medieval England* (Gloucester, Alan Sutton, 1979), p. 24.

79. Jacob, *The Fifteenth Century*, p. 492.

80. J. Calmette and G. Périnelle (eds), *Louis XI et l'Angleterre (1461–1483)* (Oxford University Press, 1961); Société de l'École des Chartes, *Mémoires et Documents*, vol. 11 (Paris, A. Picard, 1930), pp. 306–7.

81. J. Gairdner (ed.), *Letters and Papers Illustrative of the Reigns of Richard III and Henry VII*, Rolls Series 24 (2 vols, London, 1861), p. 32.

82. 'Dumque contra morem viduam a rege ductam predicaret, quem virginem uxorem ducere opportuisset'. D. Mancini, *The Usurpation of Richard III*, tr. C.A.J. Armstrong (Gloucester, Alan Sutton, 1989), pp. 62–3. More, *Complete Works*, vol. 2, p. 62.

83. Campbell (ed.), *Encomium Emmae Reginae*, p. 32.

84. Smith, *Coronation of Elizabeth Wydeville*, p. 17.

85. Sutton and Hammond (eds), *Coronation of Richard III*, p. 33. J. Leland, *De Rebus Britannicis Collectanea*, ed. T. Hearne (4 vols, London, Gregg International, 1970), vol. 3, p. 219.

86. F. Grose and T. Astle (eds), *The Antiquarian Repertory* (4 vols, London, Edward Jeffery, 1808), vol. 2, p. 236.

87. Leland, *Collectanea*, vol. 3, p. 219.

88. It should be noted that this shared livery of royalty and virginity extended even to the most powerful royal symbol of all, the crown, which was worn by figures representing virtues (almost invariably virgins as stated earlier) and by virgin-martyrs. See Kim Phillips' article in the present volume.

89. For example, in the stained glass of Great Malvern Priory the pregnant Virgin and St Elizabeth greet each other, and on the altar screen of Houghton St Giles church both of Mary's sisters are surrounded by their children while she holds Christ.

90. M. Warner, *From the Beast to the Blonde: on Fairytales and their Tellers* (London, Vintage, 1995), p. 367.

91. Ibid., p. 368.

92. Ibid., p. 104.

93. Lambert (ed.), *Records of the Skinners*, p. 82.

94. J. Huizinga, *The Waning of the Middle Ages* (New York, Doubleday Anchor, 1956), p. 203.

95. A.F. Sutton and L. Visser-Fuchs, 'The Device of Queen Elizabeth Woodville: A Gillyflower or Pink', *The Ricardian*, 11 (1997), no. 136, p. 20.

96. S. Bentley (ed.), *Excerpta Historica* (London, 1831), pp. 178–88.

97. Kantorowicz, *King's Two Bodies*, pp. 314–450.

4

A Positive Representation of the Power of Young Women: The Malterer Embroidery Re-examined

Kristina E. Gourlay

The fear of the perceived power of women and their sexuality over men has had a long and influential history in Western European thought. Throughout history, female sexuality has been viewed by male writers with hostility and suspicion as a dangerous and disruptive force capable of causing the downfall of worthy men. During the Middle Ages and preceding centuries, leading Christian theologians, philosophers, physicians, historians and poets wrote extensively on this subject.[1] Common among these writers was the tendency to attribute full blame to the women involved, never acknowledging that the men concerned were in any way responsible for the events that led to their downfall. Sermons, treatises, instructional manuals, poetry and romances included lists of celebrated men who were brought low by the apparently irresistible power of women and their sexuality, a tradition which has been called the 'Power of Women *topos*'.[2] In the thirteenth century, this tradition found new expression in the visual arts. The early fourteenth-century German embroidery known as the Malterer Embroidery has been identified as one such artistic example; however a re-reading of its images demonstrates that it is an example with a radical twist (Fig. 1). Featuring several pairs of scenes which depict traditional examples of men who have succumbed to the power of a young woman and/or love, at first sight the Malterer Embroidery appears to embody the popular hostile view towards female sexuality. However, a closer examination of the embroidery reveals an inconsistency in the conventional iconography of the *topos* which tempers such a negative interpretation, and in fact reverses it into a positive reflection of the power of women, love, and female sexuality. The Malterer Embroidery thus emerges as a visual example of the Power of Women *topos* which, rather than placing a negative value-judgment on the power of female sexuality and attributing full blame for the effectiveness of this power to women, instead does much the opposite. This approach to the theme both demonstrates a recognition of and respect for the power of young women, their sexuality and love over even the most worthy of men, and acknowledges the responsibility of men in succumbing to this power.

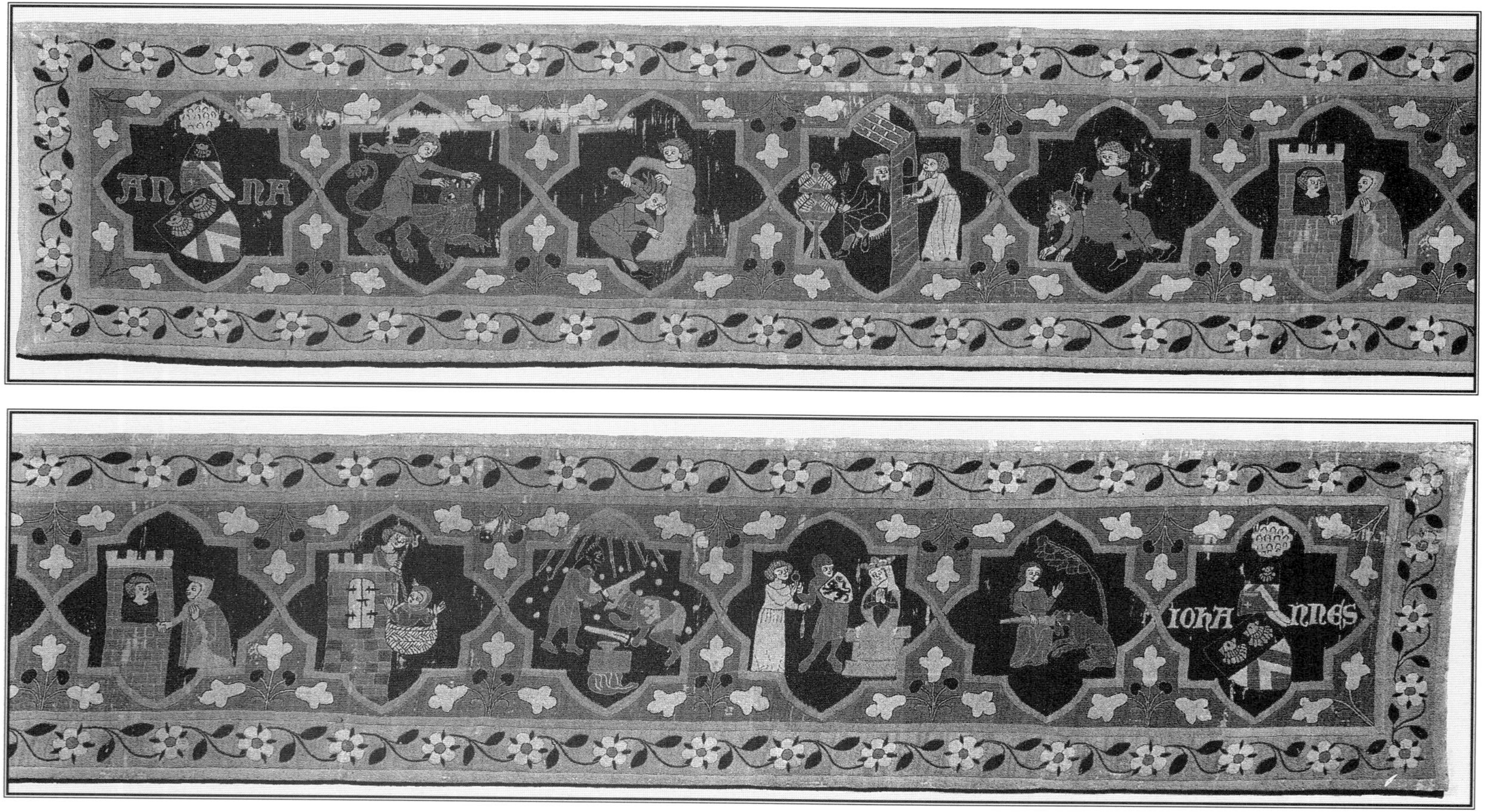

Figure 1: The Malterer Embroidery, early 14th century. Augustiner Museum, Freiburg (Breisgau).

In her recent book, *The Power of Women: A Topos in Medieval Art and Literature*, Susan Smith addresses this convention thoroughly and convincingly, tracing its history from its antique origins through to the late Middle Ages.[3] Smith defines it as '. . . the representational practice of bringing together at least two, but usually more, well-known figures from the Bible, ancient history, or romance to exemplify a cluster of interrelated themes that include the wiles of women, the power of love, and the trials of marriage . . . to prove beyond a doubt that women exercise a power that no man, however superior his mental, physical and moral endowments, can resist'.[4] She argues that, while the *topos* is best known for its moralizing and misogynist diatribes, it also became a vehicle for the expression of diverse views about women and the power that they exercise over men.[5] The tradition became firmly established during the early Patristic period when influential Christian writers such as Jerome, Ambrose and John Chrysostom made use of it in sermons, letters of advice, books of moral instruction and tracts against marriage. Citing exemplary Biblical figures like Adam, David, Samson and Solomon, who had fallen in some way through love of women, they sought to prove the dangers inherent in women and the lust they evoked.[6]

Smith maintains that the *topos* found no other expression before the twelfth century, at which point the development of the vernacular as a mode of written and oral communication in Western Europe facilitated its expansion in two very different directions.[7] The first was a dramatic increase in the circulation of the traditional use of the *topos* to support clerical anti-woman attacks, which was facilitated to a large extent by the emergence of popular preaching. Relying heavily on the use of *exempla*, popular preaching proved to be an effective tool for spreading the influence of the *topos* far beyond the limited circle of Latin-literate clerks to whom it had previously been largely confined.[8] The second was the development of the *topos* in a positive direction, enabling it to take on new meanings so that it was no longer solely a promoter of medieval misogynist views on women.

The emergence of the written vernacular, which was accessible to lay men and women of all classes who were not literate in Latin, combined with the social, economic and demographic growth of the century, also supported the formation of a new lay audience. New forms of writing and art directed at this audience evolved, particularly in the courts where patronage and vernacular literacy or exposure to such literacy was readily available.[9] In this setting, a new self-image was constructed for aristocratic society based on ideals of chivalry, *courtoisie* and courtly love, which was in turn adopted by wealthier members of the urban middle classes.[10] In the literature of courtly love, the *topos* took on a new voice, and rather than being spoken by a preacher or some other representative of orthodox Christian morality, whose only concern was to persuade his audience of the dangers inherent in the love of women, the voice of the courtly author is of the lover himself and evokes the theme not to dissuade, but to demonstrate the omnipotence of love.[11] With this shift towards a more positive use of the *topos*, illustrating the debilitating power of love rather than of female sexuality, a new series of exemplary figures drawn from chivalric romance was introduced. It was thus not unusual to find knights like Tristan, Lancelot and Gawain accompanying the more traditional biblical and pagan figures in order to illustrate that love had exercised an inescapable power throughout human history.[12] Smith stresses that this new positive emphasis did not replace the more traditional misogynist use of the literary theme, but that they were closely related, and increasingly the *topos* became the site of an interpretative contest in which reader and writer participated, attracting many different views about love, women and the powers they exercise.[13]

In the late thirteenth century, this literary theme found another medium for expression: the visual arts.[14] From around 1300 onwards, visual examples of the *topos* became increasingly popular, appearing in a wide range of artistic media, from the marginal areas of sacred spaces such as pillar capitals and misericords, to more secular objects such as marriage caskets, murals and tapestries. Paralleling their increasing popularity in contemporary textual sources, Aristotle and Virgil came to represent wise men defeated by love/women, and figures from romance came to play an important role as visual examples of men of strength and knightly virtue. Because visual representations of the Power of Women *topos* are associated with both the old tradition of focusing on the destructive powers of female sexuality, and with the more recent and concurrent move towards an acknowledgment of the independent and debilitating power of love, they invite an even wider range of interpretation than their literary counterparts. The key to interpreting the meaning of visual examples of the *topos* thus depends largely on understanding how the various *exempla* interact together.

This raises the crucial issues of the manner in which medieval texts and images are connected and how such visual images were perceived by medieval viewers. During the Middle Ages, an image did not necessarily have to illustrate one particular part of a text, but could, and frequently did, combine several scenes of narrative action into one scene. A single image could thus be not a direct translation of text into image, but rather, a symbol representing a series of events, or in fact, the whole text.[15] Such images did not even have to recall a specific text, which in many cases the artist or audience may not have known, but could evoke the general story which the viewer knew from oral sources, or even the idea that the image had come to represent.[16]

It is also important to recognize that an image or set of images could have meant different things to different people, depending on their cultural background, familiarity with the stories associated with the piece and moral outlook, and interpretations could be influenced by social context and factors such as gender, class and geography. Scholars agree that images do not have one set, unchanging meaning that is apparent to all. Instead, they maintain that viewing such images is an interactive process between image and viewer and that the meaning of any given image will be different for each viewer depending on what he or she brings to it.[17] The problem with this subjectivity, as will be seen with the Malterer Embroidery, is that it is rare for scholars to know enough about the individuals associated with a particular work of art to be able to identify what factors might have influenced their interpretation of it. It is not sufficient to know that the piece had its origins with an individual connected to a secular or sacred context because there may have been other unknown factors in their lives which may have had a greater influence on how they viewed the world, and art in particular.

The early fourteenth-century Malterer Embroidery (Fig. 1) demonstrates one use of the Power of Women *topos*. Housed in the Augustiner Museum, in Freiburg im Breisgau, the piece measures approximately 490 cm in length by 60 cm in height and is thought to have been intended to hang over a long bench.[18] It is stitched in coloured wool thread on a tan linen backing using a technique called cloister stitch which was popular in the fourteenth and fifteenth centuries among German and Swiss nuns and lay women. This method involved outlining forms and then filling them in with parallel lengths of thread fixed to the backing with tiny cross stitches.[19] The embroidery consists of a series of eleven blue quatrefoils, bordered in yellow and placed within a muted red background filled with large clusters of white lilies. These quatrefoils are in turn enclosed by a tan border edged with yellow bands, decorated by a continuous chain of white flowers with yellow centres linked by green leaves. The first and last quatrefoils, featuring the arms of the Malterer family, are stitched in blue, yellow, red, white and grey, while the remaining nine are mainly worked in brown, tan, rust, green and white. Thematically, the nine central quatrefoils are divided into four pairs and a single scene. Three of these pairs and the single scene depict famous 'love' stories commonly associated with the literary and artistic tradition of the Power of Women *topos*.

The first pair features the well known Old Testament story of Samson and Delilah as told in Judges 16:4 which was a common *exemplum* used to illustrate the power of women and their sexuality over men of strength.[20] Samson the Nazarene, renowned for his strength, fell in love with a beautiful young woman named Delilah. She, in return for the promise of great wealth, agreed to discover and provide the Philistines with the secret of Samson's great strength so that they might subdue him. So worn down by her entreaties, and not guessing Delilah's duplicity, Samson finally gave in and told her his secret: that his strength lay in his uncut hair. After lulling him to sleep in her lap, Delilah called in the Philistines, who rendered him helpless by shearing his braids, and took him into custody. In the embroidery, Samson with unshorn locks flowing, is first shown conquering a lion as described in Judges 14:6, establishing the extent of his great strength (Fig. 2). This is followed by a depiction of Delilah cutting his hair as he

Figure 2: Samson (detail, the Malterer Embroidery). Augustiner Museum, Freiburg (Breisgau).

lies in her lap, demonstrating the loss of his power in the hands of a beautiful young woman (Fig. 3).

The following two pairs of scenes depict two of the most popular stories in the Middle Ages used as visual examples of old and wise men who succumb to the power of young women and carnal desire. The first illustrates the well-known tale of Aristotle and Phyllis which became popular in the early thirteenth century.[21] According to legend, Aristotle was the tutor of Alexander the Great who became so enamoured with his beautiful wife/mistress that he neglected his imperial duties.[22] Aristotle cautioned him against this, and Alexander heeded his advice. However, the withdrawal of his attentions incurred Phyllis' wrath and she sought revenge against the philosopher who was threatening her relationship with Alexander. One morning she danced and sang enticingly in the garden before the window of Aristotle's study. As she had anticipated, he quickly became enflamed with desire and declared his love for her. She consented to return his affections, but only if he would put on a saddle and bridle and allow her to ride on his back in the orchard, where she planned to have Alexander present to witness his tutor's humiliation and hypocrisy. Firmly caught by his desire, Aristotle agreed and was ridden like a horse, much to the amusement of Alexander and fellow onlookers. In the embroidery, the elderly bearded Aristotle is first depicted abandoning his studies to caress young Phyllis' chin through his window (Fig. 4), followed by the standard illustration of the story which shows him mounted by Phyllis who actively wields a whip and steers him with a bridle (Fig. 5).

This story is followed by another tale of thirteenth-century origins in which the poet Virgil was reported to have fallen in love with the Roman Emperor's daughter. Pretending to return his love, she promised him a midnight visit to her

Figure 3: Samson and Delilah (detail, the Malterer Embroidery). Augustiner Museum, Freiburg (Breisgau).

Figure 4: Aristotle and Phyllis (detail, the Malterer Embroidery). Augustiner Museum, Freiburg (Breisgau).

tower room, which was only accessible by means of a basket elevated externally by ropes. Unfortunately for Virgil, she left him suspended half-way up, exposing him to the mockery of the Roman people who found him dangling there helplessly in the morning.[23] The embroidery depicts Virgil first clasping the hand of the maiden through her window, presumably arranging their assignation (Fig. 6), followed by a scene where the maiden, standing on top of the tower, suspends him in a basket in front of her now shuttered window (Fig. 7).

The final pair of quatrefoils are of a different thematic nature than the previous three pairs, featuring scenes illustrating what has been identified as the romance *Iwein*, although there is much scholarly debate over which part of the story the scenes represent. *Iwein/Yvain* was one of the more popular romances of the Middle Ages and versions exist in French, German, English, Norse, Swedish,

Danish and Icelandic, the best-known versions being Chrétien de Troyes' French version, *Yvain: Le Chevalier au Lion*, and Hartmann von Aue's German version, *Iwein*, both composed in the latter part of the twelfth century.[24] While the story has been interpreted in a number of different ways, an issue which will be addressed later at greater length, the basic plot is as follows. The story begins with a group of knights telling stories at Arthur's court. One story concerns the defeat of one of the knights at the hands of the defender of a mysterious magical spring which, when disturbed, causes wild and destructive storms to rage. Intrigued, Arthur proposes a visit to the spring to rechallenge the defender. Iwein, wanting the honour for himself, rides ahead and, by pouring water from the spring on a giant emerald stone, causes a frightful tempest characterized by 'a thousand flashes of lightening, followed by as many thunderclaps . . . It rained and hailed.'[25] Iwein then defeats King Ascalon, the knight who appears to defend

Figure 5: Aristotle and Phyllis (detail, the Malterer Embroidery). Augustiner Museum, Freiburg (Breisgau).

Figure 6: Virgil (detail, the Malterer Embroidery). Augustiner Museum, Freiburg (Breisgau).

the spring, and chases the mortally wounded man back to his castle. Here Iwein becomes trapped. Assisted by the Queen's lady-in-waiting Lunete, whom he had helped in the past and who now gives him a magic ring that will make him invisible and conceal him from those searching for Ascalon's killer, Iwein's predicament loses its urgency. While debating how to escape, he falls in love with Ascalon's grieving widow, Queen Laudine and, with the assistance of Lunete, marries her. He is visited a short time later by Arthur and members of his court, who issue the challenge at the spring and are surprised but happy to find him there as the new defender, Iwein is then persuaded by his closest companion Gawain not to fall into a life of marital ease and lose his honour because of love. He thus decides to leave his bride and newly won kingdom to accompany Gawain in search of honour on the tournament circuit, with the promise to Laudine that he will return to her in one year.

Iwein then becomes so caught up in knightly activities that he forgets his promise entirely and fails to return. By the time he remembers, it is too late. The enraged and hurt Laudine sends Lunete to Arthur's court where she publicly denounces Iwein, telling him to stay away from her mistress, with the result that Iwein goes mad and retreats to the forest as a wildman. The second part of the story is concerned with Iwein's return to sanity and his redemption through a series of adventures which include saving a lion who becomes his faithful companion and identifying symbol. In the end, Iwein is reunited with Laudine through a bit of trickery on the part of the resourceful Lunete, although the text is not clear as to whether they live happily ever after.

The first scene on the embroidery depicts Iwein's battle with Ascalon at the magical spring, complete with lightening and hail and large green stone (Fig. 8). Iwein is identified by the lion's head on his helmet. The second scene depicts a

Figure 7: Virgil (detail, the Malterer Embroidery). Augustiner Museum, Freiburg (Breisgau).

Figure 8: Iwein and Ascalon (detail, the Malterer Embroidery). Augustiner Museum, Freiburg (Breisgau).

seated woman with downcast eyes and hands positioned as if in prayer or supplication, who can be identified by her crown as Laudine. She is watched by Iwein, again identified by the lion on his shield, and a young woman, presumably Lunete, who grasps his elbow with one hand and holds a ring above his finger with the other (Fig. 9). This scene has proved much more resistant to identification because it does not match exactly with any one scene in the story. However, as discussed earlier and as James Rushing Jr. has emphasized in several works on *Iwein*, this should not matter, as such scenes are 'not narrative but allusions, representations of the well known tales, the pictorial equivalent of literary allusions.'[26]

The final quatrefoil is not part of a pair and depicts the popular medieval image of a unicorn lying with its head in the lap of a maiden, seated beneath a linden tree (Fig. 10). This recalls the popular story from the early medieval

Physiologus and the later bestiaries which taught that the only way to catch the fearless and invincible unicorn was to place a solitary virgin in the place it frequented. Once it had seen her, the unicorn would leap into her lap and fall asleep, at which point it could be either killed or captured for the king.[27] In the Middle Ages the unicorn was associated with many, often contradictory, things: strength, speed, worldly love, chastity, and Christ, to name only a few. The classic pose used in the embroidery also had different meanings: it could be used in a sacred context to depict the Annunciation and Immaculate Conception calling to mind ideas of virginity and chastity (Fig. 11), or it could be used in a manner which suggested physical carnality, an issue which will be discussed further (Fig. 12).[28]

The order of the scenes on the embroidery deserves a brief examination.[29] The pairs of images are arranged in chronological order beginning with an Old

Figure 9: Iwein, Laudine, and Lunete (detail, the Malterer Embroidery). Augustiner Museum, Freiburg (Breisgau).

Figure 10: The maiden and the unicorn (detail, the Malterer Embroidery). Augustiner Museum, Freiburg (Breisgau).

Testament hero, followed by a Greek, a Roman and a twelfth-century hero. The unicorn is part of a timeless legend which existed in many periods throughout history, but reached the height of its appeal in the later Middle Ages. Iconographically, the pair of Samson scenes is balanced by the Iwein pair, both heroes being known for the importance of lions in their lives. Furthermore, both were young men known for their strength and physical prowess. In contrast, both Aristotle and Virgil are older intellectuals who, according to medieval legend, fall under the influence of younger women. This juxtaposition of strength and wisdom has had a long history in the Power of Women *topos*.[30] The final scene, the unicorn and maiden image, stands alone and acts as a conclusion to the piece. It brings the eye to a halt, indicating that the series is over, yet also guides the eye back to the front of the piece by means of the unicorn's horn. Furthermore, the unicorn is iconographically connected with the Samson story in that both 'lovers' are subdued and captured by resting in the lap of their lady, thus creating an additional balance between the first and final scenes. In fact, this pairing was used subsequently at least once in the visual arts in the margins of the late fifteenth-century *Wharncliffe Hours* (Fig. 13).

These scenes raise two questions: how was the Malterer Embroidery's use of the Power of Women *topos* intended to be interpreted, and why did it include one set of scenes with no obvious connection to the theme? This topic has been long debated by art historians, and much of the debate has focused upon the family for whom the embroidery was presumably made and their purposes for doing so.

Figure 11: Tapestry: Annunciation scene. Lower Rheinland, *c.* 1500. Bayerisches Nationalmuseum, München.

Figure 12: Miniature, English Bestiary, mid-thirteenth century. Royal 12F XIII, f. 10v. Reproduced by permission of The British Library, London.

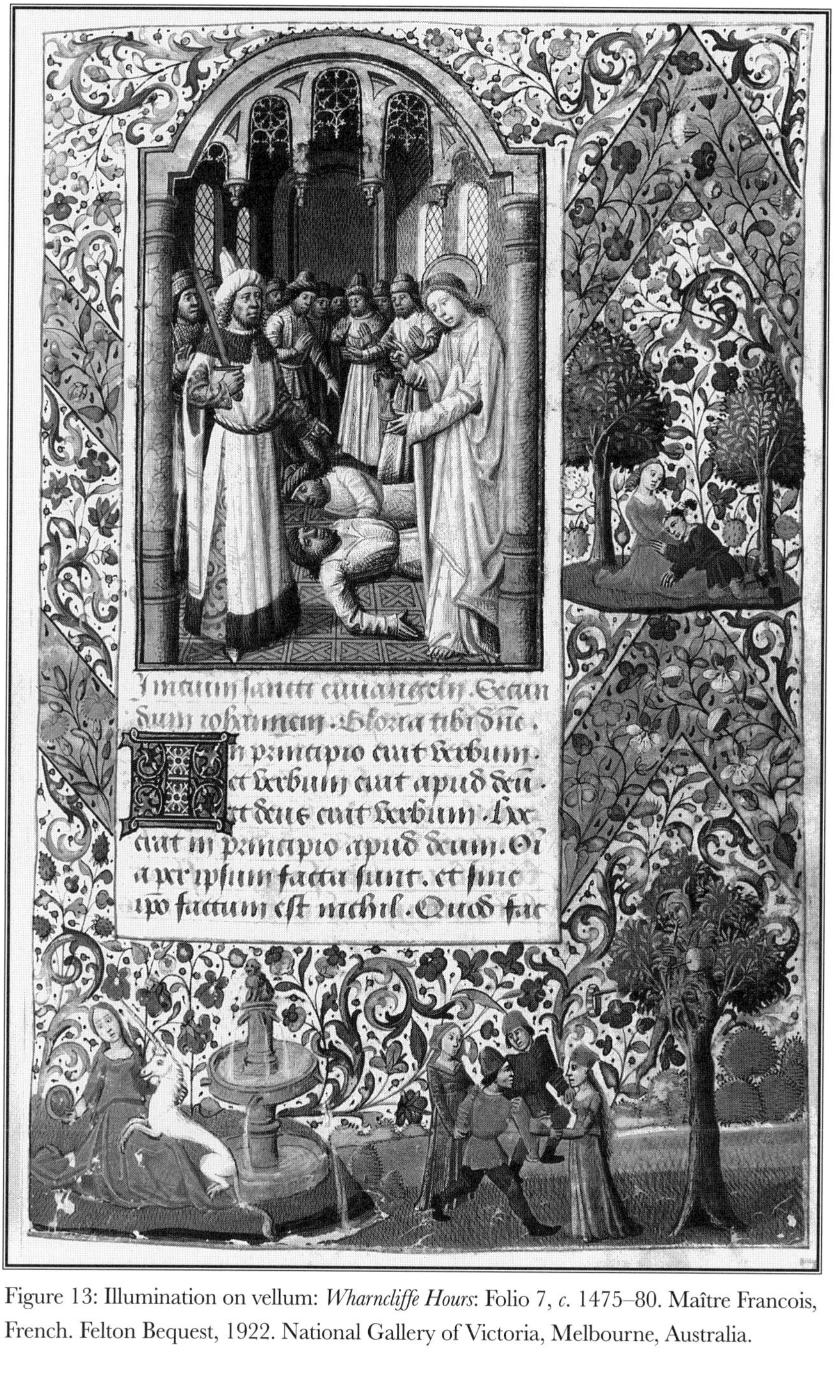

Figure 13: Illumination on vellum: *Wharncliffe Hours*: Folio 7, *c.* 1475–80. Maître Francois, French. Felton Bequest, 1922. National Gallery of Victoria, Melbourne, Australia.

It has been accepted that, based on the heraldry displayed in the first and last quatrefoil, the piece can be connected with the Malterer family of Freiburg who had gained considerable wealth and prestige by the fourteenth century.[31] Scholars have identified the 'Johannes' of the last quatrefoil as the wealthy son of Friedrich Malterer (d. 1320). Johannes lived between approximately 1295 and 1360, and family records indicate that he married a Gisela von Kaiserberg at some point before the birth of their first child Martin in 1336.[32] The identity of the Anna of the first quatrefoil is more obscure. Martin married a Gräfin Anna von Thierstein, but this probably did not happen much before the mid-1350s given his birthdate of 1336, and thus would be beyond the possible dates of the embroidery.[33] A more likely possibility is an Anna Malterer who was connected with the Adelhausen Convent, the first known location of the embroidery, and who has been identified both as Johannes' sister, and more recently, as his aunt.[34] Other scholars have speculated that Anna may have been an unrecorded first wife of Johannes. Based on the incompleteness of the family records, and the fact that a fourteenth-century Freiburg death register refers to a married woman named Anna Malterer who is not otherwise accounted for, this theory does not seem implausible.[35] Understandably, this confusion over the identity of Anna has contributed to the formulation of a wide variety of interpretations of the embroidery's meaning and to speculations as to the reason for which it was made.[36]

Herman Schweitzer was the first scholar to attempt an analysis of the Malterer embroidery in 1904.[37] He felt that the *topos* was being used as a positive testimony to love, and the embroidery must therefore have been commissioned to honour a marriage. He thus concluded that Anna must have been Johannes' first wife, based on the presence of the unidentified Anna Malterer in the death register and the fact that he felt that thirty-five, the approximate age of Johannes at his marriage to Gisela, seemed to be unusually late for a man of his class to marry for the first time. Schweitzer speculated that the embroidery was then donated to the Adelhausen Convent upon Johannes' second marriage, as Gisela would understandably not have wanted to have such a momento present in her home. In this context of marriage and love, Schweitzer sees the problematic second *Iwein* scene as Iwein winning the hand of Laudine with the help of Lunete and the magic ring that made him invisible.

Friedrich Maurer was not convinced by Schweitzer's interpretation, and in 1953 proposed much the opposite, interpreting the *topos* as a warning against carnal love.[38] He maintained an idea first put forward in 1907 by Heinrich Maurer, that Anna was Johannes' sister and a nun at the Adelhausen Convent, even though there is no clear evidence of this.[39] F. Maurer thus proposed that the embroidery was made for the convent as a gift from the siblings. From this perspective he argued that, like the other pairs, the *Iwein* scenes were intended to represent the hero at the height of his powers defeating Ascalon and then the hero humiliated by love, when Lunete denounces Iwein publicly at Arthur's court and takes back Laudine's ring.[40]

More recently, James Rushing Jr., in his extensive work on visual representations of the romance *Iwein*, disregards the previous theories as to the identity of Anna, and argues that the evidence indicates that she was the sister of Friedrich Malterer, and thus Johannes' aunt, and was somehow connected with the Convent.[41] However, he recognizes that the provenance of the embroidery cannot tell us anything conclusive about how to interpret it, because secular settings do not rule out sacred meanings and vice versa. Instead he argues that interpretations 'must be based on the work itself and our knowledge of the "Slaves of Women" *topos* that it embodies'.[42] Rushing concludes his analysis by saying that we cannot know for certain how the *topos* was meant to be interpreted, although he feels, for reasons not fully developed, that it is an allegory of play.[43]

Rushing's treatment of this subject is problematic. He attempts to force the *Iwein* images into his preconceived interpretation of the embroidery, regardless of whether they will fit, resulting in a limited and skewed interpretation of their meaning. He maintains that because the embroidery illustrates the 'Slaves of Women' *topos*, therefore the *Iwein* segments must be a part of it, and because the story does not really fit into the *topos*, then therefore the 'implied viewer' must be one who knows little of the story.[44] Again and again, Rushing stresses that it does not matter how familiar the viewer was with the *Iwein* story and its inappropriateness in this context, all they were 'expected to recognize [was] that, here, he appears as a slave of women,' and 'that he was a great knight who encountered difficulties because of a woman'.[45] For Rushing therefore, in order to understand the message of the embroidery it is better to have only a rudimentary knowledge of the story, because too much knowledge is an impediment to understanding its function in the embroidery, 'for if the entire canonical story of Yvain is considered, he does not appear to belong to the Slaves of Women at all'.[46] It is difficult to understand how Rushing can base an understanding of an image which supposedly has textual origins on *not* knowing the story behind the image well, in effect excluding those who actually may have been familiar with the *Iwein* story from what he deems to be the correct interpretation of the embroidery. It seems evident that anyone with a knowledge of a text would bring it to an interpretation of a related image, and to argue that it is necessary to deliberately suppress such knowledge to understand the image correctly is clearly problematic.

Rushing's argument also fails to suggest a reason why the patron or artist, or whoever was responsible for the choice of images, would have chosen Iwein if he or she had only wanted a general example of a knight defeated by love. Yes, he encounters difficulties that are connected with his relationship to a woman, but as we will clearly see later, those difficulties are not associated with the power of women, love or female sexuality. It seems logical that if the patron or designer had required a specific story or character to illustrate the Power of Women theme, then he or she would have picked a knight like Lancelot or Tristan, the traditional courtly representatives of the *topos*, who were easily identifiable as such. Or, if a break from tradition was desired, King Arthur himself or Erec, from the popular romance of the same name which Hartmann von Aue translated from the French in the late twelfth or early thirteenth century, would have been equally appropriate.[47] *Erec* tells the story of an Arthurian knight who 'loses' himself to love within marriage to the extent that he becomes the object of ridicule by his fellow knights in the same way that Samson, Aristotle and Virgil do. In fact, the story is specifically referred to within the text of *Iwein* as a single example of the dangers of the power of women in an effort to warn Iwein not to make the same mistake as Erec.[48]

Susan Smith arrives at the most balanced and reasonable interpretation of the embroidery. Smith's analysis does not depend on the identity of Anna, or the context in which the embroidery was made. Rather, while recognizing the presence of the Power of Women theme, she bases her interpretation of its meaning on how she interprets the individual scenes and their relation to one another, concluding that, in this case, the *topos* intermingles ideas of the power of love and the power of women in such a way that it 'endorses a model of love and desire which is legitimized only within Christian marriage, which places the value of the spirit over the value of the flesh'.[49] This is based largely on her interpretation of the final unicorn/maiden image which she explains as disclosing 'the proper outlet for . . . love and desire: Christian marriage in which desire is placed in the service of higher purposes and thereby legitimized.'[50] The power of women in the Malterer Embroidery is thus defined for Smith as '. . . their power in marriage over male sexuality. This is a message consistent with the church's doctrine concerning marriage, which discouraged carnal indulgence even within the lawful confines of marriage.'[51] In this way, Smith sees the second *Iwein* scene as the marriage between Iwein and Laudine which, rather than exemplifying womanly wiles and portraying him as a victim of the power of women, demonstrates the power of love that a beautiful woman can inspire.[52] However, her conclusion fails to take into account the fact that Iwein almost immediately abandons his wife to pursue knightly activities, neglecting this love entirely.

While Smith's argument is very convincing in most respects, I would like to propose a different interpretation of the unicorn scene and more importantly the Iwein segments of the embroidery, which I believe to be critical to interpreting the piece as a whole. Contrary to previous scholarly thought, I do not believe that the Iwein scenes were intended to act as further *exempla* illustrating the Power of Women *topos*, but rather, were meant to provide the key to unlocking how the *topos* was intended to be interpreted in this particular context. This would explain why the scenes do not seem to fit iconographically with images traditionally used to illustrate the *topos*. I will suggest that the combination of scenes presented in the Malterer Embroidery not only illustrates the power that women and young female sexuality can have over men, but also demonstrates a respect for, and even approval of, this power. Furthermore, I believe that the embroidery can be interpreted as poking some fun at the weakness of men when faced with women of beauty and strong ideas, and at the passion that such women inspire in even the wisest and most powerful of men. Finally, I will argue that the way in which the chosen subjects are represented, and in the case of *Iwein*, the story itself, demonstrates an acknowledgment of male responsibility for succumbing to this power. I thus agree with Smith that the Malterer Embroidery endorses love and desire, but in a much wider realm than that of Christian marriage alone, a realm which would seem to both acknowledge and accept carnal as well as spiritual love.

As discussed earlier, the first three pairs of scenes are clearly part of the iconographical tradition of the Power of Women *topos*. Samson, Aristotle, and Virgil are all popular literary and historical figures known for their superior strength or wisdom who are overcome with desire for a beautiful young woman and in the process are rendered helpless fools. With the popularity of this *topos* in the art and literature of the period, such a string of images would be sure to recall for most viewers the message that even the greatest of men are no match for the power of women and young female sexuality. In fact, this may have been especially true for viewers in the Freiburg area during the early fourteenth century because there is evidence that visual representations of the *topos* may have been the fashion in the vicinity at the time. In the Weberhaus in Constance, there exists a much deteriorated set of wall paintings, known today only by the incomplete watercolour copies made at their discovery in 1860. Painted between 1306 and 1316, individual roundels depict Adam, Samson, Solomon, Alexander, Virgil, Holofernes, Aristotle, Achilles, Arthur, Parzival, and Azahel, bordered by the verses of an anonymous German poem which lists these men as examples of what women, as the source of love, can do to men.[53] While there is no evidence that the paintings are connected to the Malterer Embroidery, it is possible that the patron or designer of the embroidery may have seen or heard of the wall paintings, and sought to reproduce their theme for his or her own purposes.

The final, single image of the maiden and the unicorn would also recall the message that greatness is no match for the power of young women, and in a more general fashion, this pair comes to be a common addition to visual representations of the *topos*.[54] While not a named individual hero conquered by a woman, the unicorn can be seen as a symbol of all men and the maiden a symbol of all women, and as such the scene acts as an appropriate, single-framed conclusion to the embroidery, tying it all together. Noting the presence of the linden or lime tree, the tree of love in medieval German love poetry and romances, shading the embroidery's unicorn and maiden, and the connection of the lion and unicorn as symbols of strength and chastity in the context of marriage, Smith sees this image as representing Christian marriage as a legitimate outlet for the power of women.[55] While there is little question that the unicorn/maiden pair often had specific Marian associations both in art and in the bestiary accounts, which would support Smith's interpretation, it could also have a much more erotic and sexual overtone that may have had less to do with Christian marriage than with the power of young female sexuality and its ability to overcome even the unicorn.

This arguably sexual element is apparent in several of the written versions of the legend, many of which insist that the maiden should be naked. For example, in the twelfth century, Pseudo-Hugo of St Victor adds to the traditional story that the virgin maid should be beautiful, and that she should uncover her breasts.[56] Philippe de Thaun, a twelfth-century Anglo-Norman poet, includes similar instructions in his bestiary dedicated to Adelaide, Henry I of England's queen, where the scent of the virgin's naked breasts attracts the unicorn who kisses them and then falls asleep in her lap.[57] Finally, John of San Geminiano goes one step further, recommending that in addition to being naked, the virgin should be tied to a tree. In this vulnerable position, she would attract the unicorn by her fragrant smell, causing it to lose its aggressiveness and lie down in her lap where it would lick or touch her breasts.[58]

This juxtaposition of virginity with what might be sexuality, or at least behaviour usually only enjoyed by a sexually active or lactating woman, is very interesting. While it is possible that this sort of description was intended only to create further connections with the Virgin Mary and Christ, it is also possible that putting a young maiden on display for the male mental gaze, naked and in a vulnerable position, may have been considered titillating or erotic to some, a theory supported by the more graphic visual representations.

Several extant visual representations of the story, contain an unquestionably erotic element which makes it clear that virgin or not, the maiden is evidently seen in sexual terms. For example, one late thirteenth-century version depicts the virgin naked and the hunter thrusting a spear at the unicorn whose snout is nestled between her legs (Fig. 12). It is possible that the spear passing directly through the centre of the flower decorating the hunter's shield could have been intended to represent defloration. Another pen and ink sketch dating from the late fifteenth century shows the continuity of this association, without the hunter, but with the maiden gently caressing the horn of the unicorn.[59] Most other visual representations are not as open to interpretations of this sort, but often include swords or spears thrust into the unicorn in the general direction of the maiden's open lap (Fig. 14). While I am wary of applying twentieth-century psychology to a medieval context, the possible sexual implications presented by these symbols are unmistakable.[60] In addition, many of these representations, such as the one that appears on a series of ivory boxes decorated with scenes from romance

Figure 14: Ivory casket with iron mounts, scenes of romances. French (Paris), 1330–1350. The Walters Art Gallery, Baltimore.

(Fig. 14) contain no iconographical elements that would connect the image to a sacred context. In fact, paired with Tristan and Iseult, whose love was unquestionably of a carnal nature, the context appears much the opposite.

Thus, the maiden in the Malterer Embroidery who sits under the German tree of love can be seen as the lure that the unicorn is unable to resist, and by possessing the same sexual powers as the other presumably sexually active women in the embroidery, she has provided yet another example of the power of women, one with arguably unspiritual overtones.

Given that four of the stories illustrated on the embroidery illustrate the *topos*, it would seem logical, and perhaps be expected, that the fifth and final story would also illustrate the theme. However, it does not. The *Iwein* story was never part of the existing Power of Women *topos*, visual or literary, nor does it become a part of it, as James Rushing unsuccessfully argues, without an extreme stretch of the imagination. This overturning of expectations and interrupting of thematic unity suggests strongly that the *Iwein* segments must be the key to understanding the Malterer Embroidery. Thus, by understanding what they represent and their relationship to the Power of Women theme, I hope to demonstrate how the Malterer Embroidery was intended to be interpreted.

Essential to understanding the *Iwein* segments is understanding the basic themes of the romance which would have remained in the minds of anyone familiar with the story. *Iwein*, at its most elementary level, is a story about the pursuit of knightly honour, which raises questions of what such honour involves, or perhaps should involve. A key component of this theme deals with the question of what happens when a knight abandons his responsibilities to his kingdom, wife, and more abstractly, love, for the reckless pursuit of honour on the tournament field. The text is quite clear about the result: madness. The way in which this theme is used to illustrate the importance of love and women in relation to honour, and the fact that the neglect of love is the cause of Iwein's downfall, not the power of women or love, is critical to an understanding of the embroidery.

Following Iwein's defeat of Ascalon at the magic spring, he becomes trapped inside the castle where he catches sight of the grieving, but still beautiful widow Laudine. From the start, Iwein, while enamoured of the Queen and describing his love in all the conventional, unrestrained ways, never actually gives in totally to love as is generally required and expected of the courtly lover. For example, 'Sir Iwein caught glimpses of her bare form and her hair and body were so beautiful that love robbed him of any reason to the point that he quite forgot himself and *almost* left his seat when she tore her hair and beat herself.'[61] As much as he is moved by this pathetic vision of Laudine's grief, which he himself has brought upon her in his quest for honour, Iwein is still in control. This is made even clearer further on in the episode when: 'Although the power of love had captured his mind, he still remembered one misfortune: that he could not disarm the mockery he would encounter at court when he couldn't produce any visible proof of his success and that, therefore, all his trouble would be for nothing.'[62] This is clearly not a man powerless and humiliated in the face of love and womanly wiles. My point is not that viewers would necessarily remember these specific details, but that there are enough of them to leave a general impression that Iwein is not truly in the grips of love in its most overpowering and disabling sense. Iwein is clearly rational and in full possession of his faculties and more concerned about his own somewhat skewed concept of honour than he is about love. At this point in the story, it is already becoming evident that it will not be love or women that will be the unmaking of Iwein, but his unreasonable desire for honour at all costs. Furthermore, Laudine, the supposed possessor of these irresistible and dangerous wiles, is the passive receptacle of Iwein's gaze and does nothing active to entice him – in fact, she does not even know he is present, and if she did, would have had him executed on the spot for killing her husband.

With the rather manipulative intercession of Laudine's lady-in-waiting Lunete, the couple is made to see the mutual advantageousness of their union, and are married. Iwein thus obtains his love and a means to obtain honour. However, the plot takes a sharp turn when Arthur and his knights arrive on the scene. Iwein's best friend Gawain takes him aside for a little 'man to man' talk in which he warns him of the dangers of love, specifically evoking *Erec* as an example of what call befall the unwary man:

> Now, since things have turned our favourably for you, take care that your wife's beauty does not bring you shame. Friend, watch out that you do not soon make the mistake of those who because of their wives, are condemned for sloth. Don't turn wholly to a life of ease, as Sir Erec did, who was idle for a long time because of Lady Enite. If he had not made up for it later in knightly manner, his honour would have been lost. He was a prisoner of his love. You have all you need to be satisfied, so let me tell you how to preserve your fame. Come with us and we'll take part in tournaments as before. If you should lose your knightly spirit, I would be forever sorry that I knew you.[63]

Gawain's persuasive speech continues at length, and Iwein is completely convinced. Laudine unhappily and reluctantly grants him permission to go with his friends, but only on the condition that he return in a year, and gives him a ring to seal their agreement. In effect, by leaving Laudine, Iwein is responding to love in exactly the opposite way to his predecessors on the embroidery. While Samson, Aristotle, and Virgil lose their respective strengths for the love of a woman, Iwein abandons love and resists the supposedly ever-present womanly wiles without any difficulty, in order to pursue his strengths. While the text makes it clear that leaving Laudine is a painful task for Iwein, his desire to pursue knightly adventure with his friends wins out, and his immense success on the tournament field and the prestige that this earns him does much to soothe his emotional wounds. He becomes so caught up in his knightly activities that he gives not another thought to Laudine and his promise until the specified year is well past. The power of love, women, or female sexuality clearly exercises no hold on this man.

At this point, Lunete arrives on the scene with a message from Laudine. In front of King Arthur, she publicly denounces Iwein, calling him a disloyal, traitorous liar for deserting his wife and his responsibilities for his newly won kingdom. She instructs him to stay away from Laudine and retrieves the ring which the Queen had given him as a symbol of his promise. It is this scene, where Iwein loses kingdom, wife, love and honour due to his neglect of love, which I believe is represented in the second *Iwein* component of the embroidery. While Laudine sits eyes downcast and hands held before her in sorrow or prayer, Lunete removes the ring from Iwein's finger as he looks beseechingly towards Laudine

(Fig. 9). It does not matter that Laudine is not physically present in the textual account, as the reader of the embroidery would understand that she was present there as a symbol of Iwein's loss and as a reminder that he had failed to live up to his responsibilities to women and love. Iwein is devastated by this turn of events and 'He forgot all decency, tore off his clothes until he was as bare as one's hand, and ran naked across the fields towards the wilderness.'[64] As a direct result of neglecting love, Iwein is reduced to madness.

The remainder of the story is concerned with Iwein regaining the honour he lost in abandoning Laudine through a series of adventures which involve saving various damsels in distress, which is perhaps in keeping with the importance of women in the conception of knightly honour. Iwein thus comes to represent adventure undertaken for the service of women and love. In the end, the husband and wife are reunited, although the text is ambiguous as to their future happiness.

Thus, based on an elementary knowledge of the plot of *Iwein* and its main theme, it seems clear that it would be very difficult indeed to make it fit into the traditional Power of Women *topos*. While the first three pairs of scenes demonstrate that even the strongest and wisest of men are not impervious to the powers of female sexuality and love, Iwein proves exactly the opposite, that men are fully capable of avoiding the supposedly inescapable powers of women and love and neglecting both, but that such resilience and failure to succumb to female powers results in madness and a return to an uncivilized state.

The fact that *Iwein*, clearly not connected with the Power of Women *topos* in any identifiable manner, was chosen to be included on the embroidery which is otherwise so thematically based upon the *topos*, particularly when other more appropriate images were available, suggests that the story was selected specifically for a reason. Given their unusual character, I would suggest that the *Iwein* segments were chosen by the patron of the embroidery who had a solid knowledge of the story, and thus knew that their inclusion should, to an extent, turn the *topos* on its head for anyone familiar with the tale, and call for a new interpretation. With some thought about the relationship between Iwein and the other *exempla*, it would have become clear to the viewer that what was demanded by the embroidery's iconography was more than simply an awareness and affirmation of the power of love and women, but an active responsibility to acknowledge such powers and respect them.

By returning from the antithetical *Iwein* scenes to the unicorn and maiden, which once again emphasizes the power of women, this final image can be taken to reinforce the idea that the power of women and love is very strong, and that an awareness of this fact and a moderate adherence to it is healthy; in other words, if you succumb to it you will be humiliated, if you reject it, you will go mad, so pay heed and moderate your actions accordingly. Thus, the embroidery as a whole uses the iconographical tradition of the Power of Women *topos*, combined with the antithetical *Iwein* segments, to illustrate in a positive manner that the power of women, love, and female sexuality is a potent force that must be acknowledged, recognized and respected.

While it is difficult to judge what would have been found amusing six hundred years ago, this positive interpretation is supported by the fact that the Malterer Embroidery can also be seen to have humorous undertones. A viewer who had been exposed to the biblical story of Samson and Delilah through reading or hearing an accurate translation of the Latin text and not just the potentially biased interpretation of a church official, and who also had a demanding spouse as grounds for comparison, might easily have found elements of Samson's relationship with Delilah amusing. The story attributes Samson's actual capitulation, not to his love or desire for Delilah, but simply to her constant nagging which wore him down: 'And when she had been irksome to him, and endlessly kept at him for many days, not allowing him time for rest, his spirit failed and was tired unto death.'[65] While the rest of Samson's story is not nearly so amusing, this aspect at least might have offered the opportunity for married viewers to identify with Samson's story with an irreverent smile.

The story of Aristotle suggests a similar response. The image of Aristotle being ridden provides a humorous and scandalous situation in which many norms are turned upside down: man becomes beast; youth overcomes age; sexual passion overcomes dry philosophy; nature surmounts reason; and the female the male.[66] While the image may have contained certain truths about the potential power of women and their position within the household, it would have been likely to have evoked laughter at the folly of the supposedly wise old man. In fact, at least one of the textual versions of the story puts great emphasis on the humorous nature of the story and the laughter with which Alexander greets the sight of his lover riding on the back of his tutor,[67] and the ridden Aristotle pose is later used in the visual arts as a comment on marital relations, depicting Phyllis as a housewife and Aristotle as her downtrodden husband.[68]

The Virgil story too is essentially an amusing tale where yet another wise man exposes himself to ridicule as a result of his passion for a beautiful young woman. Smith maintains that the tale seems to have been used exclusively in the spirit of the fabliaux, in order to poke fun at the follies committed by supposedly wise men in love,[69] and the embroidery's animated depiction of Virgil, hands thrown up in dismay, would support this.

The *Iwein* images are not particularly amusing in themselves, but it is possible that the story may have been intended as a satirical look at conventions of knightly honour and love, and it seems possible that at least some fourteenth-century townsfolk would have laughed at the idea of madness as a fitting punishment for a man who neglects love and honour. The unicorn, while not specifically amusing, is at least a positive image, reinforced by the absence of hunters who are often depicted slaying the helpless unicorn (Fig. 14). Thus, in addition to calling for an awareness for and respect of the power of women and love, it is possible that the Malterer Embroidery also may have been intended to poke some fun at the weakness of men when faced with women of beauty, sexual allure, and strong ideas.

Finally, I believe that the iconography of the Malterer Embroidery as a whole can also be interpreted as demonstrating that, while the power of women is strong and in many cases effective, men are ultimately responsible for succumbing to it. In the embroidery, Samson, Aristotle and Virgil are all depicted as playing active roles in their submission. Unlike most visual representations of the Samson scene which portray Samson asleep and unknowing of his fate as he is in Judges 16:19, the Samson on the embroidery is wide awake and aware as Delilah cuts his braids (Fig. 3).[70] In the few visual representations of the Aristotle legend that include a scene other than the standard ridden Aristotle, the initial image features Aristotle with Alexander. On the embroidery, however, Aristotle is depicted leaving his books to reach through the window to caress Phyllis, demonstrating his active involvement in the activities that lead up to his humiliation (Fig. 4). Virgil, who is generally only depicted in his basket, too is presented as actively arranging his ill-fated assignation with the Emperor's daughter (Fig. 6).

While all these images could also be interpreted as demonstrating the extent of male helplessness in the face of female power, which causes them to submit knowingly to their doom, the *Iwein* story dispels this notion. While the *Iwein* images themselves do not depict Iwein actively participating in his downfall, the text certainly does, and as established previously, it seems safe to assume that that the primary viewers of the embroidery would have had enough familiarity with the basic text to recognize this. In the first place, Iwein never submits to love or female power. When he falls it is because of neglect of love and women and for this, on two separate occasions, Iwein specifically admits his direct responsibility for his own downfall. After his denunciation by Lunete, Iwein is devastated, but the text is explicit that it is his fault: 'He began to hate himself, since he could blame no one else: he had been struck down by his own sword.'[71] This happens once again when Iwein and Laudine are finally reunited, and he acknowledges to her his culpability for their painful separation, saying: '. . . I lost your affection only through my own disposition.'[72] With this in support, it seems quite possible that the unusual representation of the active participation of the other figures in their downfalls was intended to admit male culpability.

Thus, I believe that the Malterer Embroidery is a less than serious illustration of the influence that women can exercise over men, acknowledging and accepting that even the strongest and most intelligent men can be subdued by love of or desire for a woman. Unlike much of the literature of the *topos* which focuses on the woman's role as seducer, emphasizing the negative impact that women, love and female sexuality can have over men, the Malterer Embroidery offers examples of men who took an active role in their seductions, and thus seems to hold men equally responsible for their amorous misadventures and for allowing desire to impair their judgment.

This leaves us with the question of who commissioned the Malterer embroidery and for what purpose. While it is impossible to know for certain, I would like to propose my own tentative conclusions. The unusual presence of the *Iwein* scenes would suggest that they were deliberately selected with a specific purpose in mind. This in turn would suggest that whoever was responsible for choosing them had a firm understanding of the *Iwein* text and how he or she thought it interrelated with the traditional Power of Women *topos*. If the use of the *topos* in the embroidery is interpreted in the manner which I have proposed as a positive and good-natured acknowledgment of the power of love and female sexuality and the responsibility of men in succumbing to this power, then I would like to speculate that it was made in honour of Johannes' marriage. One possibility is that his Aunt or sister Anna may have embroidered it for him with the help of her Sisters in the Adelhausen Convent to honour his marriage to Gisela, playfully intending to warn him to take heed of the potential powers of women. Her membership in a religious community would not necessarily have meant that her thoughts on love, marriage and sexuality were restricted to Church doctrine, as it is possible that she might have had other opportunities to be exposed to the positive and good-natured side of marital relations, such as a previous marriage or a friendship with a widowed Sister. On the other hand, it is also possible that, as Schweitzer suggested, Johannes may have had an earlier marriage to an unidentified Anna, for which the records have been lost, and that he commissioned it to show playful respect for her on the occasion of an anniversary of their marriage, by which point they would have had the time to experience the growth of love and appreciate the humour behind the images. This might help explain the fact that both sets of arms are those of the Malterer family, both because Anna may not have had her own in the first place, and because she would have taken on those of her husband upon marriage. Conversely it is possible that Anna, confident in the power she exercised over her husband, could have given him the embroidery as a teasing acknowledgment of the status of their relationship, as if to say in twentieth-century terms, 'You may wear the pants in the family, but we both know where the real power lies.'

Notes

I would like to thank Debra Hassig and Kim Phillips for their advice and support during the writing of this paper.

1. In the interest of space, I have not developed this well-known tradition fully. The interested reader should consult Alcuin Blamires, *Woman Defamed and Woman Defended: an Anthology of Medieval Texts* (New York, 1992); R. Howard Bloch, *Medieval Misogyny and the Invention of Western Love* (Chicago, University of Chicago Press, 1991); Joyce B. Salisbury, 'The Latin Doctors of the Church', *Journal of*

Medieval History, 12 (1986), 279–89; Peter Brown, *The Body and Society: Men, Women and Sexual Renunciation in Early Christianity* (New York, 1988), to name only a few of the sources available on the subject.

2. Susan L. Smith, *The Power of Women: A* Topos *in Medieval Art and Literature* (Philadelphia, 1995) and Susan L. Smith, 'The Power of Women *Topos* on a 14th-Century Embroidery', *Viator*, 21 (1990), 203–27. I am much indebted to Smith's in-depth analysis of this topic and I will use her term throughout this paper as it seems the most accurate and appropriate way to describe and define the tradition with which it is concerned.

3. For a detailed examination of the *topos* in antique and medieval literature, see Smith, *Power of Women* (1995), pp. 1–65. She directs readers to Rüdiger Schnell, *Causa Amoris Liebeskonzeption und Liebesdarstellung in der mittelalterlichen Literatur* (Bern and Munich, 1985), pp. 475–505, for an even more extensive development of this topic.

4. Smith, *Power of Women* (1995), p. 2.

5. Ibid., pp. 2–3.

6. Ibid., pp. 20–9.

7. Brian Stock, *The Implications of Literacy* (Princeton NJ, 1983), pp. 25–6.

8. Smith, *Power of Women* (1995), p. 40; Jacques le Goff, 'The Time of the *Exemplum* (Thirteenth Century)', in Arthur Goldhammer (tr.), *The Medieval Imagination* (Chicago and London, 1985), p. 78; Richard H. Rouse and Mary A. Rouse, *Preachers, Florilegia and Sermons: Studies on the 'Manipulus florum' of Thomas of Ireland* (Toronto, 1979), pp. 46–64; Franz H. Bäuml, 'Varieties and Consequences of Medieval Literacy and Illiteracy', *Speculum*, 55 (1980), 244–5.

9. John F. Benton, 'The Court of Champagne as a Literary Center', *Speculum*, 36 (1961), 551–91.

10. Smith, *Power of Women* (1995), p. 13.

11. Ibid., pp. 43–6. For background on the impact that courtly love had on the representation of women in literature, consult Joan M. Ferrante, *Woman as Image in Medieval Literature* (New York and London, 1975), pp. 65–97.

12. Smith, *Power of Women* (1995), p. 44.

13. Ibid., pp. 39 and 140.

14. Ibid., pp. 137–90.

15. Ibid., p. 109; Meyer Schapiro, *Words and Pictures: On the Literal and Symbolic in the Illustration of a Text* (The Hague and Paris, 1973), p. 9; James A. Rushing Jr., 'Iwein as Slave of Woman: the Maltererteppich in Freiburg', *Zeitschrift für Kunstgeschichte*, 55 (1992), 129.

16. Smith, *Power of Women* (1995), pp. 109–10.

17. For more information on the reading of images and their relation to texts, consult, Michael Camille, 'Seeing and Reading: Some Visual Interpretations of Medieval Literacy and Illiteracy', *Art History*, 8 (1985), 26–49; Lawrence G. Duggan, 'Was Art Really the "book of the illiterate"?' *Word & Image*, 5 (1989), 227–51; James A. Rushing Jr., 'The Adventures of the Lion Knight: Story and Picture in the Princeton Yvain', *Princeton University Library Chronicle*, 53 (1991), 31–49.

18. Smith, 'Power of Women' (1990), p. 204.

19. Ibid., p. 204.

20. For more information on Samson in the Christian tradition, consult Michael F. Krouse, *Milton's Samson and the Christian Tradition* (Princeton NJ, 1949), and for Samson and Delilah's representation in art,

particularly the art of the later Middle Ages and Renaissance, refer to Madlyn Millner Kahr, 'Delilah', in Norma Broude and Mary D. Garrard (eds), *Feminism and Art History* (New York, 1982), pp. 119–146.

21. Smith, *Power of Women* (1995), pp. 67–8. The story is believed to have originated in similar stories concerned with foolish wise men which were prevalent in the folklore of the Near and Far East. Many versions exist, the earliest being the vernacular poem *Lai d'Aristote* by the Northern French poet Henri d'Andeli, composed sometime between 1200 and 1240. Around the same time, another version of the story appeared in an *exemplum* contained in a sermon by Jacques de Vitry, and yet another in a Middle High German version called *Aristoteles und Fillis* at the end of the thirteenth century. While each of the extant versions of this story invite a somewhat different interpretation of the theme of the power of women and love, they all tell essentially the same tale of the humiliation of the great philosopher Aristotle by his surrender to carnal desire.

22. My synopsis is based on a summary of 'Li Lais d'Aristote' by Henri d'Andeli in Raymond Eichmann and John DuVal (eds and tr.), *The French Fabliau B.N. MS. 837*, vol. I, (New York and London, 1984), pp. 94–117, cross-referenced with Smith's assessment of all the versions.

23. Domenico Comparetti, *Vergil in the Middle Ages*, tr. E.F.M. Benecke (London, 1895. Reprint, Hamden, Conn., 1966), pp. 326–7. In many versions of the tale, Virgil extracted revenge on the young woman by casting a spell which extinguished all the fires in Rome which could only be re-lit by obtaining fire from the most intimate area of the maiden's body.

24. Hartmann von Aue, *Iwein*, tr. J.W. Thomas (Lincoln NB and London, 1979), p. ix. Throughout this article, I will use the spelling in the German version given that it seems most likely that this would have been the version known in fourteenth-century Freiburg. Hartmann von Aue was considered by his contemporaries to be one of the most important poets of the day, and it has even been suggested that he may have lived in the Freiburg area. William Hasty, *Adventures in Interpretation: The Works of Hartmann von Aue and their Critical Reception* (Columbia SC, 1996), pp. 11 and 14.

25. von Aue, *Iwein*, p. 62.

26. Rushing, 'Iwein as Slave of Woman', p. 129.

27. Versions of this story, to name only a few, can be found in Guillaum le Clerc, *Bestiary of Guillaum le Clerc*, tr. George Claridge Druce (Ashford, Kent, 1936), p. 44; Richard de Fournival, *Le Bestiare D'Amour* (Paris, 1860), pp. 23–4; M.C. Seymour, (ed.), *On the Properties of Things; John Trevisa's translation of 'Bartholomaeus Anglicus de proprietatibus rerum'* (Oxford, 1975), pp. 1240–1.

28. For a full treatment of the unicorn's symbolic meaning in art, consult Rüdiger Robert Beer, *The Unicorn: Myth and Reality*, tr. Charles M. Stern (New York, 1977); Jürgen W. Einhorn, *Spiritualis unicornis: Das Einhorn als Bedeutunstgräger in Literatur und darstellender Kunst des Mittelalters* (Munich, 1976); and Margaret Freeman, *The Unicorn Tapestries* (New York, 1976); see also my 'La Dame à la Licorne: A Reinterpretation', *Gazette des Beaux-Arts*, (September 1997), 47–72 for examples of a more secular use of unicorn iconography.

29. For further detail, see Smith, 'Power of Women' (1990), pp. 214–21; Smith, *Power of Women* (1995), pp. 154–68. While interesting, I am not convinced that the order of the scenes contributes as much to understanding the meaning of the embroidery as do other factors. Thus, in the interest of space, I have kept my treatment of this issue extremely brief.

30. Smith, 'Power of Women' (1990), p. 215. In the twelfth century this pairing was revised and translated into contemporary terms through the orders of clergy and chivalry. For a complete

discussion of the clerks and knights theme, see Charles Oulemont, *Les débats du clerc et du chevalier* (Paris, 1911. Reprint Geneva, 1974). As Smith notes, originally these orders were rivals, and this rivalry manifested itself in a light-hearted group of texts in which ladies debate whether clerks or knights make better lovers. The rival groups were later brought together as the two classes of men qualified to be lovers by virtue of their *courtoisie.*

31. James A. Rushing Jr., *Images of Adventure: Ywain in the Visual Arts* (Philadelphia, 1995), p. 222. This information is based on family records that surived an early fifteenth-century fire. For further information, refer to Hermann Schweitzer, 'Bildteppiche und Stickereien in der städtischen Altertümersammlung zu Freiburg im Breisgau', *Schau-ins-Land,* 31 (1904), pp. 51–4; Josef Fleckenstein, 'Bürgertum und Ritterum in der Geschichte des mittelalterlichen Freiburg', in Wolfgang Müller (ed.), *Freiburg im Mittelalter* (Bühl, 1970), pp. 77–95.

32. Rushing, 'Iwein as Slave of Woman', p. 133; Rushing, *Images of Adventure,* p. 221. They also had three other children, Margarethe, Elisabeth and Gisela.

33. Rushing, *Images of Adventure,* p. 240, n. 13.

34. The former view was proposed by Friedrich Maurer, 'Der *topos* von den "Minnesklaven"', *Deutsche Vierteljahrsschrift für Literaturwissenschaft und Geistesgeschichte,* 27 (1953),182–206, and the latter by Rushing, *Images of Adventure,* p. 222; Rushing, 'Iwein as Slave of Woman', p. 133.

35. Schweitzer as referred to by Smith, *Power of Women* (1995), p. 152; Smith 'Power of Women' (1990), p. 207; Rushing, 'Iwein as Slave of Woman', p. 133.

36. The discussion in this article summarizes only the most substantial theories on the embroidery to indicate the diversity of opinion present. The interested reader should consult Rushing, *Images of Adventure,* and Smith, *Power of Women* (1995), for more detailed summaries and a complete bibliography of sources.

37. Schweitzer, 'Bildteppiche und Stickereien', pp. 35–64, as descibed in Smith, *Power of Women* (1995), p. 153 and 'Power of Women' (1990), p. 207 and Rushing, *Images of Adventure,* pp. 220–6.

38. F. Maurer, 'Der Topos', pp. 182–206, as summarized in Smith, 'Power of Women' (1990), p. 209; Smith, *Power of Women* (1995), pp. 153–4; Rushing, *Images of Adventure,* pp. 220, 223, and 227–8.

39. Heinrich Maurer, 'Ein Freiburger Bürger und seine Nachkommen,' *Zeitschrift für die Geschichte des Oberrrheins,* ns 22 (1907), 9–51, as referred to by Rushing, *Images of Adventure,* p. 220.

40. Maurer, 'Der Topos', pp. 225–6 in Rushing, *Images of Adventure,* p. 227. Maurer seems to forget that it is not love that is the cause of Iwein's humiliation, but neglect of love, a theme which I will develop extensively in my own interpretation.

41. Rushing, *Images of Adventure,* p. 222.

42. Ibid., pp. 220 and 222.

43. Ibid., pp. 235, 239.

44. Ibid., pp. 234 and 236.

45. Ibid., pp. 234–5.

46. Ibid., p. 236.

47. Hartmann von Aue, *Erec,* tr. Thomas L. Keller (New York and London, 1987).

48. von Aue, *Iwein,* p. 89.

49. Smith, 'Power of Women' (1990), p. 227.

50. Smith, *Power of Women* (1995), p. 167.

51. Ibid., pp. 167–8.

52. Ibid., pp. 159–60

53. Rushing, *Images of Adventure*, p. 233; Smith, *Power of Women* (1995), p. 138.

54. See Smith's description and discussion of the early fourteenth-century ivory caskets with scenes from romances (*Power of Women*, 1995, pp. 168–86) and the late fourteenth-century capital from St Pierre, Caen which features Aristotle, Virgil, Lancelot, Gawain, Samson and the lion, and the lady and the unicorn (pp. 186–90).

55. Smith, *Power of Women* (1995), p. 166; A.T. Hatto, 'The Lime-Tree and Early German, Goliard and English Lyric Poetry', *Modern Language Review*, 49 (1954), 193.

56. Pseudo-Hugo of St Victor, 'De Besiis et Aliis Rebus', *Patrologia Latina* 177: 59. ('Puellam viginemque speciosam ducunt in locum illum ubi moratur, et dimittunt eam solam, cum autem ipsa viderit illud, *apert sinum suum*, quo viso, omni ferociate deposita, caput suum in gremium eius deponit, et sic dormiens deprehendiur ab insidiatoribus et exhibetur in palatium regis.') Italics are mine.

57. Philip de Thaun, 'Le Livre de Creatures', in Thomas Wright (ed.), *Popular Treatises on Science Written During the Middle Ages* (London, 1841), p. 81. ('Là met une pucele hors de sein sa mamele, / Epar odurement monosceros la sent; / Dunc vent à la pucele, e si baiset sa mamele, / En sun devant se dort, issi vent à sa mort.')

58. John of San Geminiano, *Summa de Exemplis et Rerum Simi*, Book IV, cap. 123, Lyons, 1585, p. 141. ('Venatores autem, ut dicitur, qui volunt hoc animale capere, virginem aliquam nudam ligant ad aborem, iuxta quam illud animal debet transire, quod transiens dum sentit virginei odoris fragrantiam, ita immutatur, quod omni ferocitate deposita in eius gremio recumbit: et ubera eius lambit: et sic qua si agnus mansuetus factus ligatur, capitur, et tenetur.')

59. Beer, *Myth and Reality*, p. 147. Late fifteenth-century pen and ink drawing by the Upper Rhineland Master in the Copperplate Engravings Collection of the Public Art Collection, Basel.

60. For a somewhat overstated discussion of phallic imagery in medieval art, consult M. Caviness, 'Patron or Matron? A Capetian Bride and a Vade Mecum for her Marriage Bed', *Speculum* 68 (1993), 333–62.

61. von Aue, *Iwein*, p. 71. Italics are mine.

62. Ibid., p. 73.

63. Ibid., p. 89.

64. Ibid., p. 94. The text goes on to say that 'as brave as he was and as steadfast in body as in spirit, still Lady Love enabled a frail woman to turn both upside down, for he who had been a diamond of knightly virtue was now rushing wildly about in the forest, a fool.' Given that immediately preceding this Iwein acknowledges that there is no one to blame for his predicament but himself, and the fact that Laudine, ruling her kingdom on her own for over a year and actively breaking off their relationship, is anything but frail, strongly suggests that this is an ironic reference to the power of love/women which is not further developed, and therefore should not detract from the real cause of Iwein's madness.

65. Judges 16:16–17.

66. Natalie Davis, 'Women on Top', in Natalie Davis (ed.), *Society and Culture in Early Modern France* (Stanford, 1975), p. 135.

67. Henri d'Andeli, p. 113.

68. Smith, *Power of Women* (1995), p. 198.

69. Ibid., p. 157.

70. The Samson in the *Wharncliff Hours* (Fig. 13) also has eyes open, but this too is unusual.

71. von Aue, *Iwein*, p. 94. Chrétien's text is even more explicit, saying that he is at fault because he has not acted as those in love should, not sleeping and counting the days until next able to see the beloved. Chrétien de Troyes, *Yvain: The Knight of the Lion*, tr. Burton Raffel (New Haven CT and London, 1987), p. 84, ll. 2754–60.

72. von Aue, *Iwein*, p. 149. Once again, Chrétien is even more specific, saying: '. . . I've had / To suffer for my folly, and I ought / To have suffered, it was only right. / It was folly that kept me away; I was guilty / You were right to punish me.' Chrétien de Troyes, *Yvain*, p. 202, ll. 6780–5.

5

RAPE IN JOHN GOWER'S *CONFESSIO AMANTIS* AND OTHER RELATED WORKS

Isabelle Mast

INTRODUCTION

> Là, en un selier, fist entrer, oultre son gré et par force, ladicte Perrete la Souplice, et la jeta à terre, et avala ses braies, et se mist sus lui, et s'efforça contre sa nature tant comme il pot, et pour ce que elle crioit, il la bati et feri, et la laissa.[1]

> (There in a cellar he forced her to go, against her will and by force, the said Perrete la Souplice. He threw her to the ground, and pulled down his underwear, and got on top of her, and forced himself against her private parts as hard as he could: And because she cried out, he beat her, struck her, and left her there.)[2]

> And he, which al him hadde adresced
> To lust, tok thanne what him liste,
> And goth his wey.
>
> *Confessio Amantis*, VII, ll. 4988–90[3]

Here are two descriptions of a rape, one from a historical, 'real' case, the other a literary portrayal from John Gower's *Confessio Amantis*. The first quotation focuses on male aggression and female suffering, which shows that medieval writers were able to recognize that rape is one of the most painful and destructive expressions of violence that can be used against women. The passage from the *Confessio*, in contrast, does not even convince the reader that what is being described is necessarily a rape. It could be a less serious crime such as theft. This, in turn, suggests the following questions – how does Gower portray rape in his poem and what attitude towards the victims does he take? The large number of rapes and attempted rapes in the *Confessio* suggests that this was a topic of great concern to Gower. Although realism is not likely to have been one of Gower's artistic aims, his literary involvement with this crime seems to have led to a strong interest in the suffering of its victims.[4]

This article will try to show Gower's individuality in his approach to the topic of rape. The *Confessio* was probably written in the early 1390s. It describes the confession of a lover, Amans, to Genius, priest of nature. In order to warn and instruct Amans, Genius explains the Seven Deadly Sins to him through the medium of a great many exemplary stories, many of which derived from Ovid. Amans is to understand these Sins and the stories which illustrate them, in terms of the harm which they may do to him, and to Love. It is within this context that his descriptions of rape should be understood.

The legal background to rape in late medieval England is complicated. It is often difficult to distinguish between rape as 'forced coitus' and rape as 'abduction'; the Latin *raptus* and *rapere* could mean either.[5] In this article the term 'rape' will be used to denote forced intercourse only. Gower himself never used this word – nor any other precise term. His terminology will be examined later. In 1275 the first Statute of Westminster reduced the seriousness of the crime by defining it as a trespass – as opposed to a felony. At the same time it also included official provision for the rape of matrons.[6] Only ten years later the second Statute of Westminster turns rape again into a felony, a violent crime against a person punishable by loss of life or member:

> It is provided that if a man from henceforth do ravish a woman, married, maid, or other, where she did not consent, neither before or after, he shall have judgement of life and member. And like-wise where a man ravisheth a woman, married lady, Damosel, or other, with force, although she consent after he shall have such judgement as before is said.[7]

But how common was rape in late medieval England? Carter and other historians found that only a minute fraction of the crimes brought to light were rapes. He assumes that it was seriously underreported because of the embarrassment to the victim and her family and because of possible retribution by the rapist or his family.[8] Although it is very difficult to ascertain the historical reality of rape from documentary sources, there is ample discussion of the topic in medieval literature. Gower wrote his *Confessio* at a time when rape was by no means taboo as a literary topic. Here three collections of short tales have been selected for a comparison.

The *Gesta Romanorum* contains several stories concerned with rape, two citing fictional rape laws.[9] In one of the tales the emperor decrees a law that men will be blinded if they have 'defoulid a virgine'.[10] The emperor's own son meets the daughter of a widow '& he oppressid hir, & foulid hir in flesh' and is subsequently punished by his father.[11] The 'moralitee' which concludes the story emphasizes that rape is no trivial offence, by explicitly pointing out that the eyes stand for the light of heaven and that heaven is denied to rapists (of virgins). A long generalization follows in which the rape is equated with sin. In the second rape case the emperor decrees that any man who delivers a virgin from the power of her ravisher is allowed to marry her if he wishes, or alternatively has to give his consent to any other match.[12] This seems to indicate a view of women as commodity: if a man has saved a woman from a rapist he is granted the choice no matter what the views of the woman concerned might be. In the tale, the tyrant Pompeius rapes a woman ('I-Raveshid' and 'synned with her') and then decides to kill her, but she is saved by a knight.[13] Having accepted his subsequent proposal she later consents to become Pompeius' wife as well and a judge decides that both the woman and Pompeius are to be hanged for this.[14] By making the woman prefer her rapist as a husband, this tale casts doubts on her status as victim.[15] The 'moralitee' of the tale gives an allegorical reading of the tale in which the woman stands for the soul of man. The *Gesta* shows that the crime is serious – the punishment is loss of life or member – but in neither of the stories does one hear about the emotional state of the victims. The women's feelings and opinions are ignored.

In another collection of stories, the *Alphabet of Tales*, only six out of the 800 tales are concerned with rape.[16] One feature seems common to all stories in this collection: the crime is related in a very by-the-way manner. In one tale, for instance, a gang-rape is mentioned but there are no women in the tale itself.[17] Rape is taken far more lightly than in the *Gesta*, but in both collections female characters never voice their 'own' opinions on the crime. Nor are they allowed to show their wounds, mental and physical. In the third collection, Christine de Pisan's *Cité des Dames*, not many rapes are depicted, but the crime – and the problem itself – is addressed directly:

> 'Si m'anuye et m'esgriesve de ce que hommes dient tant que femmes se veullent efforcier et qu'il ne leur desplait mie, quoyque elles escondissent de bouche, d'estre par hommes efforciees. . . .' Responce: 'Ne doubtes pas, amie chiere, que ce n'est mie plaisir aux dames chastes et de belle vie estre efforciees, ains leur est douleur sur toutes autres. Et que ce soit vray, l'ont demonstré plusieurs d'elles par vray exemple, si comme de Lucresce.'[18]

> ('I am therefore troubled and grieved when men argue that many women want to be raped and that it does not bother them at all to be raped by men when they verbally protest. . . .' She answered, 'Rest assured, dear friend, chaste ladies who live honestly take absolutely no pleasure in being raped. Indeed, rape is the greatest possible sorrow for them. Many upright women have demonstrated that this is true with their own credible examples, just like Lucretia'.)[19]

The consequences of rape, however, stay unexplored in all three collections, both within the fiction of the tales and the morals drawn by the author. Does Gower's method of description differ? In his main French poem, the *Mirour de l'Omme* (*c.* 1376-1379) he shows a moralist's view of life in his own days rather than a fictional exploration of the topic. In the *Mirour* rape is discussed only in relation to virgins.[20] The deed itself is not at the centre of the relevant sections but rather its repercussions:[21]

> As autres jofnes femelines
> De Stupre et de ses disciplines
> Sovent auci vient grant dammage:
> Quant de lour corps ne sont virgines,
> Et que l'en sciet de leur covines,
> Par ce perdont leur mariage,
> Dont met esclandre en lour lignage,
> Sique pour honte en leur putage
> Tout s'enfuiont comme orphelines,
> Dont croist sur honte plus hontage,
> Quant au bordell pour l'avantage
> De sustienance sont enclines.
>
> *Mirour*, ll. 8725–36

(Great harm often comes to young women from Rape and her followers: when they are no longer virgins in body and the secret is out, they lose their chances at marriage, bring scandal to their family; so that (like orphans) they run away for shame and, forced into brothels to support themselves, their shame increases into more shame.)[22]

The dire consequences for a victim of rape – here defined to comprise seduction, especially by false oaths, as well as forcible coitus – are realistic and not necessarily judgmental. In the *Gesta Romanorum* the 'moralitees' concerning rape take one away from the concrete crime in a way similar to the allegorizations in a work such as the medieval *Ovide moralisé*. Gower's text, on the other hand, which has the same potential, takes one towards the specific effects of rape on its victims. In general, however, there is not much material in the *Mirour* which relates to rape, especially if compared to the wealth of stories and details in the *Confessio*. It would be very difficult to decide what Gower's attitude towards the topic was if one only had the passages from the French text to go by. How does Gower describe the effects of rape on his female protagonists in his English work? Do they get up unharmed and are they happy to marry their rapists or does Gower dramatize their pain and humiliation? Can one identify an attitude peculiar to Gower by comparing his tales to their sources and analogues? Does he describe these attacks in terms of standard clerical anti-feminist and misogynistic tropes about women and their sexuality, or does he attempt a more sensitive approach, one which may have found resonance with the female component of his audience? These are some of the questions which will be answered in the course of this article through an analysis of the ways in which Gower retells the rapes of certain legendary women, several of whom are explicitly young virgins. Arguably these stories, which dramatize the loss of virginity and its concomitant loss of reputation and, implicitly, social standing, would have been of particular interest and relevance to young female readers/listeners, whether single, or married.

THE PORTRAYAL OF RAPE IN GOWER'S WORKS

This section examines Gower's language in his descriptions of rape, both in English (*Confessio*), French (*Mirour de l'Omme*), and Latin (the glosses in the *Confessio*).[23] The main questions in this context are whether Gower's way of describing this crime reflects its physical nature? Does he stereotype rape by making different occasions sound the same? Is the perspective portrayed that of the victim or the rapist? What connotations are conveyed by the expressions which he uses to describe the crime? Is there a fundamental difference between his usage of the three languages and, in particular, the three genres?

A modern reader would probably expect to find the word 'rape', or a similarly specific and unambiguous term in the *Confessio*, to refer to forced, unlawful intercourse. Gower does not employ 'rape' in the sense of abducting, seducing, or sexually assaulting women.[24] This meaning probably developed slightly later and can be found, for instance, in Osbern Bokenham's *Legendys of Hooly Wummen*: 'In ethna . . . wher . . ./Proserpina was rapt'.[25] Gower also once uses another term, 'to ravish', but again in a metaphorical sense: 'I am so ravisht of the syhte' (IV, l. 683); Amans is carried away by the sight of his Lady's face.[26] 'To ravish', from Old French *ravir*, could also express both the abduction of a woman and/or unlawful intercourse, as shown by Chaucer: 'He was aboute wiȝ maistri/For to rauisse me awai',[27] 'The queene Proserpyna,/which that he rauysshed out of (Ethna)',[28] and in *The Book of Margery Kempe*: 'And on nyghtys had sche most dreed oftyn-tymys . . . for sche was euer a-ferd to a be rauischyd er defilyd'.[29]

If 'rape' was already available, it may be that Gower avoided the above words because of their inherent ambiguity. But it is questionable whether he actually sought to distinguish the meanings. In the *Confessio* there are fifteen expressions which describe rape.[30] The one paraphrase used most often is 'to steal someone's virginity': 'That lusti tresor forto stele' (V, l. 6179), 'Hir maidenhode . . ./Was priveliche stole away' (V, ll. 6246,48), and 'Cam in al sodeinliche, and stall/That thing'(V, ll. 6750–51). The notion of theft implies a lack of consent on the woman's side; an impression, however, which has to be confirmed by the circumstances within the tale. These examples, and nearly all the other ones found in Book V, share one important aspect: Gower treats the topic of rape in general under the heading of Avarice.[31] This may seem odd to the modern reader, but it makes perfect sense within the structure of the *Confessio*. Avarice in general is indeed defined as greed for material goods, but it also has its equivalents in the world of love such as possessive jealousy, stealth, being greedy for many lovers, and rape, all of which are relevant to the confession of the lover.[32] In addition, it seems to imply that women – or their sexuality – are seen as commodities and there is certainly some substance to this suspicion. In the discussion just before the tale of Neptune and Cornix, Genius explains what 'robbery in love' means:

> Riht as a thief makth his chevance
> And robbeth *mennes good* aboute
> In wode and field, wher he goth oute,
> So be ther of these lovers some,
> In wylde stedes wher thei come
> And finden there a womman able,
> And therto place covenable,
> Withoute leve, er that thei fare,
> Thei take a part of that chaffare:
> Yee, though sche were a Scheperdesse,
> Yit wol the lord of wantounesse
> Assaie, althogh sche be unmete,
> For other *mennes good* is swete.
>
> *Confessio*, V, ll.6106–18 (my emphasis)

In Gower's time a woman's sexuality was largely thought of as a commodity, and rape was often thought of as an assault on male property. But the question is whether Gower goes beyond this, whether he talks about the woman's self-image as well as her social loss. Treating rape under the heading of avarice does not necessarily imply a trivialization of the crime. Within the *Confessio* avarice is the vice that Gower appears to detest the most and to see at the root of most division in society. In addition, it even leaves scope for another level of interpretation, that rape can be less an act of passion or sexual desire than of aggression and power, that the greed/avarice of the rapist is to dominate rather than to fornicate lecherously.[33] This is indeed one of the possible interpretations of the last line of the quotation given above where the shepherdess is unsuitable but the fact that she is another man's possession makes her an object of desire. Therefore the treatment of rape in this framework makes the deed seem no less serious.

Thus one would expect to find more expressions in Book V which have economic connotations. Gower also used the word 'to rob' which also emphasizes the connection with violence: 'Wher forto robbe he made a profre' (V, l. 6178). Other examples are *ravine*, meaning 'robbery' and 'greed' – 'Of such Ravine it was pite' (V, l. 5650) – and *bereve*, also meaning 'to rob' – 'Beraft hire such thing as men sein' (V, l. 5647).[34] Indeed all the idioms for rape used in Book V have these material nuances except for one: 'That he a Maiden hath oppressed' (V, l. 889).[35] This term is used again for the rape in 'The Tale of Lucrece': 'Wherof sche swounede in his hond,/And, as who seith, lay ded oppressed' (VII, ll. 4986–7).[36] The general meaning of 'to oppress' is 'to exert physical pressure, to crush'; its usage with the meaning 'to rape' is not confined to Gower.[37] Chaucer uses it as well in Dorigen's lament in 'The Franklin's Tale': 'Whan that she [Lucrece] oppressed was.'[38] All of these expressions, though they may have different connotations, are, however, unambiguous and exact. The reader is not in doubt about the nature of the act described, and that it is unlawful. Sometimes these expressions also convey the violence and the violation of the woman's personal sphere, particularly those idioms which use the image of robbery.

But Gower is by no means always so successful in his choice of words. The first rape in the *Confessio* – or rather an allusion to a possible rape – occurs when Neptune protects Galatea so that Polyphemus 'Ne mihte atteigne hir compaignie' (II, l. 184). This is, however, quite a common euphemism for the sexual act in general; its usage is not restricted to Gower. Chaucer, for instance, has Emelye say in her prayer to Diana 'Noght wol I knowe compaignye of man'.[39] The remaining expressions in the poem fall into two groups, the first one using the rapist's 'wille' as the main component: 'Demene hire at his oghne wille' (II, l. 1101), and 'And Phebus failen of his wille' (III, l. 1720). This is extremely close to Gower's descriptions of non-violent, mutual sexual intercourse. Gower uses highly androcentric terms like 'to have one's will' to delineate this act as in 'And yit Thobie his wille hadde' (VII, l. 5361) and 'That all his wille of hire he hadde' (I, l. 928).[40] These expressions are, as opposed to the ones discussed earlier, ambiguous, and it can only be the context of the tale which decides whether a woman is forced into sexual intercourse. The last two expressions 'And thoghte of hire his lust to take' (II, l. 1109) and 'tok thanne what him liste' (VII, l. 4989) are similar in structure and bear the same androcentric focus as the use of 'his will'.[41] Although 'lust' does not yet have its full meaning and is less negative than its twentieth-century equivalent.[42]

How does this compare to Gower's usage in French? In the *Mirour* there are two passages concerned with rape; the section about the second daughter of Lechery, Rape, and the section concerning the second daughter of Chastity, Virginity, who helps against the vice of Rape. The word used in the heading of the first section is *stupre*, which is a fourteenth-century term derived from the Latin *stuprum*.[43] *Stuprum* means 'dishonour, disgrace, lewdness, violation' and had become one of the technical terms for rape: '*Stuprum* is the felonious taking away of a woman's maidenhood.'[44] *Stupre* is a specific word which is what one would expect of a name for a personification and as such it dominates this section of the *Mirour*.[45] As rape is considered in relation to virgins, this determines the expressions used such as 'desflourie' (l. 8676) or when the rapist 'Au force tolt le pucellage' (l. 8699: Through force he takes away her virginity). But there are hardly any descriptive phrases in the passage. It is more occupied with the consequences of rape than with the act itself. The *Mirour* is rarely narrative; it is more like a listing of cases and sayings, and this affects the language used on this topic.

The second passage is about Virginity which opposes *stupre* (ll. 16825ff.). Here one does find a quite elaborate warning concerning rape:

> La femme fieble a l'omme fort,
> Ou soit a droit ou soit a tort,
> Sa force ne puet resister,
> Ainz son delit et son desport
> Souffrir l'estuet sanz nul desport,
> Si soule la porra trover.[46]

> (The strength of a feeble woman (whether she be right or wrong) cannot resist a strong man, and she must suffer without mercy his delight and pleasure if he succeeds in finding her alone.)[47]

This may not be a precise description of a rape but despite the fact that it leaves out the penetration and the dire consequences for the woman, it does convey the violence and physical nature of the crime.[48] In the same section the Biblical story of the rape of Dinah is mentioned;[49] she is 'ravist et desflouroit' (l. 16966). But – like the Middle English – this is ambiguous: it does not tell us whether Dinah was an accomplice in her abduction/rape/defloration.[50] In French, as in English, the words employed by Gower may not be enough; he may rely on the context of the narrative to clarify the situation.

In the Latin glosses of the *Confessio* one can also find the ambiguity of the term *rapere*, for instance in the Tale of Acis and Galathea where one is told that Polyphemus 'Galatheam rapere voluisset' (II, l. 101). Even if one assumes that the love-sick Cyclops wants to carry the girl off, one may assume that the end is to consummate his desire for her. As in the English text, the Latin glosses sometimes use words which are semantically associated with robbery. This is the case in the Tale of Tereus, 'Hic ponit exemplum contra istos in amoris causa raptores' (V, l. 5554: He puts forward an exemplum against those who are robbers/ravishers for love's sake) and twice in the Tale of Calistona 'Hic ponit exemplum contra istos in causa virginitatis lese predones' (He puts forward an exemplum against robbers who hurt those in the state of virginity) and 'Iupiter virginis castitatem subtili furto surripiens' (V, l. 6227: Jupiter steals by subtle stealth the virgin's chastity). The first of the two expressions in the Tale of Calistona also includes the victim in the phrase. The violent and painful nature of rape is taken into account in some of the glosses, for example in the Rape of Lucrece 'Lucrecia . . . vi oppressit' (VII, l. 4757: He overpowered Lucrece by force) and in the Tale of Apollonius when the grace of God makes sure that 'virginitatem nullus violare potuit' (VIII, l. 1424: no one could injure/pollute her virginity).[51]

In general the *Mirour* and the Latin glosses of the *Confessio* offer less material than the English tales; the glosses are only short descriptions of the contents and the French text is not concerned with narrative. None the less, one can observe some similarities in terminology and contents. The ambiguity of the term *rapere* and other comparable expressions is very noticeable. It is sometimes very difficult to decide what happens and whether it happens with the consent of the woman concerned or not. Although the ambiguity is inherent in the term itself and hence should not be attributed to Gower, it is none the less noteworthy that he did not feel obliged to clarify the situation. Perhaps he was not even aware of the confusing effect of his descriptions. The French *stupre* is certainly the most specific term used by Gower, but as it is the name of a personification, this might be due to the frame of the *Mirour* rather than to a need felt by Gower to express things in one word. Otherwise he uses periphrases to describe rape and sometimes these are definitely euphemisms. In this Gower is similar to medieval culture in general.[52] But having one 'clear' expression is not necessarily an advantage. In general a periphrase can convey more shades of meaning, more connotations than one specific term. Perhaps Gower's expressions are actually preferable to one clinical word like the modern English 'rape' which communicates none of the horror and loss of the victims. The presence of such a term in the *Mirour* certainly does not coincide with a more sympathetic attitude.

In general, Gower manages to avoid any graphic descriptions of the deed, and it would be difficult to read these passages for one's own sexual gratification or as a concession to violent sexual fantasies on the part of the audience. Rape is never aestheticized in the descriptions either. It is disturbing that the same words can be employed to delineate the act of love-making and rape and this may betray Gower's androcentric perspective. But it does not necessarily mean that there is no attempt to accommodate the victim's views. The violent and unlawful nature of the deed is part of the expressions associated with robbery and theft. Gower's way of describing rape is not repetitive; he seems to have endeavoured to find different meaningful ways of writing about this crime.

RAPE AND ATTEMPTED RAPE IN THE TALES AND THEIR SOURCES AND ANALOGUES

Numerous rapes and attempted rapes occur in the *Confessio*, and the first thing that should be mentioned is that they by no means represent all of the rapes which are related in Gower's sources. In Ovid's *Metamorphoses* there are fifty examples of rape, attempted rape, and cases of sexual coercion close to rape,[53] and there are also more rapes in other sources used by Gower such as the *Gesta Romanorum*. This shows clearly that Gower made a choice when he wrote his tales, since he could have selected many other stories to exemplify rape than the ones he made use of. One of the most fruitful ways to approach the many rapes in the *Confessio*, which cannot all be examined here, is to look first at the two most famous cases in the poem, one about a young virgin, the other about a wife. Both tales are at the same time two of his longest and most successful tales and are noteworthy because of the many deliberate deviations from their sources which Gower implemented.

The rape of Philomena – in Ovid Philomela – seems to be a particularly good starting point as it is *the* example against 'ravine' in Book V.[54] The general events of the tale are the same in all four versions considered here, Ovid's *Metamorphoses*, the medieval *Ovide moralisé*, Gower's *Confessio*, and Chaucer's *Legend of Good Women*.[55] Progne, married to Tereus, desires to see her unmarried sister Philomena, and her husband sails to her former home to invite the girl. He immediately falls in love with her and later rapes her and, when threatened with revenge, cuts her tongue out and imprisons her. Philomena gets in contact with Progne by sending her a tapestry she has woven which tells her story and, having been freed by Progne, the two sisters serve Tereus his only son for dinner, after which the gods transform all three protagonists into birds.[56]

Gower sticks to the same basic story, but also implements many changes which reveal his own attitude towards rape. The first change is the shortening of the paraphernalia of the story. The *Ovide moralisé* spends half of the story on the events before Tereus and Philomena sail off together.[57] Gower, on the other hand, lingers for only 46 lines (V, ll. 5551–96) – or less than 10 per cent – on this part of the myth.[58] Chaucer, in the *Legend*, is closer to Ovid and repeats many details, for example, the bad omens at Progne's wedding and the speeches by Pandion, and in his version, which is on the whole much shorter than Gower's, these scenes make up 45 per cent of the story![59] Gower reshapes the story so that the rape and its consequences are more central and emotionally more forceful as befits an exemplum of 'rapine'. The function of the story within the *Confessio*, as opposed to the other texts, is the rape itself.

In Gower, the rape scene is quite detailed but the penetration itself is blended out:

> And sche began to crie and preie,
> 'O fader, o mi moder diere,
> Nou help!' Bot thei ne mihte it hiere,
> And sche was of to litel myht
> Defense ayein so ruide a knyht
> To make, whanne he was so wod

That he no reson understod,
Bot hield hire under in such wise,
That sche ne myhte noght arise,
Bot lay oppressed and desesed,
As if a goshauk hadde sesed
A brid . . .
Bot whan sche to hirselven com,

Confessio, V, ll. 5634–45 and 5661[60]

Again one can note that there is very little in this description that members of the audience could enjoy if they were interested in graphic sexual scenes. As the last line from this passage makes clear, Philomena faints and there is thus no doubt about her possible enjoyment of the act.[61] This is similar in the medieval source:

Lors li fet force et cele crie
Si se debat et se detuert;
A po que de peor ne muert;
D'ire, d'angoisse et de dolor
Change plus de Áant foiz color,
Tranble, palist et si tressue,
Et dist qu'a male ore est issue
De la terre ou ele fu nee,
Quant a tel honte est demenee.[62]

Chaucer also avoids graphic detail, so much so that his scene neglects the horror of the crime:

By force hath this traytour don a dede,
That he hath reft hire of hire maydenhede,
Maugre hire hed, by strengthe and by his myght.

Legend, F, ll. 2324–26

Of course understatement can at times be more powerful than graphic detail, but this description is nearly clinically clean.

In Gower the bird-imagery foreshadows the ending of the tale but, even more, by reminding one of the death the small bird finds in the talons of the goshawk,[63] it shows Philomena's fear and the consequences of rape, namely the victim's feeling that part of her has been killed in the act.[64] But it is mainly after the rape itself that Gower goes even more his own way, showing sympathy for the victim and an insight into how a raped woman might feel. When Gower's Philomena comes back to her senses, she delivers a long speech which cries for justice and revenge:

'And if I be withinne wall
Of Stones closed, thanne I schal
Unto the Stones clepe and crie,
And tellen hem thi *felonie*;
And if I to the wodes wende,
Ther schal I tellen tale and ende,
And crie it to the briddes oute,
That thei schul hiere it al aboute.'
Confessio, V, ll.5665–72 (my emphasis)

This extract from the speech shows that Philomena is not intimidated, and her usage of the term 'felonie' shows that Gower was probably aware of the legal implications of the deed as well. It foreshadows, yet again, the transformation to come as the nightingale will do exactly what Philomena claims the birds would do in her support. Most importantly, though, the passage shows the unnaturalness of the deed. Even nature would help to shout out Tereus's crime and to announce his unworthiness, which his violation of all laws within the family has proven. If one turns to the sources one can find this partly in the *Metamorphoses*. There Philomela is also indignant and threatens:

'si copia detur,
in populos veniam; si silvis clausa tenebor,
inplebo silvas et conscia saxa movebo;
audiet haec aether et si deus ullus in illo est!'

('If I should have the chance, I would go where people throng and tell it; if I am kept shut up in these woods, I will fill the woods with my story and move the very rocks to pity. The air of heaven shall hear it, and if there is any god in heaven, he shall hear it too'.)[65]

In the French version the speech receives a totally different emphasis.The author lets the girl dwell on the fact that Tereus has broken the promises he gave to her father, to return her safe and sound. In this way the rape is turned into a crime against the father rather than the woman. It also makes Philomena appeal to Tereus to repent.[66] All in all the speech has lost most of the feeling of outrage and most of its strength.[67] Chaucer's Philomena does not speak at all after the rape, she only calls to her family for help during the act.[68] Gower also establishes the connection between Philomena's character and speech more prominently than any other of these authors; even when her tongue is cut out she is not totally silenced:

Bot yit whan he hire tunge refte,
A litel part therof belefte,
Bot sche with al no word mai soune,
Bot chitre and as a brid jargoune.

Confessio, V, ll. 5697–700

This innovation in Gower's account shows how he endeavoured to make the transformation into a bird look as fitting as possible.

The following scenes are told with rapid speed by Gower. Unlike Ovid and the *Ovide moralisé* Gower quickly comes to the second outburst of violence in the tale, the killing of Ithis and the meal. Gower presents a unique interpretation as to why this punishment was chosen by Progne.[69] It is true that Tereus 'A Sone hath, which as his lif He loveth' (V, ll. 5886–7) but there is more to it for Gower:

Bot thus his oughne fleissh and blod
Himself devoureth ayein kinde,
As he that was tofore unkinde.

Confessio, V, ll.5904–06

Gower makes a connection between the rape and the meal, between the unnaturalness of the deeds, and also seems to give the murder and the rape equal status. After this scene Gower makes the transformations as meaningful as possible by clearly explaining how the changes continue the mental states of the human beings. Tereus is a treacherous lapwing,[70] Progne is a swallow who seeks a human environment to tell wives about the adulterer Tereus, and Philomena is a nightingale who shuns people and sings about her shame.[71] Again Gower develops new paths, but an even more important difference between his and the other versions of the tale occurs after the transformations. In Ovid Philomela never speaks again after her tongue has been cut off. In the *Ovide moralisé* the nightingale Philomena is allowed to utter two words, onomatopoeic for the nightingale's song: 'Oci! Oci!' (Kill! Kill!).[72] Gower, on the other hand, gives Philomena a long complaint and tries to show how the transformation should be read as at least a partial compensation for her fate. He restores her speech and control over life. The transformations give her 'joie' (V, l. 5989) and 'merthe' (V, l. 5990) and her behaviour as a nightingale afterwards is detailed thoroughly:

For after that sche was a brid,
Hir will was evere to ben hid,
And forto duelle in prive place,
That noman scholde sen hir face
For schame, which mai noght be lassed,
Of thing that was tofore passed,

> Whan that sche loste hir maidenhiede (. . .)
> And in hir song al openly
> Sche makth hir pleignte and seith, 'O why,
> O why ne were I yit a maide?'
> (. . .) 'Ha, nou I am a brid,
> Ha, nou mi face mai ben hid:
> Thogh I have lost mi Maidenhede,
> Schal noman se my chekes rede.'
>
> *Confessio*, V, ll. 5949–55, 5977–79, and 5985–88[73]

Although the transformation of the woman Philomena into a bird has indeed delivered her from her ordeal and imminent death, one prominent feature of her suffering is a feeling of shame.[74] Gower recognizes that the innocence of the raped woman in no way prevents her from feeling such shame, though not caused by complicity.[75] She experiences shame and embarrassment because of the pollution she has suffered and also because of the public exposure of intimate details – like the nightingale who constantly tries to hide in the bushes. Despite herself she also feels guilty.[76] Thus Philomena's behaviour as a bird continues therefore her feelings as a woman. She is not used as a mouthpiece by Gower to convey the impression that women who have been raped are morally inferior or that they are to blame and therefore should feel shame. Rather he is displaying thoughtfully how a young woman could be shamefully embarrassed about the sexual pollution and common knowledge of her rape and how she might try to evade the public stare. Gower's generally sympathetic view can also be seen in the fact that the focus shifts from Tereus and his lust to the woman. In Ovid's *Metamorphoses*, the transformation of Philomena is dealt with in one line.

The Rape of Lucrece is the second famous rape case in the *Confessio*. It deals with the forcible rape of a married woman, rather than a virgin, in line with Westminster I's official provision for the rape of matrons. Lucrece's age is not specified, but it is as well to remember that 'matrons' were not necessarily elderly women. One of Gower's sources is again Ovid, but this time the *Fasti*.[77] In Ovid's account Tarquin immediately falls in love with Lucretia and returns the day after he has visited her with her husband.[78] He is warmly received by her as a guest and relative. At night he takes his sword, sneaks into Lucretia's room and says to her:

> 'nil agis: eripiam' dixit 'per crimina vitam:
> falsus adulterii testis adulter ero:
> interimam famulum, cum quo deprensa fereris.'
> succubuit famae victa puella metu.

('Resistance is in vain,' said he, 'I'll rob thee of honour and of life. I, the adulterer, will bear false witness to thine adultery. I'll kill a slave and rumour will have it that thou were caught with him.' Overcome by fear of infamy, the dame gave way).[79]

The following morning Lucretia calls her father and husband and when they see her shame and hear what has happened 'dant veniam facto genitor coniunxque coacto: 'quam' dixit 'veniam vos datis, ipsa nego.' (Her husband and her sire pardoned the deed enforced. She said, 'The pardon that you give, I do refuse myself.')[80] She immediately stabs herself and, whilst falling down, takes care to arrange her clothes to cover her.[81] Half dead, she seems to be able to hear Brutus's speech and the revolt against Tarquin breaks out on her funeral march.

Gower implemented some significant changes which illustrate his attitude towards his material and the crime committed in it. The opening of the story seems to follow the original. The most important change occurs in Lucrece's bedroom when Tarquin, armed with his sword, tries to 'persuade' Lucrece to consent to sexual intercourse. Unlike Lucretia, Lucrece awakes already in Tarquin's arms, and unlike Ovid's – and Livy's – Tarquin, Gower's villain does not play upon Lucrece's sense of honour when he threatens her into submission. He announces that he will kill her and members of her household if he is unsuccessful:

> With that this worthi wif awok,
> Which thurgh tendresce of wommanhiede
> Hire vois hath lost for pure drede,
> That o word speke sche ne dar:
> And ek he bad hir to be war,
> For if sche made noise or cry,
> He seide, his swerd lay faste by
> *To slen hire and hire folk aboute.*
>
> *Confessio*, VII, ll.4974–81 (my emphasis)

Because of the many lives under threat Lucrece swoons, and in this Gower has certainly given his heroine a much stronger excuse than Ovid.[82] These changes make quite clear that Gower wants Lucrece to look as innocent as possible. There is no consistent interpretation of this scene that could make Lucrece appear as an accomplice. It also rules out the question of even involuntary pleasure on her side.

It is illuminating at this point to compare Gower's differences from two other versions of Lucretia's rape, retold in roughly contemporary collections of stories: in Chaucer's *Legend* and Christine de Pisan's *City of Ladies*. Chaucer's account is, on the whole, closer to the original than Gower's,[83] and his Lucresse is intimidated with the same threat as Lucretia:

'As I shal in the stable slen thy knave,
And ley hym in thy bed, and loude crye
That I the fynde in swich avouterye.
And thus thow shalt be ded and also lese
Thy name, for thow shalt non other chese.'

Legend, F, ll. 1807–11

The same is true for de Pisan's heroine:

Et a brief dire, quant il l'ot assez sermonee par grans promesses, dons et offres que faire voulsist sa voulenté et il vid que priere riens ne luy valloit, il tira son espee et la manaça d'occire sa elle disoit mot et se elle ne se consentoit a sa voulenté. Et elle respondi que hardiement l'occist et que mieulx amoit mourir que s'i consentir. Tarquin, qui vid bien que riens ne luy valoit, s'avisa d'une autre grant malice et dist que il diroit publiquement qu'il l'avoit trouvee avecques un de ses sergeans. Et a brief dire, de ceste chose tant l'espoventa, penssant que on croiroit aux parolles de luy, que au paraler elle souffry sa force.[84]

(Put briefly, after trying to coax her for a long time with promises, gifts and favors, he saw that entreaties were getting him nowhere. He drew his sword and threatened to kill her if she made a sound and did not submit to his will. She answered that he should go ahead and kill her, for she would rather die than consent. Tarquin, realizing that nothing would help him, concocted a great malice, saying that he would publicly declare that he had found her with one of his sergeants. In brief, he so scared her with his threat (for she thought that people would believe him) that finally she suffered his rape.)[85]

All of the authors are unequivocal in their condemnation of the rape. All leave no doubt about the fact that it is done entirely against her will, yet Gower recognizes a possible reproach to Lucretia's behaviour and therefore creates an entirely individual version.

The rape itself is not described at all by Ovid; Gower and Chaucer both add one detail which is not in their source, namely that Lucrece/Lucresse swoons:[86]

She loste bothe at ones wit and breth,
And in a swogh she lay, and wex so ded
Men myghte smyten of hire arm or hed;
She feleth no thyng, neyther foul ne fayr.

Legend, F, ll. 1815–18

And thus he broghte hire herte in doute,
That lich a Lomb whanne it is sesed
In wolves mouth, so was desesed
Lucrece, which he naked fond:
Wherof sche swounede in his hond,
And, as who seith, lay ded oppressed.

Confessio, VII, ll. 4982–87

The next morning, when her husband, her father and her cousin Brutus have arrived, Gower confronts his readers with a woman who feels shame because of the violence that has been done to her:

Hire wofull chiere let doun falle
For schame and couthe unnethes loke. (. . .)
And sche, which hath hire sorwes grene,
Hire wo to telle thanne assaieth,
Bot tendre schame hire word delaieth (. . .)
Whan that sche sih sche moste nede,
Hire tale betwen schame and drede
Sche tolde, noght withoute peine.

Confessio; VII, ll. 5032–3, 5040–2, and 5047–9

Gower is very sensitive to the difficulties Lucrece has in expressing what has happened.[87] Again this emphasizes that hers is not a shame of complicity but a shame of pollution. There is also an awareness that her family and its reputation are implicated in this. Gower enforces this interpretation by making Lucrece reject the forgiveness of her family 'Bot sche Ö Of hem wol no foryivenesse' (VII, ll. 5058–59).[88] Lucrece has done nothing which necessitates the forgiveness of her male relatives. But the rape has destroyed a significant part of her identity as a woman and may by association besmirch the name of her family on the public stage, regardless of her actual innocence. Lucrece chooses to express this by annihilating the body that had to suffer shame; she kills herself.[89] Like Ovid's Lucretia she takes care that even in her death she will look decent and arranges her clothes whilst falling to the ground. Gower does not once mention the Christian objections to suicide, or the negative interpretation of her death proposed by St Augustine. In *The City of God* he asks 'Si adulterata, cur laudata; si pudica, cur occisa?' (If she is adulterous, why is she praised? If chaste, why was she put to death?)[90] Gower rejects this misogynistic reading and lets his heroine die with dignity and without reproach

A comparison of the rapes of Philomena and Lucrece demonstrates that both are dominated by the same themes. In both stories the victims are cleared as fully as possible. In both cases Gower tried to think himself into the position of the victim. He successfully expressed the feeling of shame which is not based on complicity, a reproach women often had and still have to endure, in addition to the pain that has already been inflicted upon them. He also makes every attempt to show the effects on the woman's identity. In the case of Philomena this is done by physical transformation, in the case of Lucrece through suicide. One of the innovations in Gower's treatment of Philomena was his attempt to compensate her for her fate. Is there any element that could reconcile Lucrece partly to her fate? When Brutus pulls the bloody knife out of her body and swears revenge we are told that:

> And sche tho made a contienance,
> Hire dedlich yhe and ate laste
> In thonkinge as it were up caste,
> And so behield him in the wise,
> Whil sche to loke mai suffise.
>
> *Confessio*, VII, ll. 5088–92

In Ovid it seems as if Lucretia might still be alive 'illa iacens ad verba oculos sine lumine movit visaque concussa dicta probare coma.' (At these words, even as she lay, she moved her lightless eyes and seemed by the stirring of her hair to ratify the speech);[91] Gower seems to try to make his Lucrece as aware as possible of the fact that her shameful rape is the cause of the end of the rape of her country by Tarquin's family.[92] In the highly political Book VII of the *Confessio* this seems as much of a compensation as any victim could hope for.[93]

Let us now turn to one of the cases of attempted rape, namely the Tale of Neptune and Cornix. This tale is *the* exemplum for robbery, entirely comprehensible in terms of the high premium which was placed on a young woman's virginity as her 'treasure':

> Which thing, mi Sone, I thee forbede,
> For it is an ungoodly dede.
> For who that takth be Robberie
> His love, he mai noght justefie
> His cause, and so fulofte sithe
> For ones that he hath be blithe
> He schal ben after sory thries.
>
> *Confessio*, V, ll. 6135–41

In the *Ovide moralisé* there is a total refusal by the author to believe the story. He does eventually relate the tale, but it is marked as a lie, a fiction. Here the girl is transformed into a bird by Pallas without asking for it:

Quant la meschine s'en fuioit
Et que Neptunus la sivoit,
Qui despuceler la cuida,
Pallas sorvint, si li aida,
Si la prist en sa compaignie.[94]

(When the girl was fleeing, and Neptune, who hoped to deflower her, was following her, Pallas came and helped her and took her into her company.)

Gower follows Ovid's original more closely, where the girl tells her tale herself:

inde deos hominesque voco; nec contigit ullum
vox mea mortalem: mota est pro virgine virgo
auxiliumque tulit.

(Then I cried out for help to gods and men but my cries reached no mortal ear. But the virgin goddess heard a virgin's prayer and came to my aid.[95])

In Gower's version of the tale the girl is also horrified by the attack of the god and 'dredende alle schame' (V, l. 6184) cries to Pallas for support to keep her 'honour' (V, l. 6291). To the modern reader it might seem as if the girl is asking for her own victimization. Why can the girl not be helped without being dehumanized? In Gower, however, this act takes on new meaning. Gower describes the girl's state of mind after the transformation as follows:

With fetheres blake as eny cole
Out of hise armes in a throwe
Sche flih before his yhe a Crowe;
Which was to hire a more delit,
To kepe hire maidenhede whit
Under the wede of fethers blake,
In Perles whyte than forsake
That no lif mai restore ayein.

Confessio, V, ll. 6204–11

There is nothing of this 'delit' in Ovid, none of the feeling of freedom that comes across when Cornix flies off in front of Neptune's eyes. The strong opposition between the black of the outer appearance and the white of her virginity, the inner state, is also new. Again the tale shows the horrors of rape very sensitively as the woman concerned prefers to inhabit an animal's body rather than stay in her own body which is about to be violated. Gower endeavours to raise our sympathy and compassion for the innocent girl by making the plea to the goddess as emotional as possible. The girl's relief after her transformation does not make her sound like a mouthpiece of the ideology that a woman's virginity is her most precious and definitive quality. Rather it conveys the horror rape holds for women; and this without actually relating a rape at all.

After Cornix's story one is immediately confronted with Calistona's fate, which is one of two examples examined here where the situation is not quite as clear as in the three previous tales. How is Calistona's virginity lost? The reader is told that Calistona's virginity 'Was priveliche stole away' (V, l. 6248). This description tells us very little about the loss of Calistona's virginity; Gower even omits to inform us whether it was done with or without her consent. The sources tell a different story. In Ovid the reader is told that after Jupiter approaches the girl in Diana's shape,

> illa quidem contra, quantum modo femina posset
> (adspiceres utinam, Saturnia, mitior esses),
> illa quidem pugnat, sed quem superare puella,
> quisve Iovem poterat?

> (She, in truth, struggled against him with all her girlish might – hadst thou been there to see, Saturnia, thy judgement were more kind! – but whom could a girl o'ercome, or who could prevail against Jove?)[96]

The *Ovide moralisé*, which stays very close to the original, makes it just as clear that the girl is being forced.[97] The situation is very similar in the Tale of Leucothoe. Phebus has fallen deeply in love with the maiden Leucothoe and Gower describes her defloration as follows:

> And thus lurkende upon his stelthe
> In his await so longe he lai,
> Til it befell upon a dai,
> That he thurghout hir chambre wall
> Cam in al sodeinliche, and stall
> That thing which was to him so lief.
>
> *Confessio*, V, ll. 6746–51

'Stall' gives some suggestion of the woman's unwillingness but the question of consent is left unresolved. In Ovid the events are very ambiguous indeed: the god gains access to the girl's room in the shape of her mother and when he reveals himself in his magnificence, the girl is terrified and drops her spindle but then accepts his embraces without protest.[98] When she faces her father she claims: 'ille vim tulit invitae' ('It was he who forced me to it! I did not wish it!').[99] The *Ovide moralisé*, on the other hand, leaves no doubt about what is happening:

Li dieux en sa forme revint;
La bele court prendre et saisir;
Par force ot de lui son plesir.
Cele a la force en gré soufferte.[100]

(The god returned to his shape, he rushed forward to grasp and seize the fair lady. With force he had of her his pleasure, she suffered through force, because of his will.)

Why does Gower in these two cases omit to show indisputably that these virgins are being raped, especially when the *Ovide moralisé* reminds him that this is the consistent interpretation of Ovid's myths? One satisfying interpretation of the material is that Gower does not feel the need to clarify the situation any further. The Tale of Calistona is the second example against robbery in the *Confessio* following The Tale of Cornix, with the words 'An other tale therupon' (V, l. 6223). The Tale of Leucothoe is an exemplum for another crime which can be committed by lovers, namely stealth 'Be weie of Stelthe to asssaie,(In loves cause and takth his preie' (V, ll. 6708–9). As it is quite clear from the frame that the sexual act is achieved without the consent of the woman – by stealth and by robbery – there is no need to make this point again in the tale. Gower seems to have felt that if the male lover 'forgets' to ask his lady for consent, this constitutes an act of violence even if there is no description of the terror of the woman concerned or of her fighting back. It also seems that these two tales focus more on the social consequences of rape rather than the physical trauma inflicted by the act itself. The first rape which is told in Book V – that of Philomena – has done this very elaborately and there is no need within the terse structure of the poem to repeat a message that has been conveyed so convincingly before. I would maintain that the stories of Calistona and Cornix, which concentrate on the violent and unsympathetic reaction of the girls' social environments, show an important part of Gower's attitude towards rape. By omitting the struggle and the violence he shows that even when the only information one has is that the woman did not explicitly consent, she is still the victim and not an accomplice; she has still been robbed.

CONCLUSIONS

The previous pages have shown that the rape scenes Gower has selected are not graphic enough to be a source of pleasure to anyone in the audience and that he certainly avoids all danger of being accused of exploiting the element of rape in these tales. But this does not mean that Gower neglects the physical nature of the crime, that he depicts it in a 'hygienic' way. There are other means of conveying the import of what has happened to the woman than a detailed description of the deed itself. In the stories where Gower concentrates on the horror of rape – as opposed to its consequences – the victims are not unchanged after they have been defiled and humiliated, nor is their attitude to their bodies. Quite on the contrary, their standing as women, within the moral strictures of their society, has been destroyed for good. Philomena's transformation and Lucrece's suicide are not only potent symbols of this but they are also presented with an inner logic that makes the events the consistent results of the stories. Gower certainly does not only pay lip-service to the fact that rape is base but he *shows* this consistently and masterfully in the suffering of the victims. There is no difference between his claim that rape has destructive effects on a woman's life and the behaviour and emotional states of the female characters in the tales. The mental violation of the women is in the foreground but the physical horror of rape is not forgotten, and one of the most sensitive and subtle examples for this is Lucrece's outer appearance after her rape:

> And caste awey hire freissh aray,
> As sche which hath the world forsake,
> And tok upon the clothes blake (. . .)
> Thei sihe hire clothes al desguised,
> And hou sche hath hirself despised,
> Hir her hangende unkemd aboute.
>
> *Confessio*, VII, ll. 5000–02 and 5021–23[101]

Gower ensures that the audience can in no way ignore the consequences of this kind of violence against women as the reader is a witness to the rape scenes; it is impossible to avert one's gaze. Details are sometimes left out to shorten the tales, and this may cause confusion in the reader as to what exactly happens in the story, whether a certain tale contains a case of rape at all. But Gower's tales show one significant difference from real-life rape and attempts by women to prove that it has actually taken place. There is no need for witnesses within the context of the story. In reality the lack of witnesses often bars women from receiving justice, but in the *Confessio* Gower as narrator presents the words and actions of the women as proof enough, leaving us in no doubt as to the guilt and innocence of the various protagonists, and forcing the reader to become witness to this.

In order to confirm the women's innocence Gower outlines the reasons why these men commit rape. The motivations cited for their deed are similar, Tereus is 'Assoteth of hire love so' (V, l. 5618), Phebus 'withoute reste is peined/With al his herte to coveite' Leucothoe (V, ll. 6720–21), Neptune ' in his herte such plesance/He tok whan he this Maiden sih' (V, ll. 6164–65), and Tarquin:

> The resoun of hise wittes alle
> Hath lost; for *love* upon his part
> Cam thanne (. . .).
>
> *Confessio*, VII, ll. 4850–52 (my emphasis)

This love can hardly be Gower's celebrated 'love honeste', but apart from the fact that the rapists are in love/lust with their victims, we do not receive any further insight into their motivation. For Gower the root of rape was the same as that of all other sins, namely passion overcoming reason.[102] For Gower love was an ambivalent force which could, if not controlled, turn a human being into animal, into a rapist, a 'wolf' (V, l. 5633, VII, l. 4984), a 'Lyon' (V, l. 5684), a 'tigre' (VII, l. 4944), and a 'tirant' (V, l. 5646, VII, l. 4959). A rapist is 'so wod/That he no reson understod' (V, ll. 5639–40); it is not the victim who is dehumanized, though the rape can break her, but the victimiser. In the *Mirour* the same loss of humanity can be observed in the rapist:

Au fin qu'il puist son fol corage
Par ce complir, lors d'autre rage,
Sicomme la beste q'est sauvage,
Qant faim luy streigne et appetite
Sa proie, ensi de son oultrage
Au force tolt le pucellage,
Q'a sa priere fuist desdite.

Mirour, ll. 8694–700

(If he cannot accomplish his mad desire, then, in a rage like a wild beast when hunger oppresses it and it is famished for its prey, he forces her virginity, which had been refused to his requests.)[103]

But does Gower's depiction of rape gives us any evidence about his attitude towards women in general? Gower realized that women are victimized not just by their rapists, but by their social environment and illustrates this in several cases. Gower seems to try to think himself into the position of the raped woman and to describe the feelings such a woman might have. He also attempts to give the women involved some kind of compensation and he is careful not to blame the victims or to criticize their behaviour. Gower certainly does not exploit the topic of rape to show woman's tempting or deceitful nature, or that she means 'yes' when she says 'no'. Gower displays a consistent vision of rape in the *Confessio*. The single stories are like parts of a mosaic which, taken together, reveal his attitude as one of sympathy and provide an awareness of the suffering as well as the consequences connected with this crime. Within the didactic framework of the *Confessio* Gower's rethinking and reworking of rape, provides an alternative paradigm of women and female sexuality, which the audience, as well as Amans, may have found instructive.

Notes

1. Louis Tanon, *Registre criminel de la Justice de Saint Martin des Champs à Paris au XIVe Siècle* (Paris, 1877), p. 88. This article has been adapted from my doctoral thesis 'The Representation of Women in John Gower's *Confessio Amantis*' (unpublished D.Phil. thesis, Unversity of Oxford, 1997). It is dedicated to Noor.

2. Translation from Kathryn Gravdal, *Ravishing Maidens: Writing Rape in Medieval French Literature and Law* (Philadelphia, 1991), p. 138.

3. All quotations by line number from the *Confessio Amantis* have been taken from the edition by George C. Macaulay, *The English Works of John Gower*, Early English Text Society, Extra Series 81–2 (1900–01).

4. Gower's version of the rape of Philomena is also discussed by Carolyn Dinshaw, 'Rivalry, rape and manhood: Gower and Chaucer' in R.F. Yeager (ed.), *Chaucer and Gower: Difference, Mutuality, Exchange* (Victoria BC, 1991), where it is used as a gloss on Chaucer's 'Troilus and Criseyde' to draw conclusions about the rivalry between Chaucer and Gower. A.S.G. Edwards, 'Gower's Women in the *Confessio Amantis*', *Medievalia* 16 (1993), argues that Gower displays a lack of interest in the female and does not treat women sympathetically in the *Confessio*. He claims that either their suffering is made little of, or that they are blamed for what they do to men. In this article I shall take issue with both of these claims.

5. A recent article, which sums up the discussion of Chaucer being accused of *raptus*, is Christopher Cannon, '*Raptus* in the Chaumpaigne Release and a Newly Discovered Document Concerning the Life of Geoffrey Chaucer', *Speculum* 68 (1993); see p. 79 for a discussion of the ways in which Westminster I and II blurred and confused the distinction between the two definitions of 'rape'.

6. Before the Statute of Westminster I there was no common agreement on the status of rape, but most commentators, such as Bracton, concentrated on the rape of virgins only. There is a notable absence in legal treatises concerning the rape of non-virgins. The rape of virgins, however, was considered a felony and punished by castration and blinding; see, for instance, G. E. Woodbine (ed.), *Bracton on the Laws and Customs of England* (Cambridge MA, 1968), vol. 2, pp. 414–15.

7. Quoted from John Marshall Carter, *Rape in Medieval England: A Historical and Sociological Study* (Lanham, 1985), pp. 36–7. Carter himself quotes the *Statutes of the Realm*, vol. 1, ed. A. Luders, T.E. Tomlins, and J. Raithby (11 vols, London, 1810–28), p. 87.

8. Carter, *Rape in Medieval England*, p. 153. Another historian who shares this view is Barbara A. Hanawalt, *Crime and Conflict in English Communities, 1300–1348* (Cambridge MA, and London, 1979), p. 106. For further general discussion of these issues see Roy Porter, 'Rape – Does it Have a Historical Meaning?', in Sylvana Tomaselli and Roy Porter (eds), *Rape* (Oxford, 1986).

9. Because of the differences between the manuscripts it is impossible to give an exact count, but out of the seventy stories of the Middle English manuscript edited by Herrtage, four are concerned with rape. Gower knew the Latin version of the *Gesta* and used it as his source but here the analogues from the medieval English translation have been used. The English translation quoted here stems from *c.* 1440. See 'Introduction' to *The Early English Versions of the* Gesta Romanorum, ed. Sidney J. Herrtage, Early English Text Society, Extra Series 33 (1879), p. xix.

10. Ibid., p. 165.

11. Ibid.

12. The 'moralitee' of the tale is confusing as it cites another rape law as having been established by God, that the deliverer *should* marry the victim.

13. Herrtage (ed.), *Gesta Romanorum*, p. 219.

14. It has to be said that there is no internal logic in the story; the motivation of the woman for preferring the man who has raped her and was about to behead her are neither explored nor explained.

15. Rape, however, is displaced as the main topic of the tale; the woman's ungratefulness towards her saviour – he received many wounds when he fought for her – and the fact that she has given her word to two men are more important. In addition, this tale seems to present a male fantasy where men can hurt, even attempt to kill women and still be sexually attractive. This kind of fantasy is, of course, one of the many possible reasons for relating stories concerned with rape.

16. An additional four tales are centred on false accusations of rape and therefore present the woman as the villain.

17. Tale no. 773 in Mary Macleod Banks (ed.), *An Alphabet of Tales*, Early English Text Society, Original Series 126–7 (London, 1904–05).

18. Maureen Cheney Curnow, 'The *Livre de la Cité des Dames* of Christine de Pisan: A Critical Edition' (unpublished Ph.D. thesis, Vanderbilt University, 1975), p. 885. The term 'vray' in the last line might be better translated with 'true' than 'credible'.

19. Translation from *The Book of the City of Ladies*, tr. Earl J. Richards (New York, 1982), pp. 160–1.

20. All quotations from the *Mirour de l'Omme* have been taken from the edition of George C. Macaulay, *The Complete Works of John Gower* (London, 1899–1902); see ll. 8665–76 for the rape of virgins.

21. It will become clear later on that the *Mirour* is more explicit about the concrete consequences of rape whereas Gower follows different objectives in the tales of the *Confessio*.

22. Translation from *Mirour de l'Omme: The Mirror of Mankind*, tr. William B. Wilson, Medieval Texts and Studies 5 (East Lansing, 1992), p. 120. Citations by line number.

23. There is no material in Gower's main Latin poem *Vox Clamantis* which relates to rape except when the term 'rapina' is once mentioned in a list of vices in Book VII, Chapter 21, l. 1201, see Macaulay, *Complete Works*.

24. Gower uses the term *rape* three times in the *Confessio* but always with the meaning 'haste' or 'to hasten', see III, ll. 517, 1625, and 1678. This usage is common in Middle English, but it is actually a different word, which is derived from the Old Norse *hrapa*.

25. Osbern Bokenham, *Legendys of Hooly Wummen*, ed. Mary S. Serjeantson, Early English Text Society, Original Series 206 (1938), p. 40, ll. 1456–57; this text was completed by 1447. This usage of the word was derived from the Latin *rapere*, meaning 'to seize, carry off', and the Anglo-Norman *raper*, and it reflects the ambiguity of the Latin term.

26. In view of some of the issues to be discussed in this section it is important to note that *ravish* also had the meaning of 'to steal'; *Middle English Dictionary* (Ann Arbor, 1956–ongoing), vol. 9, p. 177.

27. Walter H. French and Charles B. Hale (eds), *Degare* in *Middle English Metrical Romances* (New York, 1930), p. 314, ll. 886–7; this text was written about 1330.

28. All quotations from Chaucer are from Larry D. Benson et al. (eds), *The Riverside Chaucer*, 2nd edn (Oxford, 1988) and are cited by line number. 'The Merchant's Tale', IV, ll. 2229–30.

29. S.B. Meech and H.E. Allen (eds), *The Book of Margery Kempe*, Early English Text Society, Original Series 212 (1940), p. 241, ll. 7–10.

30. There are more expressions listed here than there are rapes as some of them have been described more than once.

31. In the *Mirour*, on the other hand, rape is treated under the heading of lechery.

32. See in particular V, ll. 60–105, where Amans links avarice for wealth to that for woman when he describes his lady as a 'tresor'.

33. There is, however, no conclusive evidence that Gower was aware of this possible reading, as the tales attribute the rapes to uncontrollable lust.

34. This expression is used again in 'The Tale of Apollonius' and again it has a slight economic connotation, this time as Leonin wants to sell Thaise's virginity in his brothel: 'That he with strengthe ayein hire leve Tho scholde hir maidenhod bereve' (VIII, ll. 1439–40).

35. It is interesting that this is also the only expression in Book V which is *not* used as part of the discussion of avarice as it is part of Genius's excursus on the Belief of the Greeks.

36. In this case the English mirrors the Latin expression 'Lucreciam (. . .) oppressit', gloss to VII, ll. 4756ff.

37. *Middle English Dictionary*, vol. 7, p. 241.

38. 'The Franklin's Tale', V, l. 1406.

39. 'The Knight's Tale', I, l. 2311.

40. Compare also other examples as Eneas who 'dede al holi what he wolde' (IV, l. 91) and who certainly did not force himself upon Dido. Also the case of Cornide's lover, who is so irrelevant that Gower does not even name him and yet is still the subject of the act of love-making: 'And hadde of hire al that he wolde' (III, l. 791).

41. There is a semantic difference between *lust* and *liste* as the latter is less strong than *lust*.

42. *Lust* can indeed mean 'physical/sexual desire' or 'bodily appetite', but it also has far more neutral meanings such as 'enjoyment', 'vigour', and 'fertility'; see *Middle English Dictionary*, vol. 6, pp. 1309–12.

43. A. Tobler and E. Lommatzsch (eds), *Altfranzösisches Wörterbuch* (Berlin, Stuttgart, and Wiesbaden, 1925, repr. 1973), vol. 9, p. 1043.

44. William J. Whittaker (ed.), *The Mirror of Justices* (London, 1895), p. 29.

45. See *Mirour*, ll. 8669, 8689, 8726.

46. *Mirour*, ll. 16945–50.

47. Translation from *Mirour de l'Omme*, p. 233. It should be added that *desport* means 'pleasure' as well as 'mercy' and that l. 16946 might be better translated as 'whether right or wrong' than in Wilson's translation.

48. This extract is part of a larger passage in which Gower warns virgins not to leave the house on their own as they will be without help if they should be attacked. It is describing a rape-scene but details are missing.

49. Cf. Genesis 34:1–31.

50. In the spirit of the passage the girl is certainly blamed for visiting far-away countries without being accompanied, although she may not have encouraged the advances of her 'admirer'. In the Bible, Gower's ultimate source, the feelings and actions of the girl are left unexplored as well.

51. The same term as in the Rape of Lucrece, 'oppressit', is also used in the Tale of Tereus where he 'crushes/overcomes her virginity through his violence'.

52. Gravdal, *Ravishing Maidens*, p. 2.

53. See Leo C. Curran, 'Rape and Rape Victims in the *Metamorphoses*', *Arethusa* 11 (1978), p. 214.

54. See *Confessio* V, ll. 5546–50; the tale itself follows ll. 5551ff. A very useful study of the myth in general is Patricia Klindienst Joplin, 'The Voice of the Shuttle Is Ours', in Lynn A. Higgins and Brenda R. Silver (eds), *Rape and Representation*, Gender and Culture (New York, 1991), pp. 35–64.

55. Macaulay cites Ovid as Gower's direct source; see note to V, l. 5551, but H. C. Mainzer shows that at least some details have been taken from the *Ovide moralisé*, for example the names of the birds, and therefore maintains that Gower was working with both versions; see 'A Study of the Sources of the *Confessio Amantis* of John Gower' (unpublished D.Phil. thesis, University of Oxford, 1967), p. 232.

56. Chaucer stops short after the reunion of the two sisters and leaves the revenge and the transformation out.

57. This is roughly 730 lines out of 1468 lines altogether.

58. The story has 597 lines and therefore 46 lines represent 7.7 per cent. The 'real' Ovid also spends a considerable amount of time on the events before Philomela and Tereus sail off – the episode takes up 35 per cent (87 out of 251 lines) of the tale. In addition, Ovid relates many details which Gower reduces, for instance, the long description of the festival of Bacchus (ll. 587–600) and Tereus's meal (ll. 647–666); see Ovid, *Metamorphoses*, ed. and tr. Frank J. Miller (Cambridge MA, 1916, repr. 1951). All subsequent quotations are taken from this edition.

59. The Tale of Philomena takes up only 176 lines of the *Legend.*

60. Bruce Harbert points out that Gower intensifies the pathos of the rape by expanding on a cry only mentioned in Ovid. See 'The Myth of Tereus', *Medium Aevum* 61 (1972), 211.

61. Cf. Lucrece's swooning, as will be seen.

62. Cornelis de Boer (ed.), *Ovide moralisé*, Verhandelingen der Koinklijke Nederlandse Akademie van Wetenschappen, Afd. Letterkunde, d. 15, 21 (Amsterdam, 1915–38), Book VI, ll. 3014–22, p. 353. All subsequent quotations taken from this edition. There are actually two rape descriptions in the *Ovide moralisé* which have been turned into one by Gower. The second scene in the medieval Ovid is less vague than the first one cited above:

> Car cil totes voies l'assaut,
> Si l'esforce tant et justise
> Que tot a force l'a conquise
> Et trestot son buen an a fet.

(For he attacks her anyway, he forces and dominates her so much that he conquers her by force. And he takes all his desire of her.) *Ovide moralisé*, VI, ll. 3052–55, p. 353.

63. In the *Mirour* the goshawk is the attendant of Lady Avarice: 'Si ot sur l'un des poigns assis/Un ostour qui s'en vait toutdis Pour proye', *Mirour*, ll. 906–8. (Seated on one of her fists she had a goshawk, which is always flying off for prey, Wilson (tr.), *Mirror of Mankind*, p. 16.)

64. Tereus is not only described as a bird of prey but also as a wolf (V, l. 5633) and as a lion (V, l. 5684) and some of these comparisons can already be found in Ovid where Philomela is a dove in talons and a lamb in the wolf's mouth, see Ovid, *Metamorphoses*, VI, ll. 527–30.

65. Ovid, *Metamorphoses*, pp. 326–27, VI, ll. 545–48.

66. See *Ovide moralisé*, VI, ll. 3023–48. Ovid's Philomela is much angrier, she, too, reminds Tereus of his broken promises but makes more of his marriage duties than his relationship to her father. Repentance, unsurprisingly, is not to be found in the original version.

67. This is even before the allegorical interpretation which follows right after the tale in ll. 3685–840.

68. See Chaucer, *Legend of Good Women*, F, ll. 2328–29.

69. All versions of the myth partly answer the question 'What can women do to men (. . .) What would parallel the savage violation of rape?', E. Jane Burns, *Bodytalk. When Women Speak in Old French Literature* (Philadelphia, 1993), p. 133, but Gower adds an individual point of view.

70. By this time the lapwing's falseness has become proverbial, presumably because of its association with Tereus; cf. Chaucer, 'The false lapwyng ful of trecherye', *Parliament of Foules*, l. 347.

71. In the *Metamorphoses* Ovid only names the bird Tereus turns into, namely the hoopoe. He does mention that one of the female birds flies into the woods and the other stays close to human dwellings, and in his *Fasti* he states that Progne is a swallow (II, ll. 853–56). In the *Ovide moralisé* Tereus becomes a hoopoe, and here Philomena is specified as turning into a nightingale and Progne into a swallow, but the author does not give any details why the women should turn into those birds, rather than any other.

72. The exclamation 'Kill! Kill!' refers to all rapists, see *Ovide moralisé*, ll. 3681–83. In Chaucer there is no transformation and therefore no speech. Lydgate in 'A Seying of the Nightingale' has his nightingale utter the same cry in French and the speaker in the poem interprets it as a plea to take revenge on unfaithful lovers; see 'A Seying of the Nightingale', in Noble MacCracken (ed.), *The Minor Poems of John Lydgate*, Early English Text Society, Extra Series no. 107 (London, 1911), vol. 1, pp. 222–23, ll. 11–35.

73. Harbert stresses that as a nightingale, Philomena retains the characteristics of a young girl; see Ovid, 'The Myth of Tereus', p. 213.

74. This tale, in its original context of the *Metamorphoses*, is meant as a myth of origin, but in the context of the *Confessio* it takes on other levels of meaning.

75. Ovid has combined shame with complicity as Philomela's reactions to the rape show: she speaks of her own 'crimen' (VI, l. 541) and does not dare look at her sister (VI, ll. 605–06).

76. Susan Brownmiller gives examples of the guilt felt by a rape survivor: 'For years afterward I felt it was my fault. I tried to figure out what had made him follow me. Was it the clothes I was wearing or was it my walk? It had to be my fault, you see? I was only a child – an innocent child, but I was ashamed for a long time'. From Susan Brownmiller, *Against Our Will: Men, Women and Rape* (London, 1975, repr. 1976), pp. 361–2.

77. The story of Lucretia can be found in *Fasti*, see Ovid, *Fasti*, ed. and tr. James George Frazer (Cambridge MA, and London, 1989), II, ll. 721–852. All subsequent quotations, by line number, are from this edition. Macaulay cites Ovid's *Fasti* as the main source of this tale; see note to VII, ll. 4754 ff., and also indicates the use of Livy. Mainzer confirms this although he points out that it is not possible to determine whether Gower knew Livy in the Latin original or in the French translation by Pierre Bersuire; see Mainzer, 'A Study of the Sources', pp. 138 and 240.

78. On the question whether the Lucretia material is actually tale or historical fact consult Ian Donaldson, *The Rapes of Lucretia: A Myth and Its Transformations* (Oxford, 1982), pp. 5–8.

79. Ovid, *Fasti*, p. 114, 115, II, ll. 807–10. Gower knew the *Fasti* with medieval glosses; cf. Mainzer, 'A Study of the Sources', p. 335. Livy gives exactly the same argument for Lucretia's submission: 'ubi obstinatam videbat et ne mortis quidem metu inclinari, addit ad metum dedecus: cum mortua iugulatum servum nudum positurum ait, ut in sordido adulterio necata dicatur' (When he found her obdurate and not to be moved even by fear of death, he went farther and threatened her with

disgrace, saying that when she was dead he would kill his slave and lay him naked by her side, that she might be said to have been put to death in adultery with a man of base condition). From Livy, *Livy: In Fourteen Volumes*, ed. and tr. B.O. Foster (Cambridge MA and London, 1919–59, repr. 1967), vol. 1, pp. 200–1.

80. Ovid, *Fasti*, pp. 116–17, II, ll. 829–30.

81. Ibid., ll. 833–34.

82. From a Christian point of view the fact that Lucrece does not give in to Tarquin and swoons when the lives of others are threatened, rather than being worried about her reputation, is a very consistent way out of the moral dilemma of Lucretia's 'submission'. Although in a general sense Gower would not have underestimated the value of a wife's good reputation.

83. Chaucer himself refers to Livy and Ovid 'As seith Ovyde and Titus Lyvius' (F, l. 1683) but his tale is largely based on Ovid's *Fasti*, Alastair J. Minnis, *The Shorter Poems*, The Oxford Guides to Chaucer (Oxford, 1995), p. 348. Macaulay, *The English Works*, vol. 2, note to VII, ll. 4754 ff., p. 534. This is, of course, not true in all points: Chaucer's Tarquin, for instance, does not stay in Lucresse's house as a guest but breaks into her bedroom with his sword drawn.

84. Pisan, *Cité des Dames*, II.195, pp. 886.

85. Richards (tr.), *The Book of the City of Ladies*, p. 161.

86. Both Chaucer and Gower might have realized that one possible reading of Lucretia's suicide might be that she had enjoyed the rape and both exclude this interpretation from their accounts. Later authors do indeed reproach her on this count; see Donaldson, *The Rapes of Lucretia*, p. 36.

87. This can also be found in Ovid, *Fasti*, ll. 717–20.

88. This is very similar in Chaucer's version where Lucresse says ' "Be as be may," quod she, "of forgyvyng, I wol not have noo forgyft for nothing," ' *Legend*, F, ll. 1852–53.

89. Christine de Pisan gives her Lucretia a short speech in which she explains her unease with her own body and why she commits suicide: ' "This is how I absolve myself of sin and show my innocence. Yet I cannot free myself from the torment nor extricate myself from the pain" ', Richards (tr.), *The Book of the City of Ladies*, p. 162.

90. Augustine's problems with Lucretia's decision were partly motivated by general Christian objections to suicide, but he clearly casts doubt on her innocence: Augustine, *Concerning the City of God against the Pagans*, tr. Henry Bettenson, ed. David Knowles (Harmondsworth, Penguin, 1972), I.19, p. 30. Chaucer alludes to Augustine's remarks: 'The grete Austyn hath gret compassioun Of this Lucresse' (*Legend*, F, ll. 1690–91) at the beginning of his tale without mentioning any details and Christine de Pisan does not mention his criticism either.

91. Ovid, *Fasti*, pp. 118–19, II, ll. 845–46.

92. Chaucer's Lucresse, on the other hand, dies immediately and is certainly not aware of the things happening because of her suicide.

93. Christine de Pisan seems to create some compensation as well, as Lucretia's case is the cause for the implementation of an anti-rape law, but this occurs after her death; see Richards (tr.), *The Book of the City of Ladies*, p. 162.

94. *Ovide moralisé*, II, ll. 2717–21.

95. Ovid, *Metamorphoses*, vol. 1, pp. 100–101, ll. 578–80.

96. Ibid., pp. 90–91, ll. 434–37.

97. See *Ovide moralisé*, II, ll. 1475–91.

98. See Ovid, *Metamorphoses*, IV, l. 233.

99. Ibid., I, pp. 194–195, ll. 238–39.

100. *Ovide moralisé*, IV, ll. 1417–20.

101. This passage is nearly unprecedented in Gower's source; Ovid also describes Lucretia's hair as dishevelled – 'passis . . . capillis', Ovid, *Fasti*, II, l. 813 – but the rest seems original to Gower.

102. This is literally turning men into beasts in the *Vox Clamantis* and it is an overall theme in Gower's work, not only in the *Confessio*.

103. Translation from *Mirour de l'Omme*, p. 120.

6

JOAN OF ARC: GENDER AND AUTHORITY IN THE TEXT OF THE *TRIAL OF CONDEMNATION*

Lilas G. Edwards

In an edition concerned with medieval young womanhood it seems apt to include a study of one of the most notorious young women of the Middle Ages. Throughout the centuries the historical figure that is Joan of Arc has appeared in many guises, reflecting the interests and concerns of many people and eras. A female heroine or French patriot, heretic or saint, witch or visionary, androgyne or freak, Joan has played a diversity of roles. No less diverse are the documents from which Joan is known to us. Unlike other visionary women of the Middle Ages, Joan does not come down to us in the religious, didactic and ecstatic writings that characterize so much of the mystical genre. Rather it is through inquisitorial and trial records that we know anything of Joan. The *Trial of Condemnation* records her inquisition trial in Rouen in 1431 and attempts to justify her execution as a lapsed heretic. The *Trial of Rehabilitation*, compiled thirty years after her death, was intended to rehabilitate her memory back into the body of the Church.

There are many interesting aspects of the two trials yet to be explored – such as their often conflicting constructions of the identity of Joan, and the reasons for such conflict. For this study, however, I have chosen to focus exclusively on the *Trial of Condemnation*. What is fascinating about the *Trial* is that, though intended to condemn her, there emerge within the text complex and contrasting constructions of Joan. I propose to explore, using the ideas of gender and authority as my primary tools for analysis, the multiplicity of constructions which coexist in the *Trial of Condemnation*.

BACKGROUND AND SOURCES

The life of Joan of Arc was not long, yet it was memorable. Joan was barely out of adolescence when she burst onto the scene in 1429 and claimed that there would be no salvation for the French kingdom except through her. Born in the village of Domremy in north-eastern France, Joan came from a comfortably off but not wealthy peasant family. At the age of thirteen she had her first mystical experience; Joan later told how she was frightened when a voice, whom she identified as St Michael, spoke to her in her father's garden and instructed her how to behave. From this moment Joan swore to keep her virginity for as long as it should please God.

Joan's early life was constantly disrupted by the ravages of the English and Armagnac forces in contention for the French crown.[1] In the fifteenth century, 'France' was not the unified nation it is today. Instead, 'France' referred to an area surrounding the city of Paris, the *Ile de France*. The kingdom of France consisted of several provinces whose lords owed allegiance to the king. In the early fifteenth century, the region was in a state of civil war and rife with political divisions. Power struggles for supremacy between the Dukes of Orleans and Burgundy, due to Charles VI's intermittent insanity, led to political assassinations and further divided loyalties.[2] Aristocratic infighting was compounded by the re-entry of the English in the Hundred Years' War and Henry V's overwhelming victory at Agincourt in 1415.

War had swept the land as Henry V continued to consolidate his position in Normandy from 1417. His alliance with the disgruntled Duke of Burgundy led to negotiations with King Charles VI which resulted in the Treaty of Troyes in 1420. By its terms, all the rights to the crown of France were transferred from the dauphin, later Charles VII, onto Henry V who was then married to the Valois princess, Catherine. Thus when both Henry V and King Charles VI of France died in 1422, it was the infant Henry VI, and not the dauphin, who became formally recognized as king of France. However, as historian Christopher Allmand explains, 'To many, loyal to the idea of direct succession within the royal family, this seemed wrong. To such, the dauphin became the living symbol of resistance to English rule for years to come.'[3] The fight for sovereignty of France continued. Virtually all of central and southern France sided with the dauphin; they were known as the Armagnacs. The supporters of Henry VI included the English, Burgundians and a host of other occupied towns mainly in the north including the city of Paris.

Joan of Arc was growing up in the north-eastern province of Lorraine during these troubled years. Though far removed from the centres of power, her province had long suffered from the devastation of warfare. It comes as no surprise that her voices told her of the 'misery that is in France' as a result of the war; the war undoubtedly affected her life and the day-to-day lives of her family and neighbours.

In January 1429, with the confidence of her divine mission to inspire her, Joan went to Vaucouleurs to seek an escort to see the dauphin, the future Charles VII. There she donned male clothes and, despite all odds, convinced Robert de Baudricourt, captain of the local Armagnac troops, to provide her with men for the long journey to the royal court in Chinon. Once there, according to legend, Joan won the confidence of the dauphin with a mystical sign and the assurance that God considered him the rightful and legitimate heir to the French throne. Presumably she then stated her prophecy and the purpose of her mission: to relieve the siege at Orleans and to assure the rightful anointing and coronation of the dauphin at Rheims. In April, after two weeks of questioning by a group of theologians at Poitiers, Charles the dauphin gave *Jeanne la Pucelle*, as she came to be known, arms and troops to lead to Orleans. By 8 May the siege had been raised. In July Joan's second goal was realized when Charles was crowned at Rheims, in the tradition of French kings since the days of Clovis. Thus in a few astonishing months, Joan had jolted the Armagnac faction out of the apathy and uncertainty that had characterized their cause since Agincourt and turned the tide against the Anglo-Burgundian alliance.

Despite her initial success, however, circumstances soon worsened for Joan. A series of defeats ended in her capture by the Burgundians in Compiègne in May of 1430. After six months of captivity, during which the English and the University of Paris petitioned for her possession, she was sold to the English. The English turned her over to the Bishop of Beauvais, Pierre Cauchon, to be tried by an ecclesiastical court on suspicion of heresy. Unsurprisingly, three months of interrogation by Cauchon and nearly 100 clergymen led to Joan's condemnation as a heretic by the pro-English University of Paris. After recanting and relapsing within the space of three days, Joan was declared a relapsed heretic. She was excommunicated, turned over to the secular arm, and burned at the stake in May 1431.

Much of what we know of Joan's life comes from her own testimony and the testimony of her contemporaries as recorded by the two trials. Though a woman and a peasant living in a society which marginalized both groups, Joan's special mission and the unusual events of her life ensured that there would be extensive, if problematic, recording of her life. The extant traces of Joan's life are, unlike much of medieval documentation, unusually rich and abundant, so it is not only in the writings of the chroniclers of her time or in the literature of her contemporaries that she exists. Joan of Arc is constructed most vividly in the record of her two trials. Unlike any other important woman of her period, there is a unique opportunity for the historian of Joan to listen to her own words and the words of her contemporaries – though, of course, those words are heard only through a number of filters. For the purposes of this study I intend only to examine the text of the *Trial of Condemnation*.[4]

As with any methodological approach to historical sources, there are a number of practical problems associated with the *Trial*. Like all traces of the past, the documents that surround Joan of Arc must be carefully analysed and interpreted to extract all potential meaning. It is important to remember while examining the *Trial*, or any medieval document, the language filters which could possibly influence the text.[5]

The actual conditions of the trial must affect the way that we as historians read its record, as well. Though we do have Joan's words as recorded by the scribes at the trial, they are not, obviously, in the form of a diary or memoir. Joan was tried by the Inquisition for heresy while being held in a secular prison by the English. She was fettered to her bed, continuously guarded by the roughest of English soldiers, threatened with torture and death, and interrogated with deliberately tricky and devious questions. The conditions of the trial were undoubtedly designed to break down Joan's will and confuse her to the point of incriminating herself.

For her own part, Joan seems to have been aware of the precarious circumstances she was in and she did attempt to defend herself. She deferred all to the Lord, her answers, actions, even her dress. She tried to avoid directly defying her judges – though on occasion she did so – and seems to have been looking for the answers that would save her from being condemned but, at the same time, not compromise her special relationship with God. It was an impossible dilemma; the judges would not accept the divinity of her voices and Joan could not deny them without losing her unique authority.

The trial was essentially political in motivation. Though officially an inquisition into the alleged heresy of Joan of Arc, the trial was driven and funded by her enemies, the English, who were specifically concerned with eliminating the moral and military threat she presented to their claims on France. However, it would be a mistake to dismiss the event as merely political without any attempt at further examination. Though written to condemn Joan, the documents of the original trial show her individuality and strong character, often evoking sympathy in the reader. Despite its official intention, the text of the trial contains room for multiple readings; it must be carefully examined in order to untangle those various meanings.

AUTHORITY

The *Trial of Condemnation* is just that: a document specifically concerned to condemn Joan of Arc and justify her excommunication and, ultimately, her execution as a relapsed heretic.

What is fascinating about the *Trial* as an historical source is that, though intended to condemn her, there is room for an alternative construction of Joan. The text relies on the underlying theme of authority and disobedience. Both Joan and her judges were concerned with their authority to act in their society, and more specifically to construct themselves and each other in the text of the *Trial*. Both parties claimed their authority from God. Joan's judges were explicitly interested in authority: first, their own powers as representatives of the Church and second, their perception of Joan's wrongful and disobedient denial of that authority. At the same time, it was as a visionary and divine intermediary between heaven and earth, authorized with a special mission of social reform, that Joan most strongly identified herself. It was her capacity as divinely inspired 'daughter of God' that gave Joan the credibility to embark on her mission. Her powerful association with the will of God empowered Joan to construct herself and the inquisitors in the *Trial*.

'Daughter of God'

Joan was not acting without precedent when she identified herself as a prophetic and mystical visionary inspired by God. Indeed, she was responding to and participating in a Christian tradition, rich with symbolism. In medieval Europe the sacred was everywhere; it pervaded the art, literature, politics and daily life of medieval culture. But the will of God was not perceived to be transparent. In fact, the intangible nature of human/divine communication, which provides institutions or individuals with the authority to rule or act in the name of God, was seen as difficult to control and tenuous in the best of circumstances. Who, then, truly knew the will of God? The Pope was considered the spiritual descendent of St Peter, and therefore the head of Christ's Church on earth.[6] Yet, according to Christian tradition, any individual, from the most exalted to the most humble, could be touched by the numinous light of the Almighty. After all, Christ taught that 'blessed are the meek'. Anyone could be chosen by God to serve as His tool or mouthpiece on earth. And often those chosen were women.

Because women were considered to be more corporeal and sensual than 'reason-led' men, they were more susceptible to mystical experience, particularly that type of visionary experience categorized by St Augustine as 'spiritual'.[7] Though potentially dangerous – a visionary walks a fine line between mysticism and witchcraft or heresy – mystical abilities, if accepted by the Church or the society at large, could bring respect and power to the visionary. Women, denied access to virtually all official religious authority within the Church during the later part of the Middle Ages, sought alternative ways to express their spirituality and gain their own authority.

The phenomenon of women visionaries was not new in 1429 when Joan of Arc sprang into prominence. Many women had achieved renown and respect through their transcendent relationships with the divine. A range of women visionaries, including Julian of Norwich, Catherine of Siena, Marguerite Porete, Bridget of Sweden and Margery Kempe, to name a few, make it possible to see Joan of Arc in the context of a movement: a wave of popular female mystics whose lives and visions brought them renown or infamy in their societies. [8]

Thus Joan entered a powerful, though not unproblematic, area of female visionary and Christian mysticism when she testified about her voices at the Trial of Condemnation. Joan's visionary experiences dominate a large portion of the text of the *Trial* because her inquisitors were particularly concerned to determine whether her voices came from God or whether they were the work of Satan. In her testimony Joan expressed no such uncertainty about the source of her voices. It is understandable that in the hostile circumstances of the trial Joan was reluctant to speak about her voices. She refused numerous times to take the oath concerning matters that did not 'touch her trial' and she would occasionally ask for a grace period to answer a question in order to consult her voices or gain 'leave' to speak.[9] As she herself emphasized, it was her communication with God which gave her the authority to speak on various matters. 'I have done nothing save by revelation.'[10]

Joan's voices were in constant communication with her. They came every day, and were always accompanied by a light. Joan used the presence of her divine counsel to establish her own state of grace. Her judges were very concerned about her spiritual state and tried to make her admit she might be in mortal sin, particularly without the benefit of confession. With circular logic, Joan implied that without the grace of her own purity and specialness, her voices would no longer visit her; by her presence, a presence that only she could verify, her lack of sinfulness was 'proved':

> Questioned as to whether there was any need to make confession since she believes, through the revelation of her voices, that she will be saved she answered that she does not know that she has committed mortal sin; but if she be in mortal sin, she thinks that St Catherine and St Margaret would at once abandon her.[11]

As well as providing comfort and companionship, Joan admitted that her voices gave advice, although usually nothing more specific than urging her to 'go boldly'. However, the exhortation to 'go boldly' is significant in itself; it justified, in Joan's eyes, her male dress, her warfare techniques and her actions in general. But the phrase was also strangely in contrast to her self-construction as a humble female chosen by God for a special purpose.

Early in her testimony Joan began to construct herself as a humble female obedient to the will of God, and in doing so she engaged with a long tradition of Christian humility:

> And she said that, from the age of thirteen she received revelation from Our Lord by a voice which taught her how to behave. And the first time she was greatly afraid. . . and she said further after she had heard it three times, she knew that it was the voice of an angel.[12]

In this passage, Joan clearly wanted to depict herself as 'chosen'. Interestingly, Joan's fear and misgivings reflect those expressed by the Virgin Mary at the Annunciation. In the gospel of Luke, Mary is told by the Angel Gabriel that she is 'blessed among women'. Mary is, not surprisingly, 'troubled' by the news, but the angel assures her to 'fear not'.[13] In myth and spiritual tradition, mortals often responded with trepidation when they first came in contact with the divine. Yet, once her fear had abated, the knowledge that her 'voice' was truly sent from God came to Joan from within herself; she verified the experience with her own sense, an action she considered legitimate, to her eventual cost.

In the same interrogation session, Joan's testimony leapt forward chronologically to her fateful departure for Vaucouleurs, and the Marian parallels continue. Joan pronounced that the voice then began to urge her to 'go to France' and 'that she must hurry and raise the siege of Orleans'.[14] It need hardly be stated that for a peasant woman, or any woman, to be given the divine mission to go to war was remarkable. Even for the Virgin Mary a traditionally feminine role was chosen: that of motherhood. To counterbalance the transgressiveness and rarity of her calling, Joan employed a common feminine theme of humility by declaring her own concern to the angel, 'that she was only a poor woman who knew nothing of riding or making war'.[15] This bears some similarity with the Virgin's disclaimer made at the Annunciation, when upon hearing of her own conception of Jesus she established her innocence and purity in a phrase which would influence generations of Christians: 'How shall this be, seeing I know not a man?'[16] In the text of the *Trial* it appears that Joan, like Mary, could do nothing but accept the blessing and the burden with which God chose to gift her. Moreover, by making explicit an issue that was undoubtedly at the forefront of her accusers' minds – that she was transgressing her natural female role – and then justifying it as God's plan, Joan was attempting to undercut their objections.

In the *Magnificat*, Mary's longest speech in the Bible, the Virgin exalts God's grace and strength:

> For he hath regarded the low estate of his handmaid: for behold from henceforth all generations shall call me blessed. . . . He hath put down the mighty from their seats and exalted them of low degree.[17]

When asked by her accusers why she had been chosen, in an answer brief but resonant of the *Magnificat*, Joan replied, 'It pleased God so to do, by means of a simple maid to drive back the King's enemies'.[18] On a spiritual level Joan must have known that her humble background and female body were no barrier to God's grace; indeed, the contradictions inherent in her humble and female person made his choice all the more apt.

Virginity

Joan also established her validity as a divine messenger through another powerful and classic theme in Christianity: virginity. 'Now that a virgin has conceived in the womb and borne us a child. . .the curse is broken. Death came through Eve, but life has been bestowed most richly upon women, seeing that it has its beginnings from a woman.'[19] The Church Fathers, in particular Augustine, Ambrose, and Jerome, set the stage for the Christian idealization of virginity by associating the Fall of Man with sexuality, sin and death. With sexual sin often linked with Original Sin, and therefore a result of the Fall, it stood to reason that virginity would constitute the praiseworthy ideal of Christian perfection, particularly for women who, theologically, bore the guilt of Eve's transgressions.[20] In the minds of some theologians, virginity elevated a woman to a 'manlier' state, freeing her from the feminine weaknesses of the flesh to a stronger and more rational state.[21]

By the High Middle Ages, virginity had become a 'symbol of sacred power' and carried the greatest reward. The immense popularity of the cult of the Virgin Mary, considered humanity's most powerful intercessor by the fifteenth century, as well as the veneration of the virgin-martyr saints, attests to the importance of virginity as a holy condition.

At the age of thirteen, Joan of Arc swore to remain virgin 'for as long as it should be pleasing to God.[22] Joan equated her virginity with her special relationship with her voices. Indeed, her celibacy could be seen as a sacrifice she willingly made in order to receive her voices' 'counsel' and God's grace.[23] 'Questioned as to whether, after this revelation, she believes that she cannot commit mortal sin she answered: 'As to this I know nothing; but commit myself in all things to Our Lord . . . [and asserted that] provided she keeps the vow and the promise that she made to Our Lord that she should keep her virginity both of body and soul.'[24] That Joan identified with her virginal status there is little doubt. In the Eighth Session she stated that her voices called her '*Jeanne la Pucelle*, Daughter of God.' *Pucelle* is the name that Joan gave to herself. She used it in her correspondence before her capture and it became distinctly hers in both English and Armagnac circles. According to Warner, '*pucelle* means virgin, but in a special way, with distinct shades connoting youth, innocence and paradoxically, nubility.'[25] That Joan chose an appellation that emphasized her virginal condition reveals how strongly she connected her virginity with the divine authority she received from God.

Voices

The saints which Joan identified with her voices were Michael, Catherine and Margaret. In her earliest testimony Joan did not originally name St Michael as the owner of the voice that first visited her in her father's garden, she merely states that she received 'revelation from God by a voice'.[26] Not until the Fourth Session did Joan name any of her voices and then only after pressured questioning. Perhaps she realized that her previous answers concerning her voices were too vague, insufficient to convince the inquisitors of her mandate from heaven; she needed the efficacy and power of the saints to strengthen her visionary status.

As Charles Wood suggests, 'It becomes difficult to conceive of more suitable intermediaries.'[27] St Michael is an archangel and of the same order as Gabriel, the messenger who brought the news to Mary of Christ's conception. And like Gabriel, Michael resonated in his messenger capacity as a voice from God. Michael was also the 'emblem of French resistance.' Since 1419 and the fall of the Abbey of St Denis, the image of St Michael, represented by a valiant knight with weapons drawn, had been painted on the banners of the Armagnac soldiers. As an archangel and the guardian of France, Michael symbolized both the divinity of the French cause and Joan's mystical link to God:

> Asked how she knew it was St Michael, she replied; By the speech and language of angels . . . asked how she knew that it was the language of angels, she answered that she believed it immediately; and desired to believe it. She also said that St Michael told her that St Catherine and St Margaret would come to her, and that she should follow their counsel . . . for it was by Our Lord's command.[28]

Catherine and Margaret were both virgin-martyr saints who had captured popular imagination in the thirteenth, fourteenth and fifteenth centuries, as witnessed by the frequency with which their life cycles occur in religious art and their hagiographies appear in literary sources such as *Hali Meiðhad*, *The Golden Legend* and the writings of the Katherine Group. In many ways, particularly in their virginity and extreme piety in the face of earthly authority, Joan shared similarities with these virgin saints.

St Catherine was personally closest to Joan, the 'voice' most often receiving affectionate mention in Joan's testimony. According to *The Golden Legend*, Catherine was a well-educated pagan princess who became a Christian and refused to offer sacrifice to the emperor's 'false gods'.[29] Engaging in a verbal dispute with the emperor and his men of learning, she spoke so effectively that she converted all but the emperor. The furious emperor retaliated with numerous tortures which Catherine valiantly withstood before succumbing to death in 'glorious' martyrdom. Joan of Arc was also forced to engage in a verbal contest of wills with 'learned men' and like Catherine she put her trust in God. When Joan was threatened with torture during the trial she responded with classic martyr audacity: 'Truly, if you were to tear me limb from limb and make my soul leave my body, I would not say to you anything else.'[30]

The life of St Margaret also resonated for Joan:

> Margaret the virgin . . . was bespoken in marriage to a noble youth, and both her parents gave their consent . . . but suddenly, God inspiring her, the virgin gave thought to the loss of her virginity . . . and in the middle of the night she cut off her hair, garbed herself in the habit of a man, and recommending herself to God, secretly took flight.[31]

Joan also donned the garb of a man for what she referred to as practical purposes.

Like both Catherine and Margaret, Joan rejected marriage in order to keep her virginity intact, a symbol of her purity and devotion to God. And all three were questioned by the representatives of the male-dominated power structures of their times. It is clear from the text that Joan admired Margaret and Catherine, whose 'counsel' told her to 'go boldly'. Boldness was not considered a virtue in women and yet both saints were represented as bold in their actions and in their willingness to defy authority for their personal beliefs. Joan, too, stood firm during most of the trial, at one point even giving the principle judge, Cauchon, this blunt caveat, '. . . you say you are my judge. Consider well what you do, for in truth I am sent from God, and you are putting yourself in great peril.'[32]

Joan of Arc's visionary experiences dominate a large portion of the trial because her inquisitors were particularly concerned to determine whether her voices came from God or whether they were, more likely in their estimation, the work of Satan. For Joan, her own senses and her desire to believe were enough to convince her of the veracity of the saints. Not so for the judges. Joan's judges at the trial found her verification insufficient and her refusal to submit to their evaluation heretical. Rosalynn Voaden has shown how the discernment of spirits, *discretio spirituum*, was considered the prerogative of the male clergy: arguing that the discerning of spirits is a simple concept, based on the premise that good and evil spirits, which may at first seem indistinguishable because the devil is a master of disguise, can be distinguished by those who have a gift of *discretio spirituum*. Uniting the gift of the Holy Spirit with both theological study and ecclesiastical office meant that the exercise of *discretio spirituum* was clearly appropriated by men.[33] Thus it was the jurisdiction of the Church to determine whether a vision or revelation was legitimate or not. Joan failed to follow proper visionary procedure because she verified her own visions 'without asking advice from [her] curé or from any churchman'.

Not only was Joan's self-validation of her spirits an affront to her judges, she also asserted that her relationship with God allowed her to enjoy the Mass, if necessary, without the presence of a priest. 'She said moreover that if the judges refused to allow her to hear Mass, it was in Our Lord's power to let her hear it without them, whenever it pleased Him.'[34] With these words Joan threatened the sacred role of the priest in the most holy miracle of Christianity, the consecration of the Host.

The text of the *Trial* portrays Joan as a threat to the unity and authority of the Church, and society in general. The *Trial* attempted to establish that the clergymen who interrogated Joan were authorized by God and the Church to judge her. To understand the intentions of the *Trial* to condemn Joan, we must begin with the clergy who set themselves up as her judges. They claimed their authority from the Church, and like her, ultimately from God himself. Their right as judges was built on their understanding of the Scriptures and laws of the Church. But essentially, the judges authorized themselves: 'We, the judges competent in this trial, declare and have declared Ourselves so to be, as much as required, and declare this trial ended.'[35] The Church had a long history of securing its role as divine intermediary and it would not permit unauthorized rivals. As God's emissaries on earth, the clergy had the right to determine truth and define orthodoxy; by the same token they were authorized to judge heresy. As Edward Peters reminds us, 'Orthodoxy cannot exist without authority and it is the quality of authority which defines and denounces heresy.'[36]

Heresy

In the fifteenth century, heresy was a symbol of division, a threat to the unity of Christendom and the established authority of both secular and ecclesiastical institutions. The Great Schism had revealed the conflicts between medieval hierarchies and as André Vauchez tells us, 'awakened grave doubts among the faithful'.[37] Anti-authoritarian and anti-sacerdotal movements such as Lollardy and the followers of Hus had resulted in armed uprisings which served to underscore the link between political and religious upheaval. If medieval society was held together through the populace's general submission to an 'orthodox' and definitive faith, then heresy, by definition 'heterodox', jeopardized that. Heresy was most simply the obstinate denial of authority.[38] If we accept this definition then Joan was unquestionably a heretic.

To the judges, Joan's gravest offence was her unwillingness to submit to the authority of the 'Church Militant' or Church on earth. Her stubborn refusal to acknowledge the right of the clergy to act as representatives of the Church and judge her on spiritual matters made her a 'schismatic . . . [who] perniciously erred in the faith of God'.[39] Instead Joan did the unspeakable and chose her own judge: 'I trust in my judge, that is the King of Heaven and earth.'[40] The *Trial* presented Joan with an impossible dilemma. She must have been aware of the seriousness of her circumstances and she certainly tried to answer her interrogations in such a way to save herself. She never denied outright the authority of the Church but she always deferred to God. She seemed to search for an answer that would save her from condemnation but would not compromise her own special status as visionary. Her judges would not accept her voices as divine revelation and Joan could not denounce them without losing her uniqueness and authority which justified her mission.

Joan conceded the sacred role of the Church but she always added the proviso that the Church's sanctity was second to the power of the Lord. Since she had a personal connection with God she could then, if necessary, bypass the Church. Despite the proofs and persuasions of the judges, Joan remained firm in her unwillingness to accept the clergy's authority as ultimate. In that obstinacy, in the eyes of her judges, there was sufficient sin and error for Joan to be condemned. Article Twelve summarizes the view of Joan that the judges used to establish her heresy:

> You have said that if the Church desired you to do the opposite of the commandment which you say God gave you, you would not do so for anything in the world. And that, concerning all the aforementioned matters you are not willing to refer them to the judgement of the Church on earth, nor of any man alive but to God alone . . . regardless of the fact that the article of the Faith which says that everyone must believe in the Catholic Church has been several times explained to you, and that every good Christian must submit all his deeds to the Church, especially facts concerning revelation and such-like. As for this article, the clerks say that you are schismatic, having no comprehension of the truth and authority of the Church.[41]

Like Joan herself, the clergy who presided at the trial claimed their authority from God. However, they used the well-established institution of the Church, governed by the Holy Spirit, to confirm that claim.

Power and Danger in Androgyny

The knight, or *chevalier*, of the Middle Ages was glorified as the pinnacle of medieval soldiery. Knights were warriors on horseback, celebrated in myth and legend, sanctified as protectors of the faith and 'ennobled by the practice of the profession of arms'.[42] Knighthood and chivalry were complex concepts, however, and the reality of chivalry did not always conform to the ideal. But one point is certain: the term 'knight' was strongly gendered masculine. Women were not knights. Yet throughout the *Trial of Condemnation* Joan of Arc fashioned herself with characteristics common to a knight, associating herself with the potent imagery of the medieval warrior and male ideal. Joan acquired the necessary material accoutrements of a knight: horse, clothing, weapons, and in the inquisition she defended the possession of them. But her androgynous identity shocked and outraged the judges of the trial. For those men of God, Joan's transvestism was dangerously transgressive and unorthodox, 'an abomination before God'.[43]

At the Public Admonition Joan stated emphatically, 'When I shall have done that for which I have been sent by God, I shall take women's dress.'[44] Undoubtedly Joan associated her male attire with her mission, and to accomplish her mission she needed the status of a knight. The first and most important requirement for a knight was that which provided both mobility and defined his chivalric status, namely a horse: 'She said she was then on horseback, and it was a demi-charger. Asked who had given her this horse she replied that her king or one of his people had given it to her out of the king's treasury.'[45]

Once adequately horsed, Joan also required a weapon. The miraculous circumstances by which she acquired it further demonstrate her preoccupation with chivalry. Joan recounted that her voices had informed her where she would find her sword, buried behind the altar in the church of St Catherine de Fierbois. The sword was very old but when the clergy 'rubbed it, the rust fell off without any effort'. The magical acquisition of her weapon set Joan within a knightly and romantic tradition, for it was well known that 'the chosen hero must have a magical weapon'.[46]

In the Middle Ages a heretic was someone disobedient in the face of authority. But disobedience could be associated with any act that went against the accepted norms of society. Any transgressive action was in danger of being labelled heretical if it threatened to tear the seamless robe of orthodoxy. Joan of Arc's cross-dressing was a blatant act of social deviance and her judges did not hesitate to use it to condemn her. Her male attire became the most tangible and visible symbol of her refusal to submit to the Church. Throughout the interrogation the judges repeatedly asked Joan why she wore male dress, by whose orders, and if she believed she had done 'well' or 'rightly' to dress so. Five of the original seventy articles are concerned with Joan's male dress, in particular with her blasphemy in claiming she wore it at God's direction:

> To the Thirteenth, accusing her of blasphemy (in saying that it was at God's command that she put on male clothing, 'violating canon law, to the scandal of her sex and womanly modesty, and the perversion of all decent behaviour').[47]

Joan's dress, as far as her judges were concerned, was an 'abomination' and a 'perversion of decent behaviour'. By refusing the clothing rightful to her sex, Joan denied her appropriate role as a woman. Neither wholly female nor entirely male, Joan became a monster in the eyes of her accusers. In the condensed twelve articles, the vehemence of the language underlines the severity of her transgression:

> You have said that, by God's command, you have continually worn man's dress, wearing the short robe, doublet, and hose attached by points; that you have worn your hair short . . . with nothing left that could show you to be a woman. . . As for these points the clerks say that you blaspheme God in His sacraments; that you transgress divine law . . . and you condemn yourself in being unwilling to wear the customary clothing of your sex.[48]

That Joan's male dress was the outward measure of her heresy is best demonstrated by her abjuration and relapse. On 24 May 1431, at a public assembly in the cemetery in Rouen, Joan recanted and made her abjuration. In doing so, Joan agreed that she 'would willingly wear a woman's dress and be obedient to the Church'.[49] On 28 May, however, Joan was found dressed in man's clothing. Joan's resumption of male garb was sufficient proof of her disobedience to justify the court's decision to hand her over to the secular arm for execution. 'But being persuaded by the devil, she had declared time and again, in the presence of several persons, that her voices, who had been accustomed to appear to her, had come again; and she had taken off her woman's dress and again taken man's clothing.'[50] Joan's transvestism was transgressive in itself, a dangerous and forbidden reversal of roles.

GENDER

By its very nature the *Trial of Condemnation* attempted to create a binary relationship of power and powerlessness between the accused and accusers. As we have seen, Joan of Arc was questioned, without the benefit of counsel, by a panel of theologians (as many as sixty at a given time) on the nature of her revelations, her lifestyle and dress, her childhood, her politics and more. After the Sixth Session these interrogations were moved to Joan's prison cell where she remained fettered to her bed during the remainder of her questioning. These points may seem irrelevant to the text of the *Trial* but they do help convey a sense of the power relations inherent in the text. The interrogatory structure of Joan's *Trial*, indeed, of any inquisitorial trial, sets up a hierarchy of power. The inquisitors hold a position of superiority over the accused. As Joan Wallach Scott has suggested, 'gender is a primary way of signifying relationships of power'.[51] It is not surprising then that the text constructs the main actors of the *Trial* in terms of gender. Joan is depicted as an ignorant and unlettered female who obstinately refused to accept the authority of the learned and rational men of God who were to judge her.

Of course, Joan was female and the theologians at the trial were male. But the use of gender in the text goes beyond the mere biological sex of its members. Gender, in this case, is used to establish power and justify the 'natural' order of the trial's outcome. In the *Trial* the 'meanings' associated with feminine and masculine were not one-dimensional but rich, complex, and like much medieval symbolism, ambiguous. Joan herself demonstrated the complexities inherent in a medieval study of gender. She was female yet she dressed as a man and associated herself with knighthood. She embodied androgynous qualities which were symbolically potent yet threatening to the 'natural order' of medieval society.

Despite all the sexual ambiguities which surround Joan of Arc, the text of the *Trial* makes the attempt to construct her, in the terms of a gender-based binary, as feminine. 'The biological opposition male/female is used to construct a series of [positive masculine and] negative feminine values. . . . Western philosophy and literary thought is and always has been caught up in this endless series of hierarchical binary oppositions.'[52] As Toril Moi points out, masculine and feminine have come to signify binary qualities such as strength/weakness, positive/negative, and rational/sensual. In the *Trial* Joan was gendered feminine: ignorant, led by her senses, and stubbornly headstrong. By the same token, the judges were constructed as masculine: learned, rational and righteous in their convictions.

Initially the judges offered Joan the benefit of their knowledge in spiritual and legal matters and thus set up a contrast between her ignorance and incapacity for intellection, and their erudition: 'Since Joan was not able to understand or discern many of the matters contained in her trial as to what was contrary to Our Faith and the doctrine of the doctors of the Church, they offered to give her good and helpful counsel to advise her.'[53] The theologians 'proved to her by means of a number of the authorities and examples in Holy Scripture that she ought to obey'.[54] When Joan failed to follow the advice of their superior learning, she was accused of behaving 'lightly' and 'rashly'. Her continued belief in her convictions meant that she 'wrongly' and 'incorrectly understood the Christian faith'. Only the male clergy who defined and interpreted the laws of the faith had the rational capacity and learning to understand them.

In medieval times, the symbolic dualism between male and female identified men as spirit, mind and intellect while women were associated with flesh, body and sensuality.[55] 'Flesh must be subject to spirit in the right ordering of nature'; Augustine's decree, and the definition of female as human corporeality led to the 'natural subordination of women to men'.[56] By constructing Joan as female and the judges as male, the text attempted to establish the judges' authority as proper and righteous and Joan's refusal wholly to submit to that authority as recalcitrant and perverse.

The judges at the trial urged Joan to disbelieve her own senses (sensual/feminine) and submit to the infallible knowledge (rational/masculine) of the Church:

> Therefore if such apparitions appear to you, do not believe them, but reject and cast out such follies and imaginations, in agreement with the statements and opinions of the University of Paris and the other doctors, who are conversant with and understand God's law and Holy Scriptures.[57]

In the text of the *Trial* Joan was 'charitably admonished' by the clergy numerous times and urged to submit to their superior understanding and authority. The implication was that they were acting only for Joan's own good, her salvation:

> Up to the present you have been unwilling to heed those warnings. And although in your own deeds and words there has been matter enough to find you guilty, yet the judges, desiring your salvation both of body and soul, sent to the University of Paris, the light of all knowledge and the extirpation of all error, in order that your words and deeds at your trial might be thoroughly examined.[58]

The tone of this passage is rich with paternalism; Joan should, in keeping with the correct order, submit to the theologians of the Church just as a woman was bound to submit to the protection of her husband. In the story of Genesis, as punishment for the Fall, Eve was placed under the rule of her husband.[59] As a result womankind was made subject to male domination; likewise Joan – the 'female' of the text – was expected to obey the masculine authority of the Church. St Paul's first epistle to the Corinthians further elaborates on the proper male/female relationship:

> Let your women keep silence in the Churches; for it is not permitted unto them to speak but they are commanded to be under obedience as also saith the law. And if they will learn anything, let them ask their husbands at home; for it is a shame for women to speak in Church.[60]

Not only were women to defer to and be guided by their husbands, this passage relegates women to the private realm. Writing and speaking were the exclusive province of men because men had the authority within the public sphere. In this respect, the Church, and the judges in the *Trial*, are gendered masculine. It was their 'right' and duty to guide, teach and discipline the feminine Joan; and her duty to submit.

That Joan refused to submit placed her outside the proper order of nature. By managing the trial in terms of a gender-based system which justified a hierarchy of power as the 'natural order', Joan's condemnation was assured. Gendered feminine and thus ignorant and sensual, Joan was obliged to submit to the masculine, learned and rational clergy of the Church. The fact that Joan refused to do so only made her, in the eyes of her judges, a rebellious and dangerous freak whose inversion of the right order of gender relations and power hierarchies threatened the very foundations of Christian society.

CONCLUSION

As noted at the beginning of this essay, Joan of Arc has appeared in many guises throughout the centuries, those guises reflecting the interests and concerns of others. No less diverse are the identities of Joan represented in the main document from which Joan is known to us, the *Trial of Condemnation*. Designed to condemn her, the text of the *Trial* does much more. The *Trial* contains information that can tell us much about the society and times in which it was written as well as give insight into the complexity of Joan of Arc as a subject for historical analysis. The multiplicity of this document, by its nature and the nature of historical inquiry, allows for a variety of approaches and interpretations.

Joan, despite the intentions of her judges, was able to construct herself as a chosen 'daughter of God'. In doing so, Joan was participating in a movement of visionary women who gained authority in society through their transcendent contact with God. Empowered by her sworn and holy virginity, Joan modelled herself on the humility of the Virgin Mary. Though Joan can be shown to be part of this movement of female mystics, she was also quite different. Her voices gave her the sanction, and indeed the directive, not to merely advise or prophesy but to act. Her mystical 'counsel' told her to 'go boldly', to perform a mission of action and force, an unusual endeavor in a society where women were generally discouraged to speak out in public, much less take up arms and enter the male realm of politics and war. Joan also took on the clothes and trappings of a knight and in doing so broke the bonds that bound her to a life of peasant and female submissiveness. The underlying basis of all her constructions was the divine mission from which she derived her authority.

Oddly enough, despite the ostensible intentions of those who framed the *Trial* document (or perhaps because of them) Joan's construction of herself as a 'daughter of God' whose great mission was to assume the identity of a knight and 'save' France for the rightful heir is somehow permitted by a text designed to condemn her. This ambiguity is allowed because of the text's need to construct Joan as recalcitrant and disobedient to the Church, the 'rightful' representative of God's will on earth. Joan's attempt to authorize herself as a divine messenger whose mandate from God makes her the heaven-sent deliverer of France threatened the authority of the Church. Joan's insistence on her personal communion with God, without clerical intermediaries to control and authorize the experience, was subversive to the 'men of God' who judged her.

The same testimony that Joan of Arc used to construct herself as 'daughter of God' was seen by her judges as heresy and sedition. Joan's transvestism was 'perversion' and a threat to the established order; women were forbidden to act and dress as men. For her judges, Joan's male dress was the physical proof of her disobedience.

According to the *Trial*, Joan's greatest offence was her refusal to submit to the authority of the court and the 'Church Militant'. To the clergy at Joan's inquisition, the epithet 'schismatic' was anathema; it symbolized the disorder that arose from division. Division occurs when a person or group refuses to accept the authority of the established power structure. Heresy, by its very nature, was a serious threat to the system which justified its power through religious unity. Joan, constructed as a heretic and schismatic, became a symbol of the alarming loss of authority which grew out of disobedience.

To further justify their right to judge and condemn Joan, the judges and the text of the *Trial* made use of a gender-based binary hierarchy that had its roots in an ancient Christian tradition. Gender was used to assign meaning and support a 'natural order' where feminine was submissive to masculine. Joan was constructed as 'feminine' by the *Trial* in a system where the right ordering of nature meant that mind must control the flesh and therefore feminine must be subject to masculine. By the terms of this system, Joan was expected to submit to the authority of the masculine Church and clergy. That Joan failed to submit made her, in the eyes of her judges, 'shameful' and a heretic. That she did so dressed as a man made her monstrous.

Throughout this study, authority has been the underlying theme of analysis. The nature of the *Trial of Condemnation* was founded on a principle of authority. Both Joan and the judges were concerned with their own authority: in other words, their own power to construct themselves and each other within the text of the *Trial*. Both parties claimed their authority came from God. This conflict set up a tension that is never fully resolved despite Joan's recantation, relapse and execution. To the judges, Joan's decision not to submit was evidence of her obdurate and seditious nature, ample justification for her execution. For Joan, her decision was the only choice she could have made while still maintaining her special authority.

What emerges most clearly from this study is that the *Trial of Condemnation* is not a simple text. Neither is Joan of Arc, even within this single document, a simple phenomenon. There is no uniformity of meaning to be extracted with a glance. Rather the subject of Joan of Arc within the *Trial* is rich in complexity, capable of several interpretations. The testimony which establishes Joan's authority to construct herself within the text is also used by the judges to condemn her; the reader must determine whether Joan was heretic, 'daughter of God' or, indeed, something else altogether. Joan of Arc remains an enigma.

Notes

1. Eduoard Perroy, *The Hundred Years War*, tr. W.B. Wells (New York, 1965), p. 282.

2. Ibid., p. 259.

3. Christopher Allmand, *The Hundred Years' War* c. *1300–1450* (Cambridge, 1989), pp. 28–35.

4. The text I have chosen to rely upon most heavily is a translation of the Orleans manuscript: W.S. Scott (tr.), *Trial of Joan of Arc* (London, 1956). The *Trial of Condemnation* comes down to us in a number of manuscripts. Pierre Manchon, the principle scribe, recorded the proceedings in French. This collection of notes is known as the French Minute; unfortunately, this document has never been found by modern scholars. However, there are two manuscripts, believed to be copied from the French Minute, which provide a record of the trial. The d'Urfe manuscript is contemporary with the trial and is in French; however, it is incomplete. The Orleans manuscript, though produced much later (*c.* 1500) is also believed to be a copy of the original French Minute. There is also the official report of the trial known as the 'Authentic Document', Latinized and transcribed by Thomas de

Courcelles in 1435. Three of the five copies that were made are still extant: two of the manuscripts are in the Bibliothèque Nationale and the third is housed in the Library of the Assemblée Nationale. The Orleans manuscript, MS 518, is housed in the Bibliothèque Municipale d'Orleans.

5. For example, Joan was interrogated in the vernacular but the official documents were translated into Latin. This discrepancy between the spoken and written unquestionably affects that language of the text, particularly when that translation requires the interpretation of another party, separate from the speaker. In recent times these documents have been translated into modern languages and thus each step in translation is another step away from the veracity of the original text. This is a concern that may have more relevance in the study of literature than history, but a cogent analysis of any text, whether literary or historical, needs an accompanying awareness of the dangers inherent in the hermeneutic process.

6. Matthew 16: 18–19: 'And I say also unto thee, That thou art Peter, and upon this rock I will build my church; and the gates of hell shall not prevail against it. And I will give unto thee the keys of the kingdom of heaven; and whatsoever thou shalt bind on earth shall be bound in heaven and whatsoever thou shalt loose on earth shall be loosed in heaven.'

7. St Augustine in *De Genesi ad litteram* 12:24 defined the corporeal and spiritual eyes as capable of being deceived – as are the senses. The intellectual vision, however, was a deep, inner knowing which could not be deceived. For a detailed survey of this issue and a discussion of the differences between mystical and visionary writings see Rosalynn Voaden, 'God's Words, Women's Voices: *Discretio Spiritum* in the Writing of Late-Medieval Women Visionaries' (unpublished D.Phil., University of York, 1994).

8. André Vauchez, *Laity in the Middle Ages*, ed. Daniel Bornstein and tr. Margery Schneider (London, 1993), p. 220.

9. Scott, *Trial*, pp. 71, 78, 109.

10. Ibid., p. 66.

11. Ibid., pp. 73, 85.

12. Ibid., p. 67.

13. Luke 1: 26–30.

14. Scott, *Trial*, p. 67.

15. Ibid., p. 67.

16. Luke 1: 35.

17. In its entirety, the *Magnificat* is in Luke 1: 46–55.

18. Scott, *Trial*, p. 110

19. St Jerome, Letter 22, quoted in Marina Warner, *Alone of All Her Sex: The Myth and Cult of the Virgin Mary* (London, 1976), pp. 54–5.

20. John Bugge, *Virginitas: An Essay in the History of a Medieval Ideal* (The Hague, 1975), p. 19.

21. Rosemary Ruether, 'Misogyny and Virginal Feminism in the Fathers of the Church', in Rosemary Ruether (ed.), *Religion and Sexism* (New York, 1974), p. 159.

22. Scott, *Trial*, p. 104.

23. Anne Barstow, *Joan of Arc: Heretic, Mystic, Shaman* (New York, 1986), p. 60.

24. Scott, *Trial*, pp. 113–4.

25. Marina Warner, *Joan of Arc: The Image of Female Heroism* (London, 1981), p. 22.

26. Scott, *Trial*, p. 67.

27. Charles T. Wood, *Joan of Arc and Richard III* (Oxford, 1988), p. 134.

28. Scott, *Trial*, p. 79.

29. Jacobus de Voragine, *The Golden Legend: Readings on the Saints*, tr. William Granger Ryan (2 vols, Princeton, 1993), vol. 2, pp. 334–5.

30. Scott, *Trial*, p. 151.

31. *The Golden Legend*, vol. 2, pp. 232–3.

32. Scott, *Trial*, p. 72.

33. Voaden, '*discretio sensum*', in *Discretio Spiritum*, pp. 2–3.

34. Scott, *Trial*, p. 135.

35. Ibid., p. 122

36. Edward Peters (ed.), *Heresy and Authority in Medieval Europe: Documents in Translation* (New York, 1980), p. 14.

37. Vauchez, *Laity*, p. 221.

38. See Malcolm D. Lambert, *Medieval Heresy: Popular Movements from the Gregorian Reform to the Reformation*, 2nd edn (Oxford, 1992), p. 5.

39. Scott, *Trial*, p. 159.

40. Ibid., p. 148.

41. Ibid., p. 159.

42. *Le Jouvencel*, quoted in Warner, *Joan of Arc*, p. 160.

43. Scott, *Trial*, p. 134.

44. Ibid., p. 169.

45. Ibid., p. 101.

46. Warner, *Joan of Arc*, p. 164.

47. Scott, *Trial*, p. 134.

48. Ibid., p. 156.

49. Ibid., pp. 73, 85.

50. Scott, *Trial*, p. 171.

51. Joan Wallach Scott, 'Gender: A Useful Category of Historical Analysis', *American Historical Review* 91 (1986), 1053–75, p. 1069.

52. Toril Moi, 'Feminist, Female and Feminine', in Catherine Belsey and Jane Moore (eds), *The Feminist Reader* (Cambridge, 1989), p. 124.

53. Scott, *Trial*, p. 146.

54. Ibid., p. 147.

55. Eleanor McLaughlin, 'Equality of Souls, Inequality of Sexes', in Ruether (ed.), *Religion and Sexism*, p. 157.

56. Ruether, 'Misogyny and Virginal Feminism', p. 157.

57. Scott, *Trial*, p. 160.

58. Ibid., p. 160.

59. Genesis 3: 16: 'Unto the woman he said, I will greatly multiply thy sorrow and thy conception; in sorrow thou shalt bring forth children; and thy desire shall be thy husband and *he shall rule over thee*' (italics added).

60. 1 Corinthians 14: 34–5.

7

Female Wards and Marriage in Romance and Law: A Question of Consent

Noël James Menuge

Wardship has been a popular topic for discussion among legal historians during the last twenty years at least.[1] Little has been written from the perspective of literature, however. A rich seam of wardship literature exists within the genre of romance, and until now, it is a seam that has remained untapped.[2] Romances have the potential to inform and complement legal and historical readings of wardship, and throughout this article I shall discuss the marriages of four female wards, two from romance and two from legal cases, with particular attention to the concept of 'mutual consent'. In a volume on medieval young womanhood, I think it is important to consider some of the implications of the marriage of female minors, and while this article does not by any means profess to offer an authoritative view on female wards and marriage, it does offer some alternative ways of reading the narratives created by the practice of the marriage of female wards in the late Middle Ages.

The wards I discuss are feudal; the romance wards belong only to the feudal aristocracy and royalty.[3] The material I consider includes contemporary treatises, legislation and other parallel cases, which I refer to in the endnotes, but it is the narratives generated by the romances and cases which I discuss within the main body of the article.[4] Legal sources and romances offer us alternative discourses concerning the same subject; although belonging to different genres these alternative discourses arise from within the same society. Each discourse helps to inform our reading of the other, and read together they help to inform our reading of the society from which they came. I believe that the areas of concern raised by the wardship romances may show us a point of general public contact with the legal system; this may be a place from which to explore the legal contexts in which these areas of concern are defined.[5] Used in conjunction with legal material the wardship romances may help us to gain a greater understanding of the social and legal problems faced by those medieval wards, particularly female, who were fast approaching marriageable age.

I am concerned with the issue of mutual consent because of what I see as its ambiguity, especially in the cases of young feudal female wards. By 'mutual consent', it is meant that both parties to the marriage must agree to accept the marriage of their own volition. To the modern reader it implies freedom of choice, but this is not necessarily the case.[6] At best it meant that the parties to the marriage must have agreed to accept the marriage without any undue force or pressure having been applied. It suggests the power of refusal; it suggests the recognition of an individual's right to remain unwed. In reality the differences between consent, force, and autonomous choice were more blurred. Wards were subjected to pressures in marriage, which were largely to do with the value of the ward's estate. Large sums of money could be made from the sale of wards and their marriages.[7] Arranged marriages for profit were not unusual.[8] Pressure to comply with the wishes of guardians choosing marriage partners would have been great. Mutual consent might have different meanings according to the situations of wards and their guardians. Female wards may not have been more or less vulnerable than male wards, yet they were still vulnerable. I hope to show, through the narratives I discuss, some instances of why this might be.

An idea of female autonomy is hard to represent, or even find in the sources; representation of its possible presence in sources is rare, and yet the very idea of mutual consent, and the implications of canonical majority suggest its existence. The age of canonical majority, or the age of consent, as it is also known, was decided, in effect, upon ideas of physical and intellectual maturity, or at least upon classical learning relating to such ideas.[9] This age was twelve for girls, and fourteen for boys. That a definite age for consent was decided, suggests that at these ages it was assumed that females and males were able to think and act for themselves, and that they would be sufficiently in charge of their own sexuality to decide whether or not marriage to certain partners was for them.[10] This does imply autonomy, but as I shall argue, with particular reference to Marrays c. de Rouclif,[11] I believe this is a strategy that to a certain extent allows manipulation of the marriages of young wards. Inversely, 'mutual consent' and canonical majority may in fact imply a lack of autonomy.

The cases and romance examples I consider are not necessarily illustrative of normal practice; indeed, I have selected them because of their unusual interest. The first two sources I look at suggest that some female wards may have experienced a certain level of autonomy, but were perhaps unable to act upon it. They suggest that 'mutual consent' was a principle which female wards themselves recognized, but one which was largely ignored by their guardians. The second two sources I consider are more ambiguous; they do not imply definitely either a presence or lack of autonomy, but may easily be read either way according to individual interpretations of the narratives they supply. They do, however, suggest that a female ward who was possibly under the age of consent, or within the guardianship of her blood family, would (not surprisingly) accept the wishes of her guardians without query, or more easily than a ward who had already reached the age of canonical majority. Thus mutual consent may not mean active agreement, but instead may mean unquestioned complicity.

In many cases there must have been a fine line between a ward's acceptance of her guardian's wishes, the force with which compliance was achieved, and the actual willing consent of an individual. Walker, in effect, suggests that individual wards on the whole, including females, married the partners of their choice.[12] This is not always so, especially not in the cases I consider. Some wards no doubt exercised their autonomy, and even their free choice. To varying degrees, the wards I discuss here, did not. In terms of some female wards at least, 'mutual consent' is a misnomer.

The romances I discuss are *Havelok the Dane* (Lincolnshire/north-east Midlands, *c.* 1280–1300)[13] and *William of Palerne* (south-west Midlands, *c.* 1350–61),[14] and these are discussed in conjunction with two legal cases heard in the York consistory court during the fourteenth century. These are William, son of Adam de Hopton c. Constance de Skelmanthorpe, daughter of Walter del Brome (1348) and John Marrays c. Alice, daughter of Gervase de Rouclif (1365).[15] I shall discuss in pairs the marriages of Goldborough (*Havelok the Dane*) and Constance (Hopton c. del Brome), alongside Florence (*William of Palerne*) and Alice (Marrays c. de Rouclif). I have chosen to do this because of the similarities between the female wards in these groupings, both in circumstance, and in age. The marriages of Goldborough and Constance de Skelmanthorpe involve forced marriage without mutual consent of the wards and their spouses, and both are over the age of consent when these marriages take place. The marriages of Florence and Alice de Rouclif are arranged marriages by family members; in each case the consent of the female wards and their ages are doubtful.

Canon law stressed the right of mutual consent as early as *c.* 1140.[16] In order to marry, the parties must be of marriageable age (twelve for girls, fourteen for boys), must be legally able to contract marriage (i.e. free of impediments such as consanguinity) and must be able to give their free consent to the union without 'force and fear' (see below). A ward could bring his or her guardian to court if any of these criteria were in doubt; similarly, a guardian could attempt to bring his or her ward to account if the validity of a marriage made without his permission were in question. Such disputes were immediately referred to the Church courts from the royal courts; feudal law had no jurisdiction in this area. A king, lord, or lesser guardian might exert pressure to persuade the ward to forgo his or her rights, but the fact remained that a temporal guardian could not make or unmake a marriage. Only the Church had this right.[17]

Canon law allowed for a ward's refusal of potential unions. In certain circumstances a ward could lawfully refuse a chosen marriage partner.[18] Secular legislation ensured that guardians must recognize the right of the individual to free consent in marriage, and this included the right to reasonable refusal.[19] If a marriage was enforced in spite of this, the Church courts offered the opportunity to annul the marriage if it was found that the amount of force or pressure exerted was unreasonable (reasonable force was allowed). It was considered that unreasonable force caused '*metus qui cadere potest in constantum virum/mulierum*' ('the fear that can fall upon a constant man/woman'); such unions were considered to be brought about by 'force and fear.'[20] Consider this extract from Hopton c. del Brome:

> The proctor of Constance daughter of Walter del Brome, named proctor for the same Constance against William son of Adam de Hopton . . . in the matrimonial case alleged between William the plaintiff . . . and the said Constance the defendant . . . Item he puts it that [the marriage took place] through fear, terror and force by the said Adam de Hopton, guardian of the same Constance and natural father of the said William, towards the same Constance [and William] who mutually objected and resisted and disagreed with the alleged contract [which was forced by] striking, holding, and forcing and compelling them . . . .[21]

Compare this extract with the following taken from *Havelok the Dane*:

> Godrich þe erl was swiþe wroth
> þat she swor swilk an oth,
> And seyde: "Hwor þou wilt be
> Qwen and levedi over me?
> þou shalt haven a gadeling;
> . . . þe shal spusen mi cokes knave;
> Ne shalt þou non oþer loverd have . . .
> Tomorwe ye sholen ben weddeth
> And, maugre þin, togidere beddeth![22]
> . . . Or þou shalt to þe galwes renne
> And þer þou shalt in a fir brenne.'
>
> ll. 1118–29 and ll. 1161–62

Both examples concern a young female ward who is forced into marriage by her guardian. In each case force and fear has been used. In each case the marriage appears to have been forced without the consent of the ward. In each case the ward is denied the opportunity of choosing her own marriage partner. In each case the ward is wealthy and the guardian stands to gain from the forced marriage. In each case the ward is above the legal age of consent.

The similarities are striking, and while I do not suggest that the narratives of romance wards are deliberate or exact echoes of the narratives we find in legal cases, I do suggest that the romance is a lay, or secular, version of the legal narrative. I argue elsewhere for the ingestion of the legal narrative within that of the romance, and what this might have meant for the romance audience;[23] here I wish only to bring attention to the similarities of the narratives of these two different discourses, and to suggest that the romance is perhaps a more experimental, and controlled, forum for exploring the legal and moral issues inherent within the marriage of female wards, than is the legal case, and is thus easier to read as a summary of those issues. In this sense, the narratives within the romance can help to clarify the rather more complex issues within the exceptional wardship cases that I offer for examples. The romance is not governed by the outside and unpredictable factors of legal cases; it has the unifying voice of the author to control its narratives. The individual narratives within legal cases are less controllable, and more difficult to interpret. They are based upon personal motivations and factors which we cannot always know. While this may be no different from the way in which the personal interior of the author of the romance may shape his narratives, the issue here is that such essential elements of the legal case narrative such as background and motivation (which would not be omitted in a romance) are not always present within the legal narrative. The unified authorial voice of the wardship romance supplies us with motives and explanations which we may then consider in the light of the case material, and in the light of what we know of contemporary canon and civil law. It would be useful to bear this in mind while considering the content of the following four cases.

Hopton c. del Brome concerns Constance de Skelmanthorpe, a young female ward, who is involved in a marriage dispute against her sometime guardian, one Adam de Hopton. He had previously forced her into a marriage with his nine-year-old son, William, after she had already contracted marriage with a certain John Rotherfield.[24] Constance appears to have been fifteen at the time. Adam de Hopton, her guardian, appears to have forced the marriage because of his wishes to retain her inheritance within his family.[25] The case is brought against Constance by William de Hopton when he is fourteen and she is twenty.

The threats in the passage quoted from *Havelok the Dane* are made by Godrich, the Earl of Cornwall, to his ward Goldborough, heiress to England's throne. Goldborough is twenty years of age when this happens. We have seen that Adam de Hopton allegedly forced Constance into marriage with his under-age son in a bid to retain her inheritance; in the romance passage, Godrich marries Goldborough to Havelock, temporarily in the guise of a cook's servant, in an attempt at disparagement that will ensure his similar hold upon her inheritance.[26] Adam de Hopton threatens Constance with extreme physical violence, and allegedly forces her into the union by holding and beating her. It is this, coupled with the fear that she will lose her lands, which causes Constance eventually to give in. Godrich wields a similar proprietorial and physical control over Goldborough, who complies, like Constance, with her guardian's wishes.

In spite of the threats made against her, Goldborough tries to exercise her right to refuse the union with the following oath: '"Bi Crist and bi Seint Johan/ þat hire should no man wedde/Ne no man bringen hire to bedde, /But he were king or kinges eyr,/Were he nevere man so fayr"' (ll. 1113–7). Goldborough not only wishes to maintain her virginity and guard against the shame and (public) disgrace of forced intercourse ('Ne no man bringen her to bedde'), she is also guarding against the legal implications of consummation, possible validity and resulting disparagement; perhaps she would have consented to a marriage of equal status. She is, however, unable to exercise her right to refusal, for Godrich immediately threatens her with burning and the gallows (in other words, he is threatening her with 'force and fear') if she will not follow his choice. She complies. She is given no alternative. Unbeknown to Goldborough, however, Havelok is actually heir to the throne of Denmark, so the marriage is appropriate. When this becomes apparent to her, she embraces the union with enthusiasm: ' "He beth heyman yet, als Y wene;"/ . . . She was so fele siþes bliþe / þat she mithr hire joie myth' (ll. 1260–1278).

What choice is Constance de Skelmanthorpe given? In spite of her marriage to John de Rotherfield, Adam de Hopton has maintained possession of her lands and deeds. Although of canonical majority, she is still under legal age. Adam de Hopton has refused to recognize her marriage to John, and in so doing he maintains her property while she is a minor. He drags her and his infant son to the altar, and allegedly forces them into marriage.[27] In her defence statement Constance maintains that she *refused* this union, yet, like Goldborough, she was forced to accept it. The marriage went ahead.[28]

When she is married to Havelok, Goldborough is twenty. As we have seen, she has long passed the age where she may leave her wardship and inherit her property. Nevertheless, she remains under the custody of Godrich until her marriage; the marriage itself is designed so that she will never come into her inheritance.[29] All of this is against the wishes of her father. On his deathbed Aþelwold laments her minority, that she is 'so yung þat sho ne couþe / Gon on fote, ne speke wit mouþe' (ll. 112–13). It is this minority which he fears may be a threat to her. He says he would not worry if she were already of age and in control of her inheritance. Coupled with this fear is his anxiety about her marriage. He desires that her guardian not marry her

> "Til þat she were tuelf winter hold;
> And of speche were bold,
> And þat she couþe of curtesye,
> Don, and speken of luue drurye;
> And til þat she loven mithe
> Womso hire to gode þoucte.
>
> ll. 192–97

This passage implies that a marriage brought before the age of consent is undesirable. It shows that the romance author understood the physical and psychological requirements of the age of consent. Aþelwold desires his daughter to be married *only* when she has reached the canonical age of majority, and *only* at such time as she can speak of love-making for herself; only at such time is she old enough to choose a marriage partner for herself. Thus marriage must take place only at such time as Goldborough is physically and emotionally mature. The choice, her father makes Godrich swear, must be in her hands. It must be a partner she loves. Aþelwold believes she will be able to make such decisions for herself only when she has attained canonical majority. The romance thus expounds elements of the canonical view of marriage within its narrative, and it explains the possible implications of this view for its audience.[30]

When Goldborough is married to Havelok, she has attained this age. The choice, however, is not her own, and this is one of the many points at which Godrich breaks his guardianship oath. Aþelwold has stressed that Goldborough must have *free choice*, not merely free consent. The fact that she is of canonical majority and legal age does not prevent her guardian from forcing her to do his will. As the narrative shows, legal majority did not always mean legal autonomy. Goldborough realizes this, yet there is nothing the plot will allow her to do. She is held as captive by its narrative boundaries, as she is by her guardian's machinations. These narrative boundaries must be representative of the legal difficulties female wards faced when under the guardianship of individuals such as Godrich. Constance finds herself similarly restricted, yet fights, as much as she can, for her autonomy. When the case is brought against Constance by the fourteen-year-old William, she is apparently, as I have mentioned, twenty years of age. The marriage between William and Constance appears to have taken place five years previously, when Constance was fifteen, and William nine. Constance would thus have been above the age of consent, and William below.[31] The marriage with John de Rotherfield also occurred, allegedly, when Constance was fifteen, but before the contract with William de Hopton took place. The marriage with John de Rotherfield would therefore have been valid. Witnesses testify to this validity.[32] Constance apparently fulfils the physical and psychological maturity required by the canonical definition of the age of consent, and yet is not allowed this marriage by her guardian. The actions of her guardian in ignoring the apparent validity of her first marriage, help also to explain the fears expressed by Goldborough's father. He fears that unless she is mentally and physically able to decide marriage for herself, then she will be taken advantage of by her guardian. Constance is of age; she is capable, yet her guardian still takes advantage of her. The case of Goldborough, who, when married, is also of canonical age, shows her father's fears to be well-founded, in spite of her canonical majority, and obvious maturity. By considering the content of each narrative, we may see more clearly just how difficult it is to arrive at any conclusions regarding the nature of the autonomy implied within the theoretical definition of 'mutual consent'. The apparent safeguard of a legally accepted marriage age and the implied autonomy of 'mutual consent' failed to prevent the manipulation of female wards within marriage. These cases, as I have mentioned, may not be representative of the norm, yet they do make clear some of the complexities which we must consider if we are to gain an understanding of medieval wards, guardians and marriage practice in the late Middle Ages.

Constance alleges that John de Rotherfield was murdered sometime after her forced marriage to William de Hopton. She decides for herself that her marriage to William de Hopton is invalid, and, having previously escaped from the custody of her guardian, marries a third time, to one William Bosevill. Allegedly Constance had been married to William Bosevill for ten months before William de Hopton brings his suit against her. William de Hopton claims pre-contract against the marriage to William Bosevill, and Constance claims pre-contract with John de Rotherfield against the marriage to William de Hopton. She also claims force and fear, and consanguinity (William de Hopton was first cousin to John de Rotherfield). Thus we see that the strategy of Constance to remove herself from the marriage to William de Hopton is fourfold: she was married at the time, she was forced, the subsequent union was consanguineous, and she had since contracted a further marriage. All of these allegations may in themselves have been true, but this is not their importance in her argument; they are used instead to pile up the odds against the plaintiff. Her plan appears to be to win her case on at least one point, if not on all. Constance may indeed have suffered at the hands of her guardian, yet she is constructed, both by herself, and by the material within the document, as a woman with a sound understanding of the issues at stake, as someone whose firm belief in her right to refuse marriage where she saw fit took precedence over the actions of her guardian. I have used the term 'constructed' because we must still be aware that Constance is a character within a particular type of narrative. She does not exist, for us, outside of it, and her actions will have been governed in part by factors and relationships that we can know nothing about. In this sense she is almost as textual as a romance ward.

This construction makes it easy for us to read Constance as an example of female agency in action, yet we must be wary of ascribing autonomy to her. In spite of what appears to be independence in the contracting of her first and third marriages, she is still allegedly forced into a marriage against her will, and as a consequence of her later 'autonomous' actions she is forced into court to defend herself. We only learn of her because of the consent she apparently did not give. The autonomy we may read within her narrative is one which stems from a decided lack of autonomy in her inability to prevent the marriage to William de Hopton taking place. Had she done so, we would not, in all likelihood, have heard of her at all.

The mid-fourteenth-century romance *William of Palerne* abounds in examples of marriage, most consistently where the issue of mutual consent is concerned. Florence herself is subjected to a kind of marriage attempt through force and fear before her marriage to Alphouns, although it is her marriage to Alphouns which

I shall discuss here. When Florence is eventually married to Alphouns, it is arranged by her brother, William. Florence is not consulted, nor is her mother, who had been acting as guardian until William returned to his inheritance. When William asks Alphouns to name his reward for the help and brotherhood he has shown him, Alphouns replies that he '". . . ne wilne noþing but þi suster, to be samen wedded,/to weld here as my wif al my lif-tyme"' (ll. 4740–1). William answers with enthusiasm, and offers him his kingdom as dowry: '"Bi God, sire," seide William, "þat gart me be fourmed,/ þow schalt [have] hire at þin hest, and with hire al my reaume"' (ll. 4750–1). He wonders though, that Alphouns does not mind being married so low:[33]

> '3a, worþi God,' seide William, 'welwere me þanne,
> 3if I wist þat þow woldest here to wive have:
> it were a wonderful werk 3if þou woldest evere
> meke þe in eny maner to be maried so lowe.'
>
> ll. 4742–5

Alphouns rejects the dowry, believing that he is only worthy of the wife, and not the kingdom: '"Nay, Crist forbede," seide Alphouns, "for his holi blode,/þat I were so wicked to wilne ou3t of þi gode./I ne bidde nou3t a bene worþ but þat burde one"' (ll. 4752–4). This jovial bartering is not meant to insult Florence; in effect it is courtly generosity and manners which William and Alphouns exhibit. Nevertheless it underlies an attitude that does not consider Florence as a being in her own right. It is an attitude that allows no room for possible refusal on her part. The request of Alphouns to marry Florence demonstrates another aspect of the arranged marriage. He proposes not to Florence, but to her brother, now rightful heir to the throne of Sicily. Florence is essentially another part of William's new-found inheritance; she may be given in generosity to whom he pleases. Florence's situation is merely representative of a feudal attitude towards (female) wards at this time. The author portrays the marriage bargaining in contemporary terms: Florence is a chattel. She is still a minor, and although possibly able to contract marriage for herself she is given no opportunity to do so. One might argue here for the compulsion of the narrative: that Florence's marriage to Alphouns is part of an authorial desire to resolve the plot with tidy marriages, which it is, in part. To do so exclusively, however, would be to ignore the fact that the author could easily have made Florence assent verbally to this match. He does not, which raises the issue of consent, as I have discussed it with relation to Florence.

In 1365 John Marrays brought a case against Alice de Rouclif.[34] Sir Brian de Rouclif, possibly Alice's guardian, had allegedly abducted her from her husband, John, after the apparent ratification of their marriage.[35] Her guardian *ad litem* claimed that Alice was under the age of consent when John and Alice consummated, and thereby ratified, a marriage contract which was arranged with Alice's mother Elena (who may have been her *de facto* guardian) while Alice was still below the age of consent.[36] This marriage was arranged over a large sum of money, most likely the dowry, and although witnesses for John testify that Alice gave her consent to the contract, her canonical minority at the time implies, like Florence's, her lack of direct involvement with the arrangement. While there is no dispute over her minority at the time of the contract, John Marrays complains that Alice was of canonical age when the contract was ratified, and therefore that he has been denied his conjugal rights by Sir Brian.[37] Witnesses for Alice testify that Alice was under the age of twelve when this consummation took place. Thus Alice's guardian *ad litem* argues that the marriage is invalid. Witnesses for John Marrays testify that Alice was of age, and thus John argues that the marriage should stand. The issue of Alice's canonical minority is the bone of contention, and ensures that she does not testify for herself.[38] Alice is thereby caught up in a lengthy and bitter legal argument in which many people testify for and against her, commenting on intimate details of her sexual behaviour. She is very much a pawn in a struggle which involves, at bottom, her value as a chattel.

Witnesses for John Marrays testify strongly that Alice wanted the initial contract to take place, and that she gave her consent without argument. Her 'uterine' brother, John Fische, testifies that although under-age when marriage was contracted, Alice accepted the marriage willingly, indeed happily, and was under no pressure to do so. Her 'blood' brother, Robert de Rouclif, testifies to the same.[39] Anabilla Wasteleyne, the sister of John Marrays, deposes that Alice herself requested the solemnization of the marriage to take place after she had slept with John in Anabilla's house. The words she gives for Alice are as follows:

> 'Dame, I have a secret to tell you if you will hear it . . . Dame, I should like the marriage between your brother and me to be solemnised and I ask you that you persuade him to do this . . . I am old enough and mature enough to be his wife, but not his mistress.'[40]

The alleged words which Anabilla gives to Alice serve to demonstrate her physical maturity (and therefore canonical majority), her consent to the marriage, and that sex (the reference to 'mistress') has taken place. Depositions of other witnesses for John Marrays do the same.[41] These are not words that Alice gives for herself; there may be truth in them, but they may also be a demonstration of how witnesses and plaintiffs for a cause could manipulate canonical theory for their own ends. John Marrays wins his case. The court deems that Alice was both physically and mentally capable of agreeing to ratify the marriage, and that she had indeed so done. Although her age cannot be definitely proven, the court deems that, as certain witnesses testified, she was near enough to the age of consent (*proxima pubertati*) for the court to accept the marriage as valid.[42] Her own claims are thus made redundant. That the court decides in favour of John

Marrays does not demonstrate that Alice gave her consent, nor does it demonstrate that she did not. It demonstrates only that the court deemed her able to. We are no closer to determining what degree of autonomy she may or may not have had in terms of giving her consent. What we may determine is that she was almost certainly the vehicle for legal argument over an inheritance.

The similarities between Florence and Alice may not be as obvious as those between Goldborough and Constance, yet they do exist. Both have their marriages arranged for them by family members: Florence by her brother, acting as her guardian, and Alice by her mother, acting possibly as her guardian or *de facto* guardian. In each case the marriage is an arrangement to which the ward may have given her consent, or not, and in each marriage the girl is offered as a chattel, indistinguishable from her wealth. Neither ward is given a voice of her own within each source to express her desires, and both girls appear to comply with the wishes of their immediate families. In each case the families speak for them. In the case of Florence it is her brother, and in the case of Alice it is her mother, brothers, and sister-in-law, and Sir Brian.

As I have mentioned, in each case the age of the ward is doubtful, and this is central to the case which is brought against Alice, as I have shown. It is difficult to determine Florence's age from the text. We know from the text that she was three years younger than William 'sche was ȝonger þan William bi fulle þre ȝeres' (l. 2636), but once William has made his love pact with the princess Melior it is more difficult to determine ages. William and Melior are fourteen when they declare their love for each other, so at this time Florence is eleven, and under the age of canonical majority. G.H.V. Bunt, in the introduction to *William of Palerne*, writes that between lines 1002–1066 three years pass in which Melior and William secretly share each other's love at Melior's father's court.[43] This would make William seventeen when he marries Florence to Alphouns, and therefore Florence herself would be fourteen, and above the canonical age of majority. However, I can find no evidence in these lines for the passage of three years. The only specific mention within these lines of time passing is between lines 1057–59, where the narrator tell us that 'Wiþ alle listes of love alle longe ȝeres,/priveli unparceyved þei pleyed togedere,/þat no seg under sunne souched no gile.' '[A]lle long ȝeres' could be any amount of time, not necessarily three years; it could be more or less. We might even compare 'alle long ȝeres' to the type of approximate passage of time one finds in the depositions of Marrays c. de Rouclif.[44] Without specificity we cannot be sure of Florence's age. If one year were to have passed then she would be able to give her consent; as with Alice, however, we do not know what the margin of age is. We cannot, therefore, reasonably read her consent with any certainty. The parallel with Alice is very close – Alice may in law be of age to consent, but this is a technicality – she is still so young as not to be able to exercise effective agency. This may also be the case with Florence. It seems to be enough for the author that her family decide her marriage for her.

This should come as no surprise. We know that arranged marriages were not unusual among the gentry and aristocracy.[45] We know, also, that wards were often subject to such arrangements, in a way which suggests a norm.[46] I do not think that the author of *William of Palerne* comments upon this practice in any way that suggests it was other than the norm. What I do think he is commenting upon is how the vulnerability of minor wards was exacerbated by this norm; indeed, that their vulnerability cemented the norm. The case of Alice de Rouclif demonstrates this for us plainly. It is her vulnerability as a canonical and legal minor which allows for the exploitation of her position; it is against this exploitation that Sir Brian has apparently abducted her (while no doubt sharing the financial incentive for exploitation). Florence, like Alice, may have found the arrangements desirable, but we are not told this by the individuals concerned. In commenting upon common feudal marriage practice, the author of *William of Palerne* also comments indirectly upon the relative lack of importance of the female minor within her own marriage, and this is necessarily shaped by the patriarchal thrust of feudal society. This, even without direct authorial comment, points out the blurred lines between the so-called consent of the individual, and the wishes of the family and guardian. Consent is relative; it does not mean free choice. It does not mean autonomy.

These four cases show us that the issues of consent and age of consent for female wards were perhaps more complicated than the canon legal theory suggests at a first reading. We could arrive at this conclusion by a consideration of the legal cases alone; we do not need the codified and structured narrative of the romance to help us do this. The findings of such a conclusion, however, would overlook the fact that wardship literature existed, and was widely circulated. It would overlook the fact that this wardship literature dealt with the same issues concerning wardship marriage as those that appeared within Church courts, and would overlook the fact that a wider section of the population experienced, vicariously, the wardship position, than perhaps wards themselves. While we must be aware of the dangers of interpreting a simplified narrative as actual practice, the structured and often predictable narrative of the wardship romance may also help to clarify for us what issues were deemed most interesting for attention. Concerning marriage and wardship these are, most importantly, mutual consent, control of marriage by guardians, canonical majority, ratification and the possibility of free choice, and even love, when choosing a marriage partner. This raises questions (the answers to which lie outside the scope of this article) about why these issues were deemed more interesting than others. Why was mutual consent and its attendant concept of canonical majority so important within the narrative of the wardship romance? To conclude, I offer one possible explanation for why this might have been so.

Just as canon law allowed wards the forum of the Church court as an arena for legitimate dispute over marriage, so too did the wardship romances allow a legitimate feudal framework within which to discuss and explore these issues in a more accessible manner. Romances may be scenarios of wish fulfilment; they are also powerful reminders of the existence of a critical, authorial voice within feudal society. Within the boundary of romance the issues concerning the marriages of Goldborough and Florence are perhaps as real and as important as those of Constance de Skelmanthorpe and Alice de Rouclif; in a literary sense they are as illustrative of this point as are the legal and historical cases I have used. The wardship romances explore the dynamics involved in exercising or not being able to exercise the theoretical right of mutual consent; legal cases show the emotional struggle and the logistical difficulties experienced by wards faced with desired or undesired marriages. Reading these narratives together helps to reveal the complexities of the canon and secular legal concepts with which we are dealing. Seeking answers and providing narrative interpretation is more than just a question of considering legislation and theory; it is, for us, more than just a question of consent. It is *questioning* consent.

Notes

Abbreviations: BIHR – Borthwick Institute of Historical Research; *CCR* – Calendar of Close Rolls; CP. E. – Cause Paper category E (fourteenth century); *CPR* – Calendar of Patent Rolls.

I would like to acknowledge here Felicity Riddy, Jeremy Goldberg, Rosalind Field, Alison Spencer, and Adam Menuge for some stimulating and helpful discussions about the subject matter of this article.

1. See especially S.S. Walker, 'Royal Wardship in Medieval England' (unpublished Ph.D. thesis, University of Chicago, 1966); S.S. Walker, 'Proof of Age of Feudal Heirs in Medieval England', *Medieval Studies*, 35 (1973), 306–23; S.S. Walker, 'The Marrying of Feudal Wards in Medieval England', *Studies in History and Culture*, 4.2 (1974), 209–24; S.S. Walker, 'Widow and Ward: The Feudal Law of Child Custody in Medieval England', *Feminist Studies*, 3.4 (1976), 104–6. Reprinted in S.M. Stuard (ed.), *Women in Medieval Society* (Philadelphia, 1976, repr. 1993), pp. 159–72; S.S. Walker, 'The Action of Waste in the Early Common Law', in J.H. Baker (ed.), *Legal Records and the Historian* (London, 1978), pp. 185–206; S.S. Walker, 'Feudal Constraint and Free Consent in the Making of Marriage in Medieval England: Widows in the King's Gift', *Canadian Historical Society Papers*, (1979), 97–110; S.S. Walker, 'Free Consent and Marriage of Feudal Wards in Medieval England', *Journal of Medieval History*, 8 (1982), 123–34; S.S. Walker, 'Common Law Juries and Feudal Marriage Customs: The Pleas of Ravishment', *University of Illinois Law Review* (1984), 705–18; S.S. Walker, 'The Feudal Family and the Common Law Courts: The Pleas Protecting Rights of Wardship and Marriage, *c.* 1225–1375', *Journal of Medieval History*, 14 (1988), 13–31. For other sources concerning medieval marriage, some of which discuss wardship, see especially N. Cartlidge, *Medieval Marriage: Literary Approaches 1100–1300* (Woodbridge, 1997); K. Dockray, 'Why Did Fifteenth-Century English Gentry Marry?', in M. Jones (ed.), *Gentry and Lesser Nobility in Late Medieval Europe* (Gloucester, 1986); R.H. Helmholz, *Marriage Litigation in Medieval England* (Cambridge, 1974); S.F.C. Milsom, 'Inheritance by Women in the Twelfth and Thirteenth Centuries', in M.S. Arnold and et al. (eds), *On the Laws and*

Customs of England: Essays in Honour of Samuel E. Thorne (North Carolina, 1981); S. Payling, 'The Politics of Family: Late Medieval Marriage Contracts', in R.H. Britnell and A.J. Pollard (eds), *The McFarlane Legacy: Studies in Late Medieval Politics and Society* (Stroud, 1995); M.M. Sheehan, 'The Formation and Stability of Marriage in the Fourteenth Century: Evidence of an Ely Register', *Medieval Studies*, 33 (1971), 228–63; M.M. Sheehan, 'Choice of a Marriage Partner in the Middle Ages: Development and Mode of Application of a Theory of Marriage', *Studies in Medieval and Renaissance History*, 1 (1978), 1–33; M.M. Sheehan, 'Marriage Theory and Practice in Consiliar Legislation and Diocesan Statutes of Medieval England', *Medieval Studies*, 40 (1978), 408–60; S.L. Waugh, 'Marriage, Class and Royal Lordship in England under Henry III', *Viator*, 16 (1985), 181–207; S.L. Waugh, *The Lordship of England: Royal Wardships and Marriages in English Society and Politics* (Princeton, 1988).

2. See also N.J. Menuge, 'The Wardship Romance: A New Methodology', in R. Field (ed.), *Tradition and Transformation in Medieval Romance* (Cambridge, 1999) and N.J. Menuge, 'A Few Home Truths: The Medieval Mother as Guardian in Romance and Law', in N.J. Menuge, (ed.), *Women and Law in the Middle Ages* (Cambridge, forthcoming).

3. In this paper I am concerned only with feudal wardship, and as such, shall not discuss the burghal or ecclesiastical systems of wardship, which were in many respects different to feudal wardship. For further reference to burghal and ecclesiastical wardship see especially M. Bateson, (ed.), *Borough Customs*, Selden Society (2 vols, London, 1904, 1906) and R.H. Helmholz, 'The Roman Law of Guardianship in England, 1300–1600', *Tulane Law Review*, 52 (1978), 22–57.

4. This legal context is formed by the content of various legal treatises, statutes, and legal cases. Treatises are explanatory, discursive, philosophic accounts of past law. Useful treatises include G.D. Hall (ed.), *The Treatise on the Laws and Customs of England, Commonly Called Glanvill*, (*c.* 1190) (London, 1968), and the early thirteenth-century *Bracton de legibus et consuetudinibus Anglie*, ed. G.E. Woodbine (Massachusetts, 1968). Statutes are laws which have been passed. See A. Luders, T.E. Tomlins, and J. Raithby (eds), *Statutes of the Realm, 1101–1713* (11 vols, London, 1828, repr. 1963). Those to do with wardship include Magna Carta (1215), c. 6 (*Statutes* 1: 3), the Statute of Merton (1236) (*Statutes* 1: 3), the Statute of Marlborough (1267) (*Statutes* 1: 23–4, Westminster I (1275) (*Statutes* 1: 33), Gloucester (1278) (*Statutes* 1: 40), and Westminster II (1285) (*Statutes* 2: 16). The two cases I discuss in this article, although concerning feudal wards, were heard in the consistory court in York, due to their concern with marriage litigation, over which the Church had jurisdiction. For discussions concerning wardship in common law cases see the articles by S.S. Walker, in n.1 above, *passim*. The romances within my wardship romance grouping are R. Allen (ed.), *King Horn* (New York and London, 1984); M. Mills (ed.), *Horn Child and Maiden Riminild* (Heidelberg, 1988); *Havelok the Dane*, ed. D. Speed in *Medieval English Romances* (2 vols, Durham, 1993); E. Kolbing (ed.), *The Romance of Sir Beues of Hamtoun*, Early English Text Society, Extra Series, nos. 46, 48, 65 (London, 1885, 1886, 1894); G.H.V. Bunt (ed.), *William of Palerne* (Gronengen, 1985); W. Skeat (ed.), *The Tale of Gamelyn* (Oxford, 1893). In this article I discuss only *Havelok the Dane* and *William of Palerne*.

5. For discussions of possible romance audiences see K. Brunner, 'Middle English Metrical Romances and Their Audience', in M. Leach (ed.), *Medieval Literature in Honor of Professor A. C. Baugh* (Philadelphia, 1961), pp. 219–27; C. Fewster, *Traditionality and Genre in Middle English Romance* (Cambridge, 1987); H. Hudson, 'Towards a Theory of Popular Culture: The Case of the Middle English Romance', *Journal of Popular Culture*, 23 (1989), 31–50; S. Knight, 'The Social Function of the

Middle English Romances', in D. Aers (ed.), *Medieval Literature: Criticism, Ideology and History* (Brighton, 1986); C.M. Meale, 'The Middle English *Ipomedon*: A Late Medieval Mirror for Princes and Merchants', *Reading Medieval Studies*, 10 (1984), 136–89; C.M. Meale, '"gode men / Wiues maydnes and alle men": Romance and its Audiences', in C.M. Meale (ed.), *Readings in Medieval Romance* (Cambridge, 1994): 209–27; D. Mehl, *The Middle English Romances of the Thirteenth and Fourteenth Centuries* (London, 1968); D. Pearsall, 'Middle English Romance and its Audiences', in M.J. Arn and H. Wirtjes (eds), *Historical and Editorial Studies in Medieval and Early Modern English for Johan Gerritsen* (Groningen, 1985), pp. 37–48; E. Salter, *Fourteenth Century English Poetry: Contexts and Readings* (Oxford, 1983).

6. See Walker, 'Free Consent', p. 123, in which she implies that free choice in marriage for wards was the norm. Her conclusions are drawn from marriage-fine evidence, and while this evidence may demonstrate a limited figure of wards marrying where they chose, it does not, I believe, represent a norm.

7. For example, Geoffrey of Mandeville promised King John 20,000 marks for the Countess of Gloucester and her land: *Rotuli de Oblatus et Finibus, temp. Joh.* (Record Commission), p. 520, as cited in F. Pollock and F.W. Maitland, *The History of English Law Before the Time of Edward I* (2 vols, Cambridge, 1911), vol. 2, p. 322, n. 3.

8. See especially Pollock and Maitland, *History of English Law*, vol. 2, pp. 318–22, and Waugh, *The Lordship of England*, pp. 15–18.

9. The age of consent (i.e. marriageable age) was based on the ability to procreate. See Gratian, *Glossa Ordinaria* ad X 4.2.3. in A.L. Richter and A. Friedberg (eds.), *Corpus Iuris Canonici*, 2nd edn (2 vols, Leipzig, 1922). See also K. Phillips, 'The Medieval Maiden: Young Womanhood in Late Medieval England' (unpublished D.Phil. thesis, University of York, 1997), esp. pp. 31–41 for a sound discussion of factors influencing and determining the definition of the age of canonical majority. She defines the issues in terms of physiological and psychological maturity.

10. I discuss this in further detail below with reference to my wardship examples.

11. BIHR CP. E. 89 (1365). See also n. 15, below. I would like to thank Jeremy Goldberg for some very useful discussions concerning this case.

12. Walker, 'Free Consent', esp. p. 123.

13. Speed (ed.), *Havelok the Dane*. Briefly the plot runs thus: Athelwold, King of England, lies dying. He expresses concern for the well-being and wardship of his infant daughter, Goldborough. One of the king's nobles, Godrich, is charged with her care. In parallel, King Birkabeyn, King of Denmark, lies dying, and similar conerns are expressed for the welfare of his three infant children, Havelok and his two sisters. The Earl Godard becomes their guardian. After the death of each king the guardians break their promises; Godrich imprisons Goldborough in a tower, and Godard slaughters Havelok's sisters and arranges to have him killed. Havelok escapes with the help of the fisherman Grim. His journeys take him to England, where he finds employment as a cook's servant. Meanwhile, many years have passed and Godrich plans to marry Goldborough to someone well below her station so that she cannot inherit her kingdom. He marries her to Havelok, believing him to be a common knave. After further adventures, Havelok and Goldborough regain their respective inheritances, and are revenged upon their guardians. They have many children and reign together happily for many years.

14. Bunt (ed.), *William of Palerne.* Briefly the plot runs thus: While out walking in the forest with his parents, four-year-old William of Palerne, prince of Apulia, is stolen from them by a werewolf. This is because William's life is in danger from his uncle, who plans to have the infant William and his father poisoned so that he can inherit the kingdom. The werewolf is pursued, but to no avail. He swims across the Strait of Messina, and deposits the infant William in a cave in Rome, where he is found by a kindly cowherd, who raises him as his own son. Some years later the Emperor of Rome comes across the child, and recognizing his innate noble bearing takes him home where his daughter Melior looks after him. Meanwhile, William's real father has died, and his mother and sister Florence are under siege from the King of Spain, who wants Florence's hand in marriage for his son Braundinis. Florence and her mother refuse. In Rome, William and Melior have now fallen in love, and elope with the help of Melior's maid and the friendly werewolf. It transpires that the werewolf is really Alphouns, first son and rightful heir to the throne of Spain. He was bewitched as a child by his step-mother, who wished the inheritance to go to her own son, Braundinis. William and Melior arrive in Palermo, where William rescues his as yet unknown mother and sister from siege. Reunions are made, Alphouns is taken to his father's court where his frightened step-mother transforms him once again into human shape. Alphouns asks William for Florence's hand in marriage, and William gives it. All the kingdoms are restored to peace, and the rightful heirs eventually reign.

15. BIHR CP. E. 62 (1348), and BIHR CP. E. 89 (1365) respectively. Due to time pressures the transcription and translation (which I have checked) of CP. E. 62 was very kindly undertaken by Lisa Howarth, to whom many thanks. Translated depositions from CP. E. 89 may be found in P.J.P. Goldberg (ed. and tr.), *Women in England,* c. *1275–1525* (Manchester, 1995), pp. 58–80. For ease of readers' reference, I have used his published translations. I have, however, transcribed the document for myself, and any quotations in the original language are my own. These cause papers from the York consistory court are kept in the Borthwick Institute of Historical Research, St Anthony's Hall, York.

16. J.A. Brundage, *Law, Sex and Christian Society in Medieval Europe* (Chicago, 1987), pp. 229–416; Walker, 'Free Consent', pp. 124–5.

17. Helmholz, *Marriage Litigation*, esp. pp. 90–4.

18. Waugh, *The Lordship of England*, p. 33. Waugh later gives the amusing example of William de Cantilupe, whose mother, in 1314, had obtained his marriage. She offered him the choice of two suitable brides, in the presence of Chancery witnesses. He refused; his reason was personal taste. Like Havelok, he declared he had no use for a woman as a wife. See CCR, 1313–1318, 87; CPR, 1307–1313, 94, as cited by Waugh, p. 217. Apparently William never married.

19. Statutes of Merton (1236) and Westminster II (1285). See *Statutes of the Realm* 1: 3 and 2: 16, respectively.

20. The descriptive term 'force and fear' comes from this phrase. See Brundage, *Christian Society*, pp. 335, 345, 454; Helmholz, *Marriage Litigation*, pp. 90–4. CP. E. 62 is itself such a case. See also text, above.

21. 'Noves infrascript' facit et dat procurator Custancie filie Walteri del Brome nomine procuratorio . . . in causa matrimoniali pretensa inter Willelmum partem actricem ex parte una et dictam Custanciam parte ream ex altera . . . Item ponit quod per metum terrorem et vimas per dictum Adam de Hopton ipsius Custancia curatorem ac patrem carnalem dicti Willelmi eidem Custancie invicem contradicenti et renitenti ac distensicuti huis contractum pretens' in cussos tende et illatos inducte et coacto m'ob'.' CP. E. 62 (1348).

22. The legal implication here is that if this marriage is consummated ('And, maugre þin, togidere beddeth!' l. 1129), then the marriage might prove more difficult to annul. This is surely Godrich's intention; Goldborough recognizes this, and it is likely that the audience do as well. See J.B. Post, 'Ravishment of Women and the Statutes of Westminster', in Baker (ed.), *Legal Records*; J.B. Post, 'Sir Thomas West and the Statute of Rapes, 1382', Bulletin of the Institute of Historical Research, 53 (1980): 24–30; and S.S. Walker, 'Punishing Convicted Ravishers: Statutory Strictures and Actual Practice in Thirteenth and Fourteenth-Century England', *Journal of Medieval History*, 13 (1987): 237–50. Ravishment in the sense that these articles discuss is largely abduction, not necessarily rape as we know it. Ravishment of wards by guardians is sometimes followed by marriage (not to the guardian, but to someone of his or her choosing), in some cases possibly forced. Consummation of such a marriage might result in a ruling of validity. I believe this is presented as Godrich's reasoning. Constance has obviously been abducted at some stage by her guardian; consummation with his son appears not to have been forced. Her lawyer argues that her first marriage to John Rotherfield was proved valid because consummation took place, and that therefore any consequent union with William de Hopton would be invalid: 'Item he puts it that the same John and Constance begot children together . . . he puts it that the aforesaid marriage made between them is thus proved and the carnal coupling between them confirms the contract in law legally between them . . . .' ('Item ponit quod idem Johannis et Custancia proles inter se procearunt . . . ponit quod et matrimonialem predictum inter se sic ut provitatur habitui et [m'at'] per carnalem copulam inter se habitam confirmarit negationem contractum iur' legitium inter eosdem . . . .' CP. E. 62 (1348). See also my discussion of this issue regarding Goldborough and Constance in N.J. Menuge, 'The Wardship Romance'.

23. See N.J. Menuge, 'The Wardship Romance', and N.J. Menuge, 'A Few Home Truths'.

24. Church law allowed individuals to contract marriage from the age of seven years. After attaining canonical majority (twelve for girls, fourteen for boys) they could either give their consent or dissent. If they chose dissent then it had to be given in public, and before an ecclesiastical court. Gratian, *Glossa Ordinaria* X 4.2.7, *iudicio ecclesiae*. See also Helmholz, *Marriage Litigation*, pp. 98–100 for a detailed analysis of nonage cases. It is likely that many female (and male) wards found themselves in this position but found it difficult to seek the redress of the court. The plaintiff in BIHR CP. E. 76 (1357–8), William Aungier, uses this option when he brings the case, at fourteen, to have his marriage to Johanna Malcake (the niece of his guardian) annulled. When wed, he was eight, she was ten. In CP. E. 62 Constance is twenty by the time the case is brought. William de Hopton's lawyer alleges that the marriage took place five years ago ('Item ponit quod quinto'). This would mean that William de Hopton is fourteen and therefore legally able to represent himself when he brings the suit; indeed, upon attainment of this age he would have had to acknowledge or to dissent to the marriage verbally, and publicly. See also text, below. Such verbal ratification is partly the issue in CP. E. 89, as I discuss later in the article.

25. According to Walker male heirs came of age at twenty-one, and female heirs came of age at fourteen if married, or sixteen if unmarried (Walker, 'Pleas Protecting Rights of Wardship', p. 15). According to Orme, by the end of the thirteenth century noble female wards could come out of wardship and inherit. He gives sixteen as the age at which 'a girl who had previously been in wardship could marry', N. Orme, *From Childhood to Chivalry: The Education of the English Kings and Aristocracy 1066–1530* (London and New York, 1984), p. 7. See also Pollock and Maitland, *The History of English Law*, vol. 1, pp. 319–20, and vol. 2, pp. 436–7. Pollock and Maitland are less sure about the age at

which noble female wardships were to end; they are not sure as to whether this should be at the age of sixteen, or at the time of marriage. It seems likely, however, that Constance should have come into her lands while married to John de Rotherfield (she was fifteen); however, as she was still under sixteen, if the marriage was discounted by her guardian, then he may have kept hold of her lands. What appears to have happened is an abduction of Constance, followed by the forced marriage to William. Sometime after this Constance claims that John was murdered. It might have been at this time that her lands were regained by her guardian. It is because Constance herself discounted the de Hopton marriage and remarried elsewhere that the case has been brought. Presumably Constance requires the seisin of her inheritance as she is now married, and of age. Thus must William de Hopton argue for the validity of his own forced marriage if he and his father are to retain her property.

26. Godrich believes that Havelok is a villein. In Anglo-Norman England a woman assumed her husband's status when she married ('He wende þat Havelok wer a þral; / þertou he wende haven al / In Engelond, þat hire rith was' (ll. 1098–1100). The origins of *Havelok the Dane* are Anglo-Norman. Much of early English law was taken from the Anglo-Norman and Magna Carta c. 6 (1215) states that heirs must not be disparaged in marriage, that is, married to someone of lower social standing. See *Statutes of the Realm* 1: 3.

27. See, for example, the deposition of Richard de Helay: 'And he says at the time of the contract made between William and Constance aforesaid the same juror saw the aforesaid William cry and the aforesaid Constance led by fear as it appeared to the same juror as he says, which William and Constance then were under the care and home of Adam de Hopton aforesaid . . . .' ('Et dicit quod tempore contractus habiti inter Willelmum et Custanciam predictos vidit idem iur' prefatum Willelmum flere et dictam Custanciam metu ductam prout apparuit eiden iur' dicit qui quidem Willelmus et Custancia tunc fuerunt sub cura et cognitio Ade de Hopton' predicto . . .') CP. E. 62 (1348).

28. '. . . Item he puts it that [the marriage took place] against the expressed will and wish of the said Constance. . . .' ('. . . item ponit quod et contra expressam voluntato et construsum dicte Custancie. . . .') CP. E. 62 (1348).

29. See n. 26, and text, above.

30. Canon law does not require love within marriage, merely mutual consent, without undue force. The romance example of Goldborough takes the implications of mutual consent a step further by stating that love within marriage is desirable. The implication is that if Goldborough can decide where and when to love for herself, then she is at least emotionally mature enough to make an appropriate choice.

31. As Constance was above the age of consent when the forced union took place, she could not apply to have it annulled on the same grounds available to William when he came of age. Constance chooses not to seek the redress of the courts until a case is brought against her; she chooses, instead, to ignore the marriage control of her sometime guardian.

32. See, for example, the depositions of Adam and Richard de Helay.

33. See n. 26, above, with regards to disparagement. In fact, Florence is a princess, and Alphouns is a prince. Therefore no disparagement would take place.

34. Alice is represented by a guardian *ad litem* in court, because of the dispute over her age. The office of guardian *ad litem* is different from the office of legal guardian. It is not certain in this case who Alice's official guardian is.

35. Although uncertain, it is possible that Sir Brian is, or was, Alice's official guardian, or that he may have had, or claimed, ownership over her marriage. This is suggested by the claims of Thomas de Bulmer and William Sampson that Alice's mother, Elena, took Sir Brian to court at the King's Bench. As yet I have not been able to trace this action, but it is not unlikely that she may have brought the complaint to wrest either the control for guardianship, or marriage, or both, from Sir Brian, as well as to remove Alice from his physical control. No further clue is given, however, as to the guardianship status of either Elena or Sir Brian. See Goldberg, *Women in England*, pp. 79–80.

36. Elena may have been Alice's guardian, or she may have been her *de facto* guardian, responsible for everyday care. Cases between mothers as guardians *de facto* and lords or other guardians over custody occur quite frequently in the records. See Walker, 'Widow and Ward', p. 161, where she discusses 'nutriciam'.

37. The marriage contract was originally made by words of future consent. John Marray's argument is that words of present consent were made by Alice, upon attaining canonical majority, followed by the act of consummation, thereby ratifying the marriage.

38. The court must presume that Alice is a minor until shown otherwise so as not to prejudice the outcome. Thus Alice is represented by a guardian *ad litem*.

39. See the depositions of John Fische and Robert de Rouclif, Goldberg, *Women in England*, pp. 68–9.

40. See Goldberg, *Women in England*, pp. 60–1. The Latin is as follows: *Domina, ego habeo secretum revelandum si auderem . . . Domina, ego vellem quod matrimonium esset solempnization inter Johannem, fratrem vestrum, et me, et rogo vos . . . quia ego sum in sufficiente etate constituta et satis senex ad essendum uxor sua sed non amica sua.*

41. See, for example, the depositions of Beatrix de Morland and Stephen Wasteleyne, Goldberg *Women in England*, pp. 59 and 61, respectively.

42. This was essentially based upon physical attributes. It was held that a physically mature child could achieve majority up to six months early. See *Decretales Gregorii IX.*, Lib. IV. Tit. II. Caps. VI and IX, in Richter and Friedberg (eds), *Corpus Iuris Canonici.*

43. Bunt, *William of Palerne*, introduction, p. 94.

44. Several witnesses testify as to the age of Alice by comparing her birth with other events they remember. For example, Margery, the wife of John Gregson of Clifton, calculates her age by comparing the time of the birth of her own child with the time of Elena de Rouclif's pregnancy. It is difficult to determine the specificity of age from such information.

45. See, for example, the correspondence of the Stonor, Paston, and Plumpton families: C. Carpenter (ed.), *Kingsford's Stonor Letters and Papers, 1290–1483* (Cambridge, 1996); N. Davis (ed.), *Paston Letters and Papers of the Fifteenth Century* (2 vols, Oxford, 1971–6); T. Stapleton (ed.), *Plumpton Correspondence*, Camden Society Publications, Original Series 4 (London, 1839). See also Dockray, 'Why Did Fifteenth-Century English Gentry Marry?' for an explanation of the complexities of such marriage.

46. See especially Waugh, *The Lordship of England, passim.*

8

Pigs and Prostitutes: Streetwalking in Comparative Perspective

P.J.P. Goldberg

> *No one shall keep pigs which go in the streets by day or night, nor shall any prostitute stay in the city.*[1]

So begins a York ordinance of 1301, made as part of a series in response to the problems created by the temporary location of the royal court in the city. Concern with wandering pigs, the cause of some particularly nasty accidents as any perusal of coroners' rolls demonstrates, was a perennial urban phenomenon; the concern was not with the keeping of pigs per se, and thus the possible health hazards so caused, but the failure of some owners to keep their animals suitably constrained. The civic concern to keep prostitutes outside the city is no more remarkable since this appears to have been common policy in many English towns throughout the later Middle Ages. The York injunction was indeed specifically reiterated in 1482.[2] The perdurance of this policy through the later fourteenth and fifteenth centuries contrasts strikingly with the policy of institutionalization of prostitution within civic brothels found in some regions of Continental Europe. It is the purpose of this present chapter to explore this English pattern in more depth and to locate it within a broader cultural framework by comparison with these other regions of Europe.

In 1301 the city authorities of York must have been concerned to forestall an influx of 'misgoverned' women in the wake of the royal court. What is remarkable about this ordinance is that two very different concerns are treated in the same paragraph, even the same sentence. They could just as well have constituted separate ordinances. Whereas to the modern reader there is little obvious connection between pigs and prostitutes, there evidently was in the minds of the medieval framers of this ordinance. The juxtaposition is not a matter of convenience, not least because the sanctions imposed for breach of this ordinance are very different according to whether it is a pig or a woman that is at fault. Rather the juxtaposition is ideological.

According to the medieval trope of identifying the seven vices with specific animals, the pig was sometimes held to be symbolic of gluttony or even of anger, but was not infrequently used to represent lust.[3] The pig and the prostitute were thus linked by a common association with lust. But the connection goes further. The pig was notorious for wandering freely through the streets, hence the symbolism of the reward of the trotters to whomsoever captured an escaped animal. To wander around like a Tantony pig was proverbial, but was also behaviour that respectable women were specifically warned against. Indeed it was said of that archetypal prostitute, the harlot of the book of Proverbs, that 'her feet will not abide within the home'.[4] The pig and the prostitute were thus again connected through their transgressive wandering.

The juxtaposition of pig and prostitute is thus deliberate and, within the conventions of a magisterial discourse clearly influenced by clerical notions of vice, entirely logical. The movements of pigs and of prostitutes plying their trade through the streets are both seen as transgressive and a threat to the moral order. The solutions required by the ordinance are similar in their ends if not their means. By killing the runaway pig, and cutting off the trotters that were the means of the pig's transgression, the wandering pig is, literally, removed from circulation (and of course a dire warning is sent to all who keep pigs to see that they are securely kept at home and off the streets). The penalty for any prostitute who 'keeps a brothel and resides within the city' was temporary imprisonment, but more significantly 'the bailiff who takes her shall have the roof timbers and the door of the building in which she is lodged'. There was thus material reward, and hence incentive, for both the captor of the wandering pig and of the woman of the streets. The removal of the roof beams and the door would likewise have served as a warning to landlords not to let their property to suspect women, but the immediate effect would have been to deprive the prostitute once apprehended of a home and shelter. In this way the stated policy of denying prostitutes accommodation within the city would have been effected.

The sanctioned dismantling of property is not peculiar to York and once again suggests certain parallels likely to have been to the forefront of the minds of the framers of the ordinance, for like sanctions had been used against Cathar heretics in the South of France. At Bristol in 1344 an ordinance was issued that prohibited lepers and prostitutes from living within the city walls.[5] As with the York ordinance just discussed two different categories are consciously juxtaposed within the same sentence. Here again the sanction for prostitutes who transgressed against the ordinance was the removal of the doors and windows of their houses by officers of the mayor. Heretics, lepers, and prostitutes thus appear to have occupied the same mental category, one that is again constructed through a clerical discourse of sin and fornication. Whereas heresy was imagined as spiritual fornication, leprosy was thought to be sexually transmitted and lepers were believed to be sexually voracious. All three groups posed a threat to the social fabric through their contact with other residents that could be controlled only through exclusion.[6]

Two further aspects of the York ordinance of 1301 merit discussion. The first concerns the association of prostitutes and of pigs because both posed a threat when wandering the streets at large. The concern was not with the phenomenon of brothels or of prostitution as such, but with the way in which the prostitute, by plying her trade through the streets, posed a moral threat.[7] The point I wish to make is that prostitution was associated not so much with specific, enclosed locations, namely brothels, but with streetwalking. This perspective is confirmed by an (undated) fourteenth-century Bristol ordinance concerned to ensure that the prostitute was readily identifiable from other sorts of women when plying her trade. This demanded 'that no prostitute wander about town without a striped hood'. (A similar ordinance is found for London in 1382.)[8] Though it would be possible to read this legislation as seeking to stigmatize prostitutes at all times, regardless of whether they were soliciting or otherwise, it seems more logical to read it as signifying that the prostitute was understood to solicit by 'wandering about town'. Much the same reading may be applied to sumptuary ordinances designed to prevent prostitutes dressing in costly and showy attire such as are found in London in 1351 and 1382.[9] If prostitutes did not regularly solicit in public places then such regulation would hardly be necessary.

The second aspect to be addressed is that the ordinance constructs a category of 'prostitute' as if this were an unproblematical identity. The London ordinance of 1382, just referred to, warns us that this is not so since it was to be applied to 'all common prostitutes *and all women commonly reputed as such*' (my emphasis). It may be that the York ordinance, fashioned as it was to meet the needs created by the removal of the royal court to York, implicitly understood all women coming in the wake of the court and found walking the streets to be prostitutes. It may also reflect the harsh economic climate of the early years of the fourteenth century which provided few opportunities to women to support themselves independently such that some may indeed have made their livelihood for at least a part of their lives primarily from commercial sex. However, the corollary of the observation that commercial sex operated on the basis of prostitutes soliciting in public places – the street, the churchyard, the public house – rather than being confined within a brothel to which clients resorted – the pattern found in parts of southern Europe from the later fourteenth century and the product of a very different ideology – is that women engaging in commercial sex could also pursue other lines of employment, either simultaneously or between periods of prostitution.[10]

An examination of two extant and overlapping act books for the Capitular court of York, which record presentments before the court for fornication and adultery between 1358 and 1495, adequately demonstrates the point.[11] The cathedral Chapter exercised spiritual jurisdiction over an area around and to the north of York Minster. This included some areas of cheap rented housing that was let to, among other groups of single women, some of whose names occur both within surviving rentals and in the act books. Not infrequently these women are presented for fornication with vicars choral or other lesser Minster clergy, though this in part is simply a reflection of this geography.[12] A proportion of the presentments, particularly where both parties were described as servants, probably had nothing to do with commercial sex but followed from courtship relations that had not (or not yet) resulted in marriage. Indeed in some instances one or both parties acknowledged a contract of marriage when answering in court.[13] A few presentments reflect abuse of female servants by their masters.[14] Certain names, however, occur more frequently and in respect of several different sexual relationships. This suggests that they relate not to sexual activity associated with courtship, but to commercial sex. Only occasionally are any of the women so presented described as '*communa meretrix*' (common prostitute), although this itself is not a significant observation since the court was concerned to police the sins of fornication and adultery rather than commercial sex.[15] What is striking about this evidence is just how few are the names that recur repeatedly over any given period of years.

One of the advantages of the act book evidence is that it allows us to know something of the clients as well as the sex workers. Within a sample of 166 presentments for fornication or adultery involving women resident within York over the ten-year period 1441–51, the names of some 45 different ordained clergy, mostly vicars choral or chantry priests employed within the Minster, are presented as against some 59 laymen.[16] Whereas most of the lay males presented are named only once, many of the clergy are presented more frequently, thus the 45 clergy account for 86 presentments, but the 59 laymen for only 79 presentments. Among habitual users of the sexual services of women outside marriage, here defined as males presented three times or more within the sample, we find ten clergy (accounting for 43 presentments), but only four laity (accounting for 12 presentments).[17] The conclusion that follows is that although some lay males regularly sought sexual services outside of marriage, most demand came from clergy. This is not to say that a larger number of lay males did not also occasionally look for sexual services outside of marriage. Presumably some men visiting the city on business sometimes also used the services of local women selling sex. For example, our sample includes a Lincoln man presented for having sex with one Maud Bliburgh who was herself presented on two further occasions for sexual relations with two different clergymen.[18]

It is evident that even frequent users of sexual services offered by women did not always turn to prostitutes in the sense of women who regularly sold their bodies to any man desirous of her services – common women in contemporary parlance. The vicar choral William Norton, for example, was several times presented for sexual relations with a woman variously called Marion Hogeson, Johnson, Scott, and possibly Thomson. This woman is presented in relation to no other man which may suggest she was in effect Norton's mistress over a couple of years rather than a 'common prostitute'.[19] Of the 108 women in our sample, only 12 can be surmised with any confidence to have engaged in commercial sex.[20] A further ten women were presented in relation to more than one man, in six instances including clergy and hence in relationships that could not have resulted in marriage, but even if some of these instances were associated with the exchange of money, it would be inappropriate to dub these women who only occasionally sold their bodies prostitutes.[21] It follows that only a minority of the women presented were engaged in commercial sex and that the numbers that might be described as prostitutes were very few indeed.

The twelve women identified as engaging in commercial sex between them accounted for forty-four presentments, i.e. rather more than a quarter of the total. Of these, twenty-seven were in respect of clergy. A few women, indeed, clearly looked primarily to a clerical clientèle. Margaret Phillip, for example, was presented in respect of five different clergy and Joan Cryspyn and Joan Walker in respect of three. On the other hand Alice, the wife of William Crakse was presented in respect of five laymen, three of them described as fishers. The implication is that some women engaging in commercial sex catered primarily or even specifically for the clergy, from whom there was particular demand for sexual services, but an implicitly smaller group of women may have catered primarily for laity. We may note, for example, that in 1424 an Elizabeth Frowe was presented as a procuress acting for the Austin friars and Joan Scryvener likewise for friars and priests.[22] It may even be that we have a hint here of a hierachy among women selling sex since clergy, as men with no family responsibilities, presumably had more disposable income than may have been true of the fishers and the minstrel's servant entertained by Alice Crakse.

It is apparent even from this brief analysis that the 'common prostitute' is a fairly elusive phenomenon. Even of the ten women tentatively identified as engaging in commercial sex within our ten-year sample period, only Margaret Clay, Margaret Phillip, and Joan Cryspyn appear to have pursued active careers as sex workers and so may usefully be termed prostitutes.[23] Numbers of other women may have occasionally sold their bodies, but they scarcely constituted career prostitutes. Clergy appear to have formed a significant part of the clientèle for commercial sex and some seem regularly to have used the services of women who sold sexual services on either a regular or occasional basis, though some clergy preferred long-standing concubinage relationships with women who did not make their bodies available to other men and hence cannot be described as prostitutes. We may suggest somewhat speculatively that the demand for commercial sex was too small to support large numbers of women as professional sex workers, but also that most women who engaged at some point in their lives in commercial sex did so to supplement their livelihood or out of particular need rather than as a career move. In one rare and telling example from 1458 Robert Pykebane, presented for illicit sex with one Alice Dornade, claimed that he had supplied her with two tunics, but that when he had called at her house to ask for payment she had claimed that she could not give him money, but offered her body instead.[24]

If we put the sale of sexual services alongside what else is known about women's work in later medieval England, we can pursue the above reading a stage further. Although the wives and widows of artisans, i.e. those who managed their own workshops, may have enjoyed a comparatively stable labour identity, other townswomen, particularly the wives of labourers or women living on their own probably followed a variety of employments in order to get by. This pattern may often be obscured by such occupational bye-names as spinster or sempster (seamstress). Petty retailing of one form or another, reflected in the ubiquitousness of the bye-name huckster, was, however, a form of economic activity in which women were particularly conspicuous. We may also observe that a number of areas of women's economic activity represent extensions of their domestic roles as nurturers and providers of food, drink, and clothing, namely the nurse, the midwife, the vendors of blood puddings or of pies, the tapster (barmaid), the laundress, the dressmaker, the seamstress, the retailer of second-hand clothing and so on. Casual prostitution readily occupies this mould. It represents both a form of petty retailing, the provision of a service, and it is an extension of the role of wives in providing for the sexual needs of their husbands.

From the perspective of civic government, prostitution was often associated with a a sub-economy of petty thieving and the illicit retailing of ale[25]. The act book evidence reinforces this perspective and again suggests that the full-time professional prostitute is a rather elusive phenomenon. Thus in 1444 it was said of Marion Jakson, one of our small sample of women known to have engaged in commercial sex, that she kept a tavern at unauthorized hours and received suspect persons.[26] The Coventry ordinances of 1492 likewise conflate the retail of ale and the sale of sexual services by bracketing tapsters and harlots within the same paragraph, a conflation that clearly had some justification in relation to actual experience.[27] It is further suggested from presentments for defamation. Joan Pokellyngton, for example, in 1422 allegedly called her neighbours in Grape Lane, a notorious locale of commercial sex, 'false thieves and priests' whores'.[28] A well-known London case from 1385 concerns a procuress who incited her servant to steal a breviary from a chaplain who had used her services for two nights.[29] Similarly Annes Crokys and Alice Staneyge were respectively presented at Nottingham in 1515 'for baudre and reyseyvng off oder menys goodes theyftely' and 'for bawdre and kepyng off oder mennys prentys at caredys [cards] and oder gammys for money'.[30] The Capitular Act Book contains some suggestive evidence that goldsmiths, who may in effect have acted as pawnbrokers but would in any case have been well placed to dispose of items of value, may sometimes have been involved in the sex industry. The goldsmith Medard Leonard was, for example, presented for keeping a common prostitute in his house in 1453. Unfortunately she is not named.[31]

This last observation alerts us to the role of pimps, procuresses, and private, small-scale brothels in the lives of at least some of the women who engaged in commercial sex.[32] The act book evidence allows us to identify certain names that occur repeatedly in connection with procuring, although again numbers are small. Margaret Clay of Goodramgate, for example, was presented at various times as a procuress for a decade or more from the mid 1450s. She employed as 'servants' or lodged a handful of women, presumably for the purposes of prostitution. Certainly Joan Burton and probably Margaret Bugtrot, who lodged with Margaret in 1456 and 1466 respectively, engaged in commercial sex. She can also be identified as a prostitute in her own right and indeed represents one of the small number of women so identified within our sample and hence suggests a career structure whereby professional prostitutes came to be increasingly involved in procuring as they became older.[33] But Margaret Clay seems atypical. So far as the act book evidence allows us to observe, few women engaging in commercial sex seem to have been attached to a particular procuress or pimp and few probably worked in any house that might be described as a brothel. In some instances what appear to be brothels may in fact be little more than boarding houses that profited from providing a venue for illicit sex.[34] Moreover most women who engaged in commercial sex probably did so over a comparatively short span of years and, we may surmise, whilst still comparatively young.[35] Such a pattern is itself a corollary of the observation that few of the women engaging in commercial sex saw this as their main source of livelihood. Those few who did may well have continued to sell their bodies and to have managed other less experienced women over a rather longer period of time.

Despite the dangers inherent in drawing conclusions from a source that is not specifically concerned with prostitution or its organization, it would seem most women who provided sexual services in return for payment did so on an essentially freelance basis and alongside, or between periods of alternative employment. This is reflected in the occupational bye-names associated with some of these women and from the tendency by the late fifteenth century of governing elites to associate particular kinds of female employment, such as laundry work, the retail of ale, or spinning with prostitution.[36] The evidence that outsiders are noticeable among women actively engaged in commercial sex may likewise indicate that prejudice prevented their finding more legitimate forms of employment. Thus we find one Marion Scot working in the sex industry in York during the early years of the fifteenth century and in Hull a Joan Frensshewoman was presented for keeping a brothel in 1450.[37] The presence of Dutch or Flemish women elsewhere, as in the stews of Southwark, may imply a demand for the 'exotic', but also a traffic in women from economically depressed regions.[38] To reiterate: for those who could normally find other means, prostitution represented only an occasional form of employment, and one that might be practised alongside other activities, rather than as a vocation. Only some women were actually employed in brothels, although more may have used particular premises as venues for illicit sex. Actual soliciting, however, probably took place more often in certain 'public' places rather than at the doorways of known 'brothels'.

Certain alehouses or taverns seem to have functioned as recognized places for soliciting. Thus John Derby, a vicar choral, was presented in 1472 as one who frequented John Betson's tavern night after night and who talked to prostitutes. The same John Derby had been presented two years earlier for sexual relations with a tapster at the Hart in Coney Street and was to be presented again in 1474 as frequenting the Bear in Colliergate.[39] Another vicar choral, John Wait, was presented in 1480 for having spent the night at the Angel in Goodramgate rather than within the official Bedern residence of the vicars.[40] Similarly, in 1422 a London jury reported that a plot of land behind the 'Pye' in Queenhithe was used by thieves, prostitutes, and pimps, and a parliamentary petition of 1433 complained that inns and taverns in Southwark High Street were being run as brothels.[41] If we put this evidence alongside our earlier observations concerning the association of tapsters or barmaids with commercial sex, then the role of the drinking house in the sex trade seems to be fairly clearly established in both actuality as in contemporary perception.

The role of churchyards as places for soliciting is a little harder to establish, but it is suggested from a London coroner's jury verdict of 1301 that a woman was allegedly solicited and then murdered at a corner of the churchyard of St Mary Woolchurch.[42] The Capitular Act Book contains the names of a number of women said to be living in graveyards, but presumably in cheap rented chantry property which was often built onto graveyards. Thus Joan Skeldyng of St Andrew's cemetery was presented in 1492 for illicit sex with six men including a deacon and was described the same year as being '*quasi meretrix*', and Joan Long, who was presented in relation to three men in 1486, was described as living within ('*infra*') the same cemetery. It must be possible that they used the churchyard behind their rented rooms as places in which to solicit clients.[43]

It is, of course, the third locale for soliciting, namely the street, that is actually the hardest to demonstrate beyond the circumstantial evidence already presented. We do have the example of Simon Skynner who allegedly exposed himself when with Isabella Horner 'along the wall until inside the said woman's house' where the couple had illicit sex, but there is no evidence that Isabella was prostituting herself.[44] What is apparent is that certain streets in late medieval York were associated with commercial sex. Thus Aldwark, Grape Lane, St Andrewgate, Swinegate, and areas immediately adjacent appear again and again within the two act books.[45] It follows that any man turning off the main thoroughfares of Petergate or Goodramgate or their immediate extensions would have found himself in streets whose tenants included significant numbers of women who engaged at least periodically in commercial sex. It is a logical extension of this observation to suggest that any woman standing meaningfully at an entranceway or walking the street without obvious occupation would in fact have been soliciting. To speculate further, even women sitting or standing at a doorway sewing or spinning may potentially also have been tacitly advertising their sexual services.[46]

Thus far, using fifteenth-century York as a case study, we have attempted to establish that the sex industry in late medieval England was largely unregulated and that few of the women involved were professionals in the sense that their livelihood solely depended either on selling their own bodies or those of the women they managed. Brothels, so far as they existed, were small, private, and ephemeral; the sort of more substantial civic brothel, run as a public amenity that are to be found in some Continental cities hardly existed.[47] Lastly, we have suggested that the clients of prostitutes particularly comprised clergy, perhaps especially the so-called clerical proletariat who did not have the resources of their parochial counterparts to support housekeepers or live-in servants.[48] It is much harder to identify lay clients; they certainly included married men, but here again a small number of persistent users of the services of prostitutes are conspicuous.[49]

To maintain that these observations contrast with those described for other parts of Europe, and hence that England was different, is unsatisfactory. Later medieval Europe was not culturally homogenous and it is possible to locate this English evidence within a broader model of cultural diversity. There is, however, a much more substantial literature on medieval prostitution pertaining to the more southerly regions of Europe than there is of the north-west.[50] The reason for this is simple. The work of historians largely reflects the availability of evidence. For prostitution the evidence mostly exists in the form of regulation and of institutions. It follows that histories have been most readily written in respect of those regions for which there is evidence of regulation and of public brothels. Northern towns have preserved their archives to differing degrees, but they are hardly uniformly defective. If these towns put significant amounts of energy into the regulation of prostitution, we would in all likelihood know about it. We may thus conclude that not only does evidence for regulation appear much more common in southern Europe, in all probability it was.

This is the picture that emerges for the end of the Middle Ages from such southern cities as Narbonne, Toulouse, Avignon, Palermo, and Florence. The attempted concentration of prostitution within civic brothels was also civic policy in the cities of south-eastern France, Switzerland, and southern Germany such as Dijon, Basel, Augsburg, Nuremberg, Frankfurt, and Ulm. If we move a little further north-west to Strasbourg, however, the picture becomes cloudier. Here a civic brothel operated alongside a sanctioned 'red light' district, but it is evident that prostitutes in fact operated throughout the city.[51] In Paris private brothels operated within a number of districts, including the rue Glatigny within the Cité itself, but numbers of freelance prostitutes also plied their trade through various districts of the city.[52]

Much the same pattern of non-institutionalized prostitution seems to have characterized the cities of Flanders, the female sex workers of Ghent for example soliciting their clients within the recesses of the city walls.[53] Cologne seems not to have operated or sanctioned civic brothels, but rather pursued, during the fifteenth century at least, a policy of containment with only modest success. For example, in 1445 an attempt was made to confine prostitution within two streets under the supervision of the civic executioner, and during the same century action was periodically taken against pimps and procuresses.[54] Similar episodic policies can, likewise, be found in many English towns. They represent ad hoc responses conceived in essentially policing terms rather than fully articulated policies of regulation and management; in the culture of north-western Europe, the sex industry was constructed not as a civic amenity but rather as periodic nuisance. We have here, then, clear evidence of regional cultural difference in respect to prostitution. It is possible to suggest some explanations for these differences.

One approach is to ask in what other respects can we describe cultural difference, for prostitution does not operate in a vacuum and so cannot be understood without reference variously to the attitudes of different social groups to sex and sexuality, to economic factors, to the employment of women and gender relations, and to perceptions of civic government and civic governors. This is to set a very demanding agenda that is beyond the scope of this essay. Certain ideas may, however, be outlined that can subsequently be tested or challenged. My first observation is that north-western Europe was probably characterized by distinctive household and marriage patterns by the later Middle Ages. So far as we can see, both women and men tended not to marry before their twenties, though this was probably more marked in urban society, and they tended to marry at similar ages. Likewise they normally lived in households that comprised no more than one married couple and was restricted to 'nuclear' kin, i.e. parents and children, but which, especially in urban society, might also include young, unmarried strangers working as servants. The corollary of this last observation is that parents permitted their offspring to leave home as adolescents and certainly before such age as they might marry. Finally, we may note that just as girls were drawn into positions as servants, so older women were comparatively conspicuous in the labour markets of this region, perhaps especially in the decades following the Black Death.[55]

This combination of social factors differentiates north-western Europe from other regions. This is neither to imply that this region was itself culturally homogenous, nor that all these characteriztics were unique to this one region, nor even that the rest of Europe was culturally homogenous.[56] The observation does, however, allow us to pose a specific question, namely can the absence of regulation or of evidence for the existence of public brothels within this region be explained in terms of these particular social parameters? At the same time we may ask what it was about the cultures of the Languedoc, of Dijon, of Augsburg, or of Florence that created the need for regulation and for brothels, at least before the early sixteenth century, on which records modern scholars have based their studies. Obviously there is no single answer to this second question. For example, it is hardly possible to discuss the topic of prostitution in a Florentine context without reference to contemporary concerns with homosexuality. Similarly Rossiaud's study of Dijon highlights a subculture of male youth groups and gang rape.[57] Despite these observations, and painting with a very broad brush, we may still suggest some cultural similarities. In respect of marriage, in southern societies where the payment of dowry extended to the lowest echelons of society we can describe a pattern of late marriage for men, but early and near universal marriage for women, and hence comparatively marked age difference between spouses. Children seem regularly to have remained in the natal home until marriage – in the case of some sons, even after marriage – and daughters seem to have been held subject to the authority of a father or, if the father was no longer living, of a brother according to an ideology of honour much more pronounced than that found in north-western Europe.[58] Perhaps as a corollary, and again in contrast to north-western Europe, women appear to have been much less conspicuous within the 'public' economy of waged work.[59]

One of the more marked differences between the societies of north-western Europe and those of more southerly climes would thus appear to be the degree of autonomy allowed to young people, especially young women. Whereas in north-western Europe adolescents and young adults frequently left their natal homes prior to marriage and, particularly in towns after the Black Death, found positions as servants, this was not the norm elsewhere. The Tuscan catasto of 1427, which was compiled on a patrimonial rather than a household basis, probably underenumerates servants, but it still serves to demonstrate that children normally remained at home until they married. Daughters, moreover, invariably did marry, usually at some point in their later teens. As Klapisch-Zuber and Smith have shown, female servants were invariably women who lacked male protection, be they poor widows or orphan girls. These last were given over to the 'protection' of a householder for a period of years on the understanding that he would stand in for the deceased father and provide a dowry that they might marry. They were, however, a vulnerable group, open to sexual exploitation, because their lack of close male kin was seen as a loss of honour. Service was thus not so much an option, but a last resort.

It would thus appear that the preservation of female honour, construed in respect of young women as virginity, allowed little scope for female agency in the making of marriages. The family's honour was indeed bound up with that of the daughter and it was a father's duty to stand guardian of his daughter's chastity, to set aside an appropriate dowry on her behalf, and to arrange as best a marriage as he might. On the death of the father that duty passed to a young woman's male siblings.[60] Within this cultural milieu daughters would have been sexually inexperienced prior to marriage and would have had no romantic attachments other than to men chosen for them as husbands. Sons, on the other hand, were not bound by the same requirements of pre-marital chastity and, moreover, tended to marry at a rather later age than their brides, if at all.[61] Arguably they needed a sexual outlet, but one that would not be a danger to 'honest' women or to public order. This was a perspective that is rooted in canonical tradition going back to Augustine, namely that prostitution prevents greater evils associated with sexual licence, violence, and even homosexuality; just as the palace must have a sewer pit so the well-ordered city must have a brothel.[62]

The southern European pattern of provision of brothels as civic amenities is not, however, to be explained solely in terms of demand for female sexual services on the part of males. Certainly this demand may have been greater than in north-western society since males were both encouraged to prove their virility prior to marriage, but equally were debarred from sexual relations as part of courtship. It may even be that married males were encouraged to see sex with their wives solely in terms of procreation and hence to look to prostitutes in order to find pleasure. The sexual needs of men could, however, have been met equally as effectively by women operating outside of regular, in the sense of regulated, brothels, yet to have sanctioned this, civic authorities would have had to permit prostitutes to share the streets with 'honest' women. Such potential contact between women whose conduct was seen as dishonourable and other women, who by their nature were perceived as unstable and easily led astray, could hardly be tolerated. The voracious sexuality of the prostitute was simply too dangerous to be allowed to stray beyond the confines of the brothel. To return to the medieval analogy of the sewer, the brothel served to protect the city from contamination by the women whom the brothel contained.

Though there is good evidence that prostitution was never contained solely within civic brothels in those regions for which the institution has been described, it is apparent that between the late fourteenth and early sixteenth centuries this was the ideal. This ideal was determined by a magisterial ideology of sexuality and honour such as has just been described. There is no evidence to suggest that a like ideology shaped civic regulation in England or elsewhere in north-western Europe. The evidence for a civic brothel at Sandwich is not evidence for a like ideology. Rather the case of Sandwich should be understood alongside those of Southampton, which clearly operated a rather stricter regime of policing prostitutes, and Southwark, for which a set of later fifteenth-century regulations uniquely survives.[63] The particular case of Southwark may here provide the clue. The brothels or 'stews' there fell outside the jurisdiction of the City of London. (Southwark in fact formed part of the liberty of the bishops of Winchester.) By its very location, however, Southwark was dependent upon its far larger neighbour just the other side of the Thames. Indeed Thames boatmen plying between the Middlesex and Surrey banks regularly brought clients to and from the stews. It follows that any London regulation of prostitution must be understood in the context of the presence of the Southwark stews just the other side of the river. More importantly, however, the clientèle for these stews cannot have come primarily from within Southwark itself or even from elsewhere in Surrey. Rather they would have come in the first instance from London, but whether London residents or merely persons passing through we can only surmise. The capital, together with the neighbouring vill of Westminster, would have seen large numbers of people, but particularly adult males passing through on business related to trade, the law, or government; no doubt for some the proximity of a sex industry offering the exotic attractions of Flemish prostitutes would have been too strong a temptation.[64] London, like Sandwich and Southampton, was also a port. As such it accommodated large numbers of foreign mariners and merchants, a few of whom were resident for extended periods, but most of whom would have stayed only briefly. Unlike such major east coast ports as Lynn, Boston, Hull, and Newcastle, whose trading links tended to lie with the Low Countries, Northern Germany, and the Baltic region, London also had links with more southerly regions of Europe, including the Iberian peninsular and Northern Italy. The trade of Sandwich and Southampton, which acted as outports for London, was likewise much more exclusively with regions of Europe to the south of these ports.[65]

It follows that London saw a regular turnover of non-native speaking adult males who were apart from their wives or other female companionship and who came from cultures where brothels were institutionalized and women going about the streets unchaperoned might be thought of as 'available'. It is the contention here that the brothels of Southwark, and the equivalent facilities at Southampton and Sandwich, evolved or were created to meet the particular needs of this group and to contain any threat to order that the presence of such groups of, to use contemporary terminology, 'alien' males might otherwise pose. Certainly we do not have to look far to find evidence that native xenophobia led to friction with foreigners – the attacks on Flemings in London during the Revolt of 1381 are but one example – but disputes over women, particularly where local women were mistakenly solicited for sex, must always have occurred.[66] The provision of brothels after the fashion of those found in more southerly regions of Europe would have served the double function of keeping foreign mariners off the streets, and hence out of trouble, and of protecting local women.[67] The location of the brothels in Southwark further ensured that foreign mariners did not need to pass through the streets of the capital on their way there and back.[68]

There is another point of difference reflected in the provisions of the Southwark brothel customary.[69] These seem to have been more concerned to protect the women working within them – or even working out of them – from exploitation by the brothelkeepers (or stewmongers using contemporary terminology). The preamble to the ordinances stresses how the women 'ought to have theire free goynng and comyng atte theire owne libertees' and this freedom of movement is the subject of the first ordinance.[70] Implicitly this freedom was being eroded at the time the ordinances were drawn up, but the intent of the ordinances is both clear and very different from the ideology that underpinned the civic brothels of southern Europe. Rather than containing women within the brothel and hence ensuring that their identity as professional prostitutes was absolute, the Southwark ordinances were concerned to prevent such an identity being imposed on the prostitutes.[71] Indeed the repeated use of the term 'singlewoman' in the customary is not, as Karras has argued, a euphemism for prostitute, but rather a conscious assertion within a legal document of the independent status of the women who worked in the stews vis-à-vis the stewmongers who managed them.[72]

To take the observation a step further, the regulations against women boarding within the stewhouse can hardly be construed as an attempt to suppress the stews themselves or even to prevent prostitution. Rather they may reflect the way in which the stews functioned as a resort or venue for illicit sex which might be used by numbers of women who engaged in commercial sex, whether regularly or infrequently. This is reflected in the sad case of Isabel Lane allegedly taken against her will to the Southwark stews on four separate occasions to provide sexual services to an unnamed gentleman, but also in the finding from the 1381 poll tax returns that the brothels apparently employed very small numbers of women, although a few women who may be identified as prostitutes lived outside the brothels, but within the borough.[73] In this respect the Southwark stews appear more like the informal private brothels found elsewhere in England than their southern European counterparts.

Brothels as clearly identifiable public utilities exempt from the normal sanctions against illicit sex thus appear to have been a specifically southern European idea. That civic government even in these regions had frequently to contend with illicit prostitution does not detract from this distinctive ideological position.[74] Brothels are found exceptionally in England in ports frequented by mariners and merchants from this same region. Indeed only that at Sandwich, set up at civic expense and staffed by a brothelkeeper (or bawd) and his wife and employing four prostitutes, seems directly comparable to the model described by Otis for the Languedoc.[75] The very vocabulary of brothel and of prostitute, shaped as it has been by writings relating to southern European institutions, is unhelpful in a north-western context. Few women appear to have made their livelihood solely from selling their bodies and it may be surmised that most women who can be identified as sex workers sold sex only periodically so as to supplement other forms of livelihood and while still comparatively young.

Brothels may in fact have been little more than venues where illicit sex was tolerated or where individual sex workers lodged. Like the harlot of the Book of Proverbs whose feet would not abide within the house, the women who sold sex in north-western Europe during the later Middle Ages were essentially streetwalkers. It was only in the honour and shame culture of southern Europe that prostitutes, like nuns, were cloistered.[76]

Notes

Abbreviations: BIHR – Borthwick Institute of Historical Research; YML – York Minster Library; PRO – Public Record Office.

1. M. Prestwich, *York Civic Ordinances, 1301*, Borthwick Papers, 49 (1976), p. 16. The pertinent injunction is reprinted in P.J.P. Goldberg (ed.), *Women in England* c. *1275–1525* (Manchester, 1995), p. 210.

2. The lapse of time between the two ordinances may well be significant since magisterial concern with prostitution in later medieval English towns seems to have been most acute at times of economic dislocation. R.M. Karras, *Common Women: Prostitution and Sexuality in Medieval England* (New York, 1996), pp. 18–19; P.J.P. Goldberg, *Women, Work and Life Cycle in a Medieval Economy: Women in York and Yorkshire* c. *1300–1520* (Oxford, 1992), p. 150; L.C. Attreed (ed.), *York House Books 1461–1490* (2 vols, Stroud, 1991), vol. 1, p. 261; Goldberg (ed.), *Women in England*, p. 213.

3. For example the author of *Jacob's Well* compares the lecherous man or woman to swine: A. Brandeis (ed.), *Jacob's Well*, Early English Text Society, Original Series 115 (London, 1900), p. 159. The civic brothel at Sandwich is referred to as the 'hog house' in a document of 1485: W. Boys (ed.), *Collections for a History of Sandwich* (2 vols, Sandwich, 1792), vol. 2, p. 678. I am grateful to Cordelia Beattie for these references.

4. For a discussion of this point see P.J.P. Goldberg, 'Women', in R. Horrox (ed.), *Fifteenth-Century Attitudes: Perceptions of Society in Late Medieval England* (Cambridge, 1994), pp. 112–31.

5. F.B. Bickley (ed.), *The Little Red Book of Bristol* (2 vols, Bristol, 1900), vol. 1, pp. 33–4; Goldberg (ed.), *Women in England*, p. 210.

6. I am indebted to Patricia Cullum for discussion of these issues.

7. Here I differ from Ruth Karras who argues that the concern of this ordinance focused on the brothel: Karras, *Common Women*, p. 18.

8. '*Item quod nulla meretrix vadat in villa absque capucio stragulato*': Bickley (ed.), *Little Red Book*, vol. 2, p. 229; Goldberg (ed.), *Women in England*, pp. 210–11. Interestingly the Bristol injunction is sandwiched between other ordinances concerned with cleanliness.

9. H.T. Riley (ed.), *Memorials of London and London Life in the XIIIth, XIVth, and XVth Centuries* (London, 1868), pp. 267, 458–9.

10. The role of the street, the alehouse, and the churchyard as places for soliciting are discussed later in the article.

11. YML, M2(1)f; BIHR, D/C AB. 1. It should be noted that the act books record *ex officio* presentments in respect of sexual sin, notably fornication and adultery, although numbers of persons are also presented as pimps or procuresses. They are thus not primarily concerned with commercial

sex and so throw light on prostitution only tangentially. Because the Dean and Chapter exercised spiritual jurisdiction only in a specific part of the city the record is unlikely to provide more than a partial picture of commercial sex within the city and may be biased towards recording clerical clients because the court had jurisdiction in an area which, being by the Minster, was unusually heavily populated with clergy, particularly the unbeneficed chantry priests and vicars choral attached to the cathedral church. On the other hand numbers of the names presented are associated with locations that fall outside the strict geographical jurisdiction of the court and there is a striking tendency for names of women engaged in commercial sex found in other sources also to be noted in the act books. For example the notorious Cherrylips complained of by her Micklegate neighbours and so reported in the York house books for 1483 is also found in the Capitular act book under the previous year: Attreed (ed.), *York House Books*, vol. 2, pp. 708, 723; BIHR, D/C AB. 1, f. 221v. For these reasons we may have some confidence that the source is at least partly representative of broader patterns within the city rather than just the specific circumstances of a small clerical enclave.

12. Included within the liberty of the Minster were the Bedern college, where the vicars choral lived communally, and, from the later fifteenth century, St Williams College, which housed the Minster's numerous chantry priests.

13. For example, Emma Giliot claimed a contract of marriage with Robert Thoresby when presented for fornication in 1374: YML, M2(1)f, f. 14.

14. For example, in 1445 the skinner Thomas Hyrste was presented for illicit sex with one Maud Clarke, but also with his servant Katherine: BIHR, D/C AB. 1, f. 106.

15. Margaret Phillip and a certain Elienor were for example described as common prostitutes in 1447 and 1450 respectively, and two further women were labelled '*meretrix*' in 1492. Two other women presented in 1492 are described as '*quasi meretrix*', but it is unclear what distinction is here being made: BIHR, D/C AB. 1, ff. 111, 114, 230v, 231. Karras further points out the ambiguity of the term '*meretrix*' which is used in relation to illicit, but not necessarily commercial sex: Karras, *Common Women*, pp. 10–12. Canon legal commentators likewise stress promiscuity and reputation rather than commercial exchange when discussing prostitution: J.A. Brundage, 'Prostitution in the Medieval Canon Law', in V.L. Bullough and J.A. Brundage (eds), *Sexual Practices and the Medieval Church* (Buffalo NY, 1982), p. 150.

16. The sample is taken from BIHR, D/C AB. 1, ff. 100–15. It is possible that the record slightly overstates the number of individual clients due to problems of nominal linkage. For example, in a few instances servants are not identified by second name, and the name Thomas Raynald occurs five times as a priest, but once as a fisher. In this last instance they have been treated as two different persons, but there are reasons for suspecting a recording error.

17. One of these men, Richard Franke, fisher, seems still to have been using the services of prostitutes more than twenty years later to judge from a presentment dated 1477 where he is described as married: BIHR, D/C AB. 1, f. 215.

18. Ibid., ff. 103, 106, 112.

19. Ibid., ff. 106, 108v, 110, 111, 112.

20. The actual number of women in our sample is almost certainly less than the number stated here since one woman was not named at all, a further four are given no second name, and seventeen are identified only in relation to an employer or former employer rather than by second name. It

follows that some women identified first as a servant may be subsequently identified by their second name and hence have been erroneously counted twice. A few women were also known by more than one second name. In a few instances nominal linkage may be suggested, e.g. Joan, the servant of Amy Semyster may have been the same as Joan Banyster noted at a slightly later date since both names are presented in connection with sexual relations with the vicar choral Thomas Skyres, but, in the absence of alternative sources, most of the Christian names of the women in the sample are too common for such identifications to be made with any confidence: BIHR, D/C AB. 1, ff. 100, 119, 110v. The criteria for identifying commercial sex are necessarily somewhat subjective, but I have counted those women who are presented in respect of sex with at least three different men, usually over a period of time. I have not counted Margaret Sawer in this category because, although presented in respect of sexual relations with three different men, all laity, she was presented on only one occasion and hence possibly as a byproduct of a courtship dispute.

21. Obviously some women may have been presented at other times outside our short sample period, though a fuller analysis of the data has yet to be attempted. Equally we may assume that even those women regularly engaged in commercial sex were only occasionally presented within the Church court, but these observations need not detract unduly from our overall findings.

22. BIHR, D/C AB.1, f. 67

23. This observation is based on a wider reading of the evidence than the sample alone.

24. BIHR, D/C AB. 1, f. 141v.

25. Cf. Karras, *Common Women*, pp. 15–16.

26. BIHR, D/C AB. 1, f. 105v.

27. M.D. Harris (ed.), *Coventry Leet Book*, Early English Text Society, Original Series 134–5, 138, 146 (London, 1907–13), p. 545. The ordinance runs 'Also that no person of þis Cite ffrohensfurth kepe, hold, resceyve nor fauour any Tapster, or Woman of evell name, fame or condicion to whom eny resorte is of synfull disposicion, hauntyng the synne of lechery . . .'. The marginal entry reads 'For Tapsters & harlottes'. This was part of series of ordinances designed to cleanse the city at a time of profound economic disclocation: see Goldberg, 'Women', p. 120. A like connection was made in a Lynn ordinance of 1465 which attempted to exclude common tapsters and common women from inns: D.M. Owen (ed.), *The Making of King's Lynn*, Records of Social and Economic History, New Series, no. 9 (London, 1984), p. 268. Women with the bye-name 'Tapester' are found among those presented for fornication with vicars choral in the York Capitular Act Book and in 1470 one Phillipa Pryce, tapster of the Bull in Coney Street, was presented for fornication with a deacon: BIHR, D/C AB. 1, ff. 178v, 179, 191, 192, 193v.

28. Ibid., f. 63. Grape Lane, an area of cheap rented accommodation just off the prosperous thoroughfares of Stonegate and Petergate, was known as Grapecuntlane in contemporary sources: ibid., f. 241v.

29. Riley (ed.), *Memorials*, pp. 484–6.

30. W.H. Stevenson (ed.), *Records of the Borough of Nottingham* (3 vols, Nottingham, 1882–5), vol. 3, pp. 243–4. Presentments of this type are fairly common over a long period of time. For similar presentments at Lynn in 1309 see Owen (ed.), *Making of King's Lynn*, p. 419.

31. The connection may further be suggested from the possible association of the goldsmith William Snawschill with commercial sex. Members of his household including his wife were

presented in respect of illicit sex a number of times within our sample. His was thus either a dysfunctional household in which William as head failed to exercise discipline over its members, or he was a pimp. The second interpretation depends on the observation that his servant Alice was presented for fornication with Thomas Burneby, a vicar choral who is also presented in relation to women known to be engaging in commercial sex, and that Joan Snawschill was presented for adultery with John Kendale, a servant in the household of the Earl of Northumberland who also had illicit sex with Agnes Lymberd, again a woman known to have been involved in commercial sex: BIHR, D/C AB. 1, ff. 100, 103, 104, 107, 107v, 112v, 114v, 119.

32. If the numbers of female servants over fifteen years noted in respect of the Southwark stewmongers in the 1381 poll tax returns is an accurate guide, even the brothels of Southwark employed only two or three prostitutes each: M. Carlin, *Medieval Southwark* (London, 1996), tab. 0.1, p. 212; PRO E 179/184/30.

33. BIHR, D/C AB. 1, ff. 112v, 119v, 125v, 127v, 129, 129v, 132, 132v, 142, 155v, 156v, 175v, 177, 178, 178v.

34. Some of the persons noted as procurers or procuresses within the Capitular act book seem only to have been facilitating established and long-standing illicit sexual relationships that neither constitute prostitution nor render their homes brothels in the conventional sense. For example Margaret, wife of William Wasshyngton and John Esyngwald had an affair over a number of years in respect of which Isabel Johnson of Aldwark, Joan Foster of Goodramgate, and Richard Kay of Stonegate are noted as procurer or procuresses. (Margaret was also presented in 1453 for illicit sex with three priests and John likewise in 1458 for illicit sex with an unnamed daughter of Robert Luter, described as his concubine. In the last instance the notorious Margaret Clay is named as procuress.) BIHR, AB. 1, ff. 120, 121, 121v, 142, 144. Cf. Karras, *Common Women*, p. 75.

35. It is seldom possible identify the women who engaged in commercial sex by age, but whereas some may be recorded as servants in the households of known procuresses, few are married. By analogy with other life-cycle servants, we would expect these women to be somewhere in their teens or early twenties. Karras cites various examples of young girls allegedly initiated into prostitution under duress. Deposition evidence relating to the ages of women acting as jurors in impotence cases within the York consistory provides further evidence in so far as at least some of these women engaged in commercial sex (and hence brought professional expertise to their work which involved attempting to arouse sexually the allegedly impotent husband by erotic stimulation). It may be that the evidence is biased towards those women who were professional sex workers. Of the seven (apparently unmarried) female jurors in a cause of 1432, one was said to be fifty, two forty (clearly approximate ages), two thirty-six, one thirty, and one twenty-six years. Of these Joan Laurence was presented for fornication in 1431 and 1432 while resident in Aldwark, but may also have been likewise presented in 1412 in Bishophill. If so, she would then have been about sixteen. (Of the other women only Joan Semer can plausibly be linked to the act books.) Of the three jurors whose depositions are recorded in another cause of 1441, two were stated to be forty-one, and one Joan Savage, eighteen years. (I have noticed the names of none of these six women in contemporary act books, but the name of one of the women, namely Katherine Lightfote, is certainly suggestive.) Goldberg, *Women, Work, and Life Cycle*, p. 154; Karras, *Common Women*, p. 55–64; BIHR, CP.F.111, 175, 224; BIHR, D/C AB. 1, ff. 83v, 85v, 87v; YML, H2/1 f. 4v; YML, VC 6/2/51, 53.

36. Harris (ed.), *Coventry Leet Book*, p. 219; Karras, *Common Women*, p. 54

37. BIHR, D/C AB. 1, ff. 37, 38, 47v, 75, 77, 79v; E. Gillot and K.A. MacMahon, *A History of Hull* (Oxford, 1980), p. 88.

38. Cf. Karras, *Common Women*, pp. 56–7. My observation is influenced by the modern analogy of the trafficking in women from the former Eastern bloc.

39. William Wansford, another vicar choral, was presented at the same time for frequenting the Bear and also for suspected fornication with the landlord's daughter. Derby was still frequenting the Bear in 1480: BIHR, D/C AB. 1, ff. 193v, 202v, 208v, 220.

40. Ibid., f. 220v.

41. A.H. Thomas (ed.), *Calendar of Plea and Memoranda Rolls of the City of London 1413–1437* (Cambridge, 1943), p. 138; Carlin, *Medieval Southwark*, p. 218.

42. R.R. Sharpe (ed.), *Calendar of Coroners' Rolls of the City of London 1300–1378* (London, 1913), pp. 7–8. This pattern is also suggested from Geremek's work on Paris: B. Geremek, *The Margins of Society in Late Medieval Paris*, tr. J. Birrell (Cambridge, 1987), pp. 90, 92, 213, 221.

43. Alice Marchill, presented for illicit sex with a priest, was similarly described as having a room in the cemetery of St Lawrence's church: BIHR, D/C AB. 1, ff. 225, 227v, 230v, 231.

44. '. . . *id symon emisit virgam suam per murum usque in domum dicte mulieris in scandalum pluriorum*': ibid., f. 244.

45. Another fragmentary act book for the Spirituality of Bishophill, which covers the period April 1426 to May 1427 only, suggests that Bishophill, located off Micklegate in the part of the city south-west of the Ouse, was likewise associated with commercial sex: YML, M2(1)e.

46. The fifteenth-century customary of the Southwark brothels includes the telling clause (B13), '. . . if therbe any woman that liveth by hir body that spinneth or cardeth . . . or elles cast any stone, or make any countenance to any man goyng by the wey . . .': J.B. Post, 'A Fifteenth-Century Customary of the Southwark Stews', *Journal of the Society of Archivists*, 5 (1977), p. 425.

47. This point will be explored in more depth later in the article.

48. Parochial visitations suggest that parish clergy were sometimes suspected of living in concubinage with their housekeepers and even to have fathered children by them. Such arrangements may have been quite common and only reported where other tensions existed between parishioners and their priests. In 1519, for example, the churchwardens of Humberstone (Leics.) settled their differences with their vicar when he agreed to remove one Margaret Buckle from his house following intervention by the vicar general: M. Bowker (ed.), *An Episcopal Court Book for the Diocese of Lincoln 1514–1520*, Lincoln Record Society, 61 (1967), p. 87.

49. The clients of brothels in a southern European context were supposed primarily to be younger unmarried lay males and the limited evidence suggests that the unmarried male certainly constitued a significant part of the clientèle: J. Rossiaud, *Medieval Prostitution*, tr. L.G. Cochrane (Oxford, 1984), pp. 38–42.

50. The two best-known monographs are L.L. Otis, *Prostitution in Medieval Society: The History of an Urban Institution in the Languedoc* (Chicago, 1985) and Rossiaud, *Medieval Prostitution*. Both implicitly claim from their main titles a universality that is entirely spurious. (This is true of the original title of Rossiaud's work as much as of the English translation.) Only more recently have these studies been joined by R.M. Karras's monograph on prostitution in later medieval England: Karras, *Common*

Women. This is a much more nuanced study than her earlier article ('The Regulation of Brothels in Later Medieval England', *Signs* 14 (1989), 399–433) which attempted to fit the English evidence into a mould shaped by the work of Otis and Rossiaud, but some relics of this influence remain and are reflected in the emphasis on evidence drawn from London and Southwark.

51. D. Nicholas, *The Later Medieval City* (London, 1997), pp. 275–6; Otis, *Prostitution in Medieval Society*; M.E. Wiesner, *Working Women in Renaissance Germany* (New Brunswick NJ, 1986), pp. 97–100, 102–3.

52. Geremek, *Margins of Society*, pp. 87–94.

53. D. Nicholas, *The Domestic Life of a Medieval City: Women, Children, and the Family in Fourteenth-Century Ghent* (Lincoln NB, 1985), p. 276

54. E. Ennen, *The Medieval Woman*, tr. E. Jephcot (Oxford, 1989), pp. 194–6.

55. This position is argued at much greater length in Goldberg, *Women, Work, and Life Cycle*. Cf. also L.R. Poos, *A Rural Society After the Black Death: Essex 1350–1525* (Cambridge, 1991), pp. 111–228. Clearly a number of these points are contentious. See for example the debate between Poos, Smith, and Razi in Z. Razi and R.M. Smith (eds), *Medieval Society and the Manor Court* (Oxford, 1996).

56. The aristocracy, for example, seem to have exercised a high degree of control over the marriages of their children and in a significant number of cases to have married children, especially daughters, at more youthful ages than are compatible with a north-western marriage regime.

57. R. Trexler, 'La Prostitution Florentine au XVe siècle: Patronages et Clientèles', *Annales: ESC*, 36 (1981), 983–1015; Rossiaud, *Medieval Prostitution*, pp. 11–37. Rossiaud may be correct to suggest that the toleration of officially regulated brothels was in part a response to a perceived threat of disorder and violence, just as Trexler points to the desire of Florentine civic government to wean men off homosexual practices by introducing them to the pleasures of heterosexual sex, but these attitudes must be seen as part of a broader pattern and cannot of themselves explain essentially similar civic responses to prostitution. It is moreover apparent from the status of the victims of gang rape that the youth groups described by Rossiaud were policing in a particularly brutal way sexual mores intrinsic to the culture and hence that such sexual violence owed nothing to the availability or otherwise of public brothels. Cf. N.Z. Davis, 'The Reasons of Misrule', in N.Z. Davis, *Society and Culture in Early Modern France* (Cambridge, 1987), pp. 97–123, 296–309.

58. R.M. Smith, 'The People of Tuscany and Their Families in the Fifteenth Century: Medieval or Mediterranean?', *Journal of Family History*, 6 (1981), 107–28. Rheubottom, from his work on the Italian immigrant patriciate of Ragusa, has argued convincingly that the distinctive Mediterranean marriage regime characterized by late marriage for males, but early for females may partly be explained by the cultural requirement that sons delay their own marriages until their sisters had been betrothed and their dowries provided for. The concern here is that the virtue of women at marriage, and hence the honour of the family, was guaranteed by the protection of close male kin: D.B. Rheubottom, '"Sisters First": Betrothal Order and Age at Marriage in Fifteenth-Century Ragusa', *Journal of Family History*, 13 (1988), 359–76.

59. This is not to imply that within the much less well documented sphere of the familial economy, particularly perhaps within peasant society, women's labour (other than in respect of reproduction and childrearing) was not regularly drawn upon. Such working patterns did not challenge the cultural requirement that women remain under male protection.

60. Cf. Rheubotham, '"Sisters First"', pp. 359–76; C. Klapisch-Zuber, *Women, Family, and Ritual in Renaissance Italy*, tr. L.G. Cochrane (Chicago, 1985), pp. 178–260; R.M. Smith, 'Geographic Diversity in the resort to marriage in Late Medieval Europe: Work, Reputation, and Unmarried Females in the Household Formation Systems of Northern and Southern Europe', in P.J.P. Goldberg (ed.), *Woman is a Worthy Wight: Women in English Society* c. *1200–1500* (Stroud, 1992), pp. 16–59.

61. Cf. S. Chojnacki, 'Measuring Adulthood: Adolescence and Gender in Renaissance Venice', *Journal of Family History*, 17 (1992), 371–95.

62. Rossiaud, *Medieval Prostitution*, pp. 80–1; Brundage, 'Prostitution in the Medieval Canon Law', p. 151; Karras, *Common Women*, p. 6.

63. The regulations form a customary used in conjunction with the leet court in order to police the stews. As Post observes, they probably date to the late fifteenth century in their present form since they contain the word 'displesure' within the preamble, but he argues that they contain older material. In practice the brothelkeepers seem regularly to have been fined within the leet court supposedly for breach of these regulations, but in effect by way of a licensing fee: Post, 'A Fifteenth-Century Customary', pp. 419–20; Carlin, *Medieval Southwark*, p. 217. The brothel at Sandwich was established in 1473 and new ordinances were drawn up in 1494: Boys (ed.), *Collections*, vol. 2, pp. 677, 680. For evidence of regulation at Southampton see Karras, *Common Women*, pp. 36–7. Unfortunately no ordinances are known to survive there, but sanctioned brothels seem to have existed only from the last quarter of the fifteenth century. It is thus apparent that this level of regulation in these three boroughs is a later fifteenth-century phenomenon and goes hand in hand with evidence for greater civic concern with and policing of prostitution and associated transgressions elsewhere. Cf. M.K. McIntosh, 'Local Change and Community Control in England', *Huntingdon Library Quarterly*, 49 (1986), 219–42.

64. For prostitution in Westminster see G. Rosser, 'London and Westminster: The Suburb in the Urban Economy in the Later Middle Ages', in J.A.F. Thomson (ed.), *Towns and Townspeople in the Fifteenth Century* (Gloucester, 1988), p. 55.

65. In particular we may note Genoese trade through Southampton and Florentine trade through both ports: J.L. Bolton, *The Medieval English Economy 1150–1500* (London, 1980), pp. 255, 286, 312.

66. For attacks on Flemings and Lombards in London in 1381 see R.B. Dobson (ed.), *The Peasants' Revolt of 1381*, 2nd edn (London, 1983), pp. 162, 210, 387.

67. The naming of the civic brothel at Sandwich the 'galye' is highly significant since this is clearly an allusion to the vessels worked by north Italian mariners: Boys (ed.), *Collections*, vol. 2, p. 677; Karras, *Common Women*, n. 16, p. 156.

68. Presumably the same was true of the Rue de Glatigny, the most central concentration of brothels in Paris, which was next the Port Saint-Landry: Geremek, *Margins of Society*, p. 89.

69. These are edited in Post, 'A Fifteenth-Century Customary', pp. 418–28.

70. Ibid., p. 423.

71. Cordelia Beattie has suggested to me in a private communication that the concern here is to allow the women to leave and repent in line with clerical teaching.

72. Karras argues that such a euphemistic usage only became established 'by the early sixteenth century', but she makes a like connection in her discussion of the usage of 'singlewoman' in the Southwark customary: Karras, *Common Women*, pp. 41, 52.

73. P.E. Jones (ed.), *Calendar of Plea and Memoranda Rolls of the City of London 1437–1457* (Cambridge, 1954), pp. 13–14; Carlin, *Medieval Southwark*, pp. 212, 219, 222.

74. For an example of the comparative ineffectiveness of the Venetian civic government to enforce its own ideology see G. Ruggiero, *Binding Passions: Tales of Magic, Marriage, and Power at the End of the Renaissance* (New York, 1993), pp. 48–50.

75. Boys (ed.), *Collections*, vol. 2, pp. 677–8, 680.

76. The analogy is one that medievals recognized in the use of the term 'abbess' to describe the leaseholders of public brothels in parts of France: Rossiaud, *Medieval Prostitution*, pp. 4–5; Otis, *Prostitution in Medieval Society*, p. 60.

INDEX